well plated

EVERY DAY

Recipes for Easier, Healthier, More Exciting Daily Meals

well plated EVERY DAY

Erin Clarke

Photography by Matt Armendariz

AVERY

an imprint of Penguin Random House

New York

AVERY

an imprint of Penguin Random House LLC
penguinrandomhouse.com

Most Avery books are available at special
quantity discounts for bulk
purchase for sales
promotions, premiums,
fundraising, and educational needs. Special books or book
excerpts also can be created to fit specific needs. For details,
write SpecialMarkets@penguinrandomhouse.com.

Library of Congress Cataloging-in-Publication Data
Names: Clarke, Erin, author.
Title: Well plated every day : recipes for easier, healthier,
more exciting daily meals / Erin Clarke.
  Includes index.
Identifiers: LCCN 2023052095 (print) | LCCN 2023052096 (ebook) |
  ISBN 9780593545300 (hardcover) | ISBN 9780593545317 (ebook)
Subjects: LCSH: Quick and easy cooking. | One-dish meals. |
  LCGFT: Cookbooks.
Classification: LCC TX833.5 .C544 2024 (print) | LCC TX833.5 (ebook) |
  DDC 641.5/12—dc23/eng/20231122
LC record available at https://lccn.loc.gov/2023052095
LC ebook record available at https://lccn.loc.gov/2023052096

Printed in China
10 9 8 7 6 5 4 3 2 1

Book design by Ashley Tucker

To everyone who's cooked for someone they love,
most especially when they least felt like it.
Everyday love is the best kind of love.

And to Ben, my first and biggest fan.
I'll never be able to thank you
enough. I love you, today
and every day.

**blueberry
cornmeal crisp**
page 309

contents

peach and crispy prosciutto panzanella page 117

introduction

I didn't intend to write this book. You see, I gave (at least what I thought was) every ounce of myself to my first book—my stories, my favorite ideas, my heart and soul. You loved it, and my literary career was complete. Mic drop. Done.

But then, I started an innocent note on my phone. We were at a little restaurant in Scottsdale, and I had a combination of flavors so interesting, I had to write them down (Brie with a strawberry jalapeño salsa—see page 70). Then, we were in Istanbul and I was eating baklava, enamored with the trifecta of honey, orange, and pistachio, and I began to wonder how the combo would work in a savory application (Sheet Pan Honey Orange Pistachio Salmon and Broccoli, page 130). Then, we hosted friends for dinner where I winged a Mexican-ish "lasagna," and everyone wanted the recipe (yet another entry—Stacked Butternut Squash Black Bean Enchiladas, page 217).

And then, and then, and then . . . pretty soon all these ideas written on this highly unofficial, definitely-not-a-book list looked a lot like . . . my next book, the one you are holding in your hands.

You see, even when we think we've poured out our all, with the right inspiration, we can feel energized and creative again.

I had the luxury to wait until my cup was refilled to create these recipes, a privilege that does not apply at hangry o'clock, when your family is demanding dinner. We all need to eat, and coming up with meals day after day (after day after day) gets tiresome. Let me help.

From Balsamic Berry Chicken Thighs (page 183) to Caprese Cauliflower Melts (page 226), the recipes you'll find here are the ones that make me most excited to cook, the ones I can't wait to share with friends, and the ones I turn to when it's been a long day but *gosh darn it we have to eat. AGAIN.* **They're the recipes I want every day.**

In this book, you'll find an assortment of wholesome recipes for every meal, with a particular emphasis on all-in-one main dishes, an area where we could all use a little more help (and on busy days, a pep talk). In addition to being weeknight attainable—with the exception of the slow cooker recipes and the occasional marinade, the majority of the mains are ready in an hour or less—these recipes are *special*.

Whether it's a touch of crunch (Bam Bam Noodles, page 203), an unexpected burst of citrus (Sweet Citrus Chicken and Rice, page 155), or the final sprinkle of bacon you didn't know you needed (Loaded Broccoli Potato Cheddar Chicken Skillet, page 159), each recipe offers you a little something extra that sets it apart.

The special touches also make these company-worthy meals, not because they are fancy, but because they are (1) delicious, (2) memorable, and (3) 100 percent doable, even for new cooks and even at the last minute. All the better for inviting friends to join the fun!

Making a pan of Baked Ziti–Style Cauliflower (page 166)? Call your neighbor and see if she's free. Have a pot of BTP (Better Than Panera) Creamy Chicken and Wild Rice Soup (page 251) on the stove? Add some bubbly, and it sounds like an impromptu girls' night to me. No white tablecloth, advance notice, or three-course meal required (though if you happen to have some Cowgirl Cookies, page 303, around, I suspect no one will object). After all, if the best part of a meal is the people you share it with, why not choose recipes that make it easier to get people around the table more often?

In Well Plated fashion, I added healthy touches throughout, all of which *add to*, not detract from, the recipes. Another reason this book is meant for every day is because I've packed in the foods we need on the daily—whole grains, fresh fruits and veggies, and lean protein—wherever it made sense and didn't compromise flavor. Making Crispy Chicken Schnitzel (page 184)? I'll help you roast cabbage right along with it so you can check off those veggies. Love pasta? Try this Creamy Harvest Chicken Pasta (page 163), which sneaks in butternut squash and whole grains.

My initial list of ideas grew far too long for one book, and I've given you the best of the best—along with all my top cues, suggestions, and even substitutions so you can make each recipe with confidence and success.

I can't wait for you to try these recipes, to delight yourself when you taste them, to bask in the applause. I want you to feel great about what you're feeding yourself and to look forward to your leftovers for lunch. And most of all, I can't wait for you to enjoy them with people you love, any time. Any day. **Every day.**

XO ERIN

start here
(yes, this means you!)

Whether you've been cooking your entire life or your roommate gave you this cookbook as a not-so-subtle hint, there are a few things we should talk about so that these recipes turn out as they should. No one (least of all me) wants you to waste precious time and ingredients, so let's chat!

1. The First Step in Any Recipe Is READ THE RECIPE. All the way through. From start to finish. BEFORE you begin cooking. This is the first and golden rule, and the one home cooks are most guilty of breaking. Reading the recipe first gives you essential insights into how it will flow, ensures you are prepared for steps that come in quick succession, alerts you to steps that take time (no one wants to be surprised partway through cooking when the chicken needs to marinate for two hours), and generally makes cooking more relaxing and fun.

2. See #1. Repeat until reading the recipe first is second nature. You're going to start to like it, promise.

3. No Fluff Stuff. I respect your time and resources too much to fill my recipes with unnecessary steps and ingredients. If a spice can be skipped, I either didn't include it or I'll label it as optional. If there's a shortcut available, I'll let you know (and chances are I already took it when I wrote the recipe). Thus, when I say to use a separate bowl to mix, or on the off chance you have to add an extra spice to your cabinet, it's because it's critical to creating the most delicious food.

4. Every Oven (and Stove) Is Unique. As a recipe developer, I can tell you that this appliance variation, like lines at the DMV, is an infuriating but unavoidable part of life. Purchase an oven thermometer (a cheap one will do) so you can tell if your oven runs hot or cold, as well as if it's actually done preheating when it says it is (mine takes several minutes longer). Know that your model of stove and even the kind of pan you are using can affect your cook times. Cook not only with the clock but with your eyes, ears, and nose. I've given you as many cues as I can to help you along the way.

5. You're the Boss. While I strongly encourage you to follow the recipes as written the first time (*especially* the desserts), I'm not so self-absorbed as to think everyone shares the same (ahem, *my*) palate. If you've been cooking my recipes for a while, you know I love Dijon mustard (its tang and zippiness lend a certain *je ne sais quoi*) and the sharpest cheddar (why settle for medium sharp?), and I can always find an excuse to add garlic. If you aren't a fan of these flavors, dial them down. The reverse is true too! Want more heat? Add extra red pepper. Garlic freak? Go as wild as you dare (or your date will excuse).

6. Have Fun! Put on a cute apron, pour some wine, turn on the music—whatever makes you happy. Don't take cooking (or yourself) too seriously. If dinner is a disaster, you'll have a great story to tell later, and emergency pizza is only a phone call away.

some of my favorite ingredients

Kosher Salt. This is my hill, the one I will die on: **use kosher salt!** Kosher salt has a better, truer flavor than iodized (table) salt, which tastes metallic thanks to additives that keep it free flowing. Kosher salt grains are larger than table salt, so if you do use table salt in these recipes, you'll need to use less. I use Morton kosher salt because it's so widely available in grocery stores. If you use Diamond Crystal, which has a larger grain than Morton, you'll want to add more. One tablespoon of Diamond Crystal is about 1½ heaping teaspoons of Morton.

Flour. For those of you who prefer to cook by weight, 1 cup of flour in this book weighs 125g. One of the great conundrums of our time is that no one can agree how much a cup of flour weighs. King Arthur Flour lists 120g for 1 cup, Bob's Red Mill lists 136g, and you can find everything in between. If you aren't weighing, use your measuring cup to fluff up the flour in the bag to make sure it isn't at all compacted. Scoop it gently into your cup, then level it off with a knife.

Pure Maple Syrup. In addition to its inferior taste (and suspect ingredient list), imitation maple syrup, sometimes called pancake syrup, will not perform properly in these recipes. Use the real deal. I love amber or dark maple syrup, which has more intense flavor than golden, the lightest variety.

Farro. If this book inspires you to try one new ingredient, I hope it's farro. A variety of wheat, it's delightfully chewy, nutty, and nutritious. You can add it to soups (like Red Wine Mushroom Farro Soup, page 257) and salads, and it makes a nice change of pace from rice in risotto-inspired recipes like Summery Baked Farro with Zucchini and Tomato (page 279) and Cozy Baked Farro with Butternut Squash (page 283).

Brown Rice. Using whole grain brown rice in place of white rice is an easy, effortless way to increase the nutritional value of your dishes. Unless otherwise specified, all recipes in this book use long grain brown rice.

Old-Fashioned Oats. Also called rolled oats or "regular" oats, rolled oats start out as whole oat groats and are steamed and rolled flat. Quick oats start the same way but are rolled even thinner and then cut into smaller pieces so they cook faster. I prefer rolled oats most of the time, because they have a heartier texture and are far less prone to getting mushy. If you can swap quick oats in a recipe, I'll let you know.

Whole Wheat Pasta. Another easy whole grain swap that makes your cooking more nutritious. My favorite brand is DeLallo; because its flavor and texture is so similar to regular pasta, no one notices the swap.

Turkey or Chicken Sausage. You'll always find a pack of precooked chicken or turkey sausage links in my freezer. Sliced and pan-fried so the edges are crisp and the centers are hot and juicy, they are an easy way to add lean protein to pasta, like Creamy Harvest Chicken Pasta (page 163). Look for these in the refrigerated section, usually near the other packaged deli meats.

Greek Yogurt. My holy grail of healthy swaps. Whether it's adding creaminess to casseroles (like Croque Madame Casserole, page 33), tenderness to baked goods (Chocolate Chip Cherry Bread, page 48), cooling off Warming Chickpea, Kale, and Butternut Squash Soup (page 248), or standing in for sour cream on top of Slow Cooker Pork Tinga Tacos (page 191), plain Greek yogurt is a wonder at lightening up recipes while keeping them tasting indulgent. If you want to enjoy it for breakfast but it's too tart for your liking, add a drizzle of honey. It's tastier (and better for you!) than most prepackaged flavored yogurts at the store.

freezer breakfast
burritos, 3 ways
page 27

breakfast and brunch
wake up happy

I believe there is a morning person deep down inside all of us, just waiting to be coaxed out with a warm serving of Cinnamon Roll Baked Oatmeal (page 23) or a fat slice of egg-topped Croque Madame Casserole (page 33) with its perfect runny yolk begging to be broken with a fork. And if neither resonates? Fake it with a caffeine-infused Morning Person Coffee Banana Smoothie (page 40).

As much as I adore mornings (yes, that's me in your kitchen humming with what my husband has deemed to be an obnoxious dose of a.m. enthusiasm), I do not always relish—and rarely have time—to fix an involved breakfast. Banana Crunch Pancakes with Peanut Butter Drizzle (page 59) are *divine*; if every day were Saturday (*wouldn't that be nice?*), I'd eat them every day. Unfortunately, I can't control the cosmos like that, which is why, in addition to more "special occasion" breakfasts like Smoked Salmon Frittata (page 36), it's important to have a cache of healthy breakfasts you can whip up *fast* (any of the smoothies on pages 38–41), as well as make-ahead options you can grab on the fly: Freezer Breakfast Burritos (page 27), Oatmeal Anything Breakfast Bars (page 47), and honestly, most of this chapter.

Whether you bound out of bed at the sound of your alarm or hit snooze as many times as your partner will allow before they file for divorce, these scrumptious, wholesome breakfast recipes will give you a tasty reason to look forward to your day. **Every day.**

**cranny apple
oatmeal muffins**

page 54

mountain morning breakfast bake

ACTIVE TIME:
40 minutes

TOTAL TIME:
1 hour 15 minutes

YIELD:
Serves 6 to 8

1 large sweet potato, scrubbed and ½ inch diced (about 2½ cups)

2 tablespoons extra-virgin olive oil, divided

1 teaspoon kosher salt, divided, plus additional to taste

½ teaspoon ground black pepper, divided

1 pound ground turkey sausage, removed from its casing if needed

1 small red onion, ½ inch diced (about 1 cup)

1 medium red bell pepper, ½ inch diced (about 1 cup)

12 large eggs

½ cup reduced-fat milk

½ teaspoon dried oregano

½ teaspoon onion powder

1 cup shredded pepper Jack cheese (about 4 ounces), divided

2 to 3 tablespoons chopped fresh chives (optional for serving)

2 ripe medium avocados, sliced or diced

While I didn't immediately take to skiing, I was instantly enamored with the "skier's breakfast." A hearty meal to fortify you for an energetic day on the mountain, the typical skier's breakfast includes some combination of eggs (scrambled or fried), meat (bacon or sausage), and starch (potatoes or more potatoes). Whether or not you frolic in the wintery outdoors on a cold morning, no other breakfast is quite as satiating. My version is this nutritious, super-satisfying egg bake with roasted sweet potatoes, zesty turkey sausage, and pepper Jack cheese, plus avocado for healthy fats and good measure. You can prep it entirely the night before, and it reheats like a dream. Serve it for a brunch crowd before your own adventures, or enjoy slices warmed up for healthy meal prep.

1. Place a rack in the center of your oven and preheat to 400°F. Coat a 9 by 13-inch baking dish with nonstick spray. On a large rimmed baking sheet, place the sweet potatoes. Top with 1 tablespoon of the oil, ½ teaspoon of the salt, and ¼ teaspoon of the black pepper. Toss to coat, then spread into an even layer. Roast until the sweet potatoes are tender when pierced with a fork, about 20 minutes, tossing once halfway through. Reduce the oven temperature to 350°F.

2. Meanwhile, in a large skillet, cook the sausage over medium-high heat, breaking apart the meat into small pieces, until the sausage is browned and cooked through, about 8 minutes. With a slotted spoon, transfer the sausage to the prepared baking dish and spread into an even layer.

3. Add the remaining 1 tablespoon oil to the skillet and reduce the heat to medium. Add the onion and bell pepper. Cook, stirring occasionally, until the vegetables begin to soften, about 5 minutes. Remove from the heat.

4. In a large bowl, whisk together the eggs, milk, oregano, onion powder, and remaining ½ teaspoon salt and ¼ teaspoon black pepper.

5. Scatter the sweet potatoes and sautéed vegetables evenly over the sausage, then sprinkle with half of the cheese. Gently

recipe continues

pour the egg mixture over the top. Sprinkle with the remaining cheese.

6. Bake the casserole for 30 to 40 minutes, until the eggs are set in the center (use a butter knife to check) and the edges are slightly puffed and lightly browned. Sprinkle with chives, if using, and let rest a few minutes before serving. Slice and serve with avocado alongside or on top, with a pinch of additional salt to taste.

speed it up

Jump ahead to assembling and baking by swapping the sautéed vegetables and roasted sweet potatoes with leftover roasted vegetables from dinner the night before (for inspiration, see Every-Night Roasted Vegetables on page 262 of *The Well Plated Cookbook*).

do ahead

The beauty of this casserole is that it can be assembled to the point of baking and refrigerated overnight. Let your baking dish stand at room temperature while the oven preheats.

Egg casseroles freeze like a dream. Slice the baked, cooled casserole into squares, then freeze individually. Let thaw overnight in the refrigerator and reheat in the morning.

market swaps

Consider this casserole a guideline for your breakfast desires (or whatever is lurking in your produce drawer). Swap the sausage for ground chorizo for a kick or meatless crumbles for a vegetarian take, change up the cheese, or sub your roasted or sautéed vegetables of choice.

cinnamon roll baked oatmeal

ACTIVE TIME:
30 minutes

TOTAL TIME:
1 hour 15 minutes

YIELD:
Serves 6

For the Baked Oatmeal

2 tablespoons unsalted butter

2½ cups old-fashioned oats or quick-cooking oats

2 tablespoons flaxseed meal (optional)

1 tablespoon ground cinnamon

1 teaspoon baking powder

¼ teaspoon kosher salt

⅛ teaspoon ground cardamom (optional)

2 cups nonfat milk or milk of choice, at room temperature, plus additional for serving

1 large egg, at room temperature

½ cup unsweetened applesauce, at room temperature

⅓ cup pure maple syrup

1 teaspoon pure vanilla extract

½ cup finely chopped raw pecans or walnuts

2 tablespoons turbinado, demerara, or similar coarse sugar

The majority of my school-free summer mornings as a kid began with a can of Pillsbury cinnamon rolls and *The Price Is Right*. By the fourth grade, I could, with astonishing accuracy, quote you the price of washing machines, RVs (depending upon if they were four- or six-wheelers), and eight-piece mahogany dining room sets. What I'm saying is I'm an expert—on cinnamon rolls. This Cinnamon Roll Baked Oatmeal, made over with wholesome oats, applesauce, pure maple syrup, and flaxseed, has all the cozy flavors of a laid-back morning when the only place you need to be is your couch. I love to bake this in a deep pie dish to make it look like a giant cinnamon roll and show off the swirl (because, fun!), but a 9-inch square baking dish will work just as nicely.

1. Place a rack in the lower third of your oven and preheat to 350°F. Coat a deep 9-inch pie dish (or a 9 by 9-inch baking dish) with nonstick spray. In a large microwave-safe bowl, melt the butter in the microwave at medium power (alternatively, you can melt it in a heatproof bowl set over a pan of simmering water). Set aside to cool.

2. In a separate large bowl, whisk together the oats, flaxseed meal (if using), cinnamon, baking powder, salt, and cardamom (if using).

3. To the bowl with the cooled butter, add the milk, egg, applesauce, maple syrup, and vanilla. Whisk to smoothly combine. If the butter solidifies, place the bowl in the microwave and heat it in 10-second bursts, just until it melts. Add the wet ingredients to the bowl with the dry ingredients, then stir gently to combine. The batter will be very loose and wet.

4. Pour the batter into the prepared dish. Use a spatula to prod the oats into an even layer, then sprinkle the pecans, followed by the turbinado sugar, evenly over the top. Bake for about 40 minutes, until the oatmeal is golden at the edges, the edges spring back lightly when touched, and the center still has some give but does not feel mushy when lightly pressed.

5. While the oatmeal bakes, prepare the swirl: In a small bowl, melt the butter in the microwave at medium power (alternatively, you can melt it in a heatproof bowl set over a pan of simmering water). Whisk in the powdered sugar, milk,

recipe and ingredients continue

For the Swirl

2 tablespoons unsalted butter

½ cup powdered sugar, plus additional as needed

2 teaspoons nonfat milk or milk of choice, plus additional as needed

1 teaspoon pure vanilla extract

and vanilla. The glaze should be thick but pourable. Add more powdered sugar 1 tablespoon at a time to thicken, or milk 1 teaspoon at a time to thin, until your desired consistency is reached. Once the oatmeal is out of the oven, immediately drizzle the glaze over the top in a swanky swirl shape. Let cool 5 minutes, then serve hot, adding a pour of milk on top of individual servings if desired.

pro tip

For this recipe (and many recipes in general), I recommend flaxseed meal, which is made of ground flaxseeds and has a speckly, flour-like consistency, making it excellent for incorporating into baked goods. Whole flaxseeds are nice for texture, but because they are difficult to digest, you won't reap the same nutritional benefits that you can from flaxseed meal.

do ahead

The night before, assemble the oatmeal up to the point of adding the turbinado sugar; cover and refrigerate. In the morning, remove it from the refrigerator and preheat your oven. Uncover, sprinkle with the sugar, and bake as directed.

variation

Make It Dairy Free: For the oatmeal, use a nondairy milk, as well as coconut oil or a nondairy butter substitute instead of butter; for the swirl, omit the butter (or use a nondairy substitute) and use nondairy milk.

freezer breakfast burritos, 3 ways

ACTIVE TIME:
1 hour

TOTAL TIME:
1 hour 15 minutes

YIELD:
8 burritos

For the Base Recipe

1 cup frozen unseasoned diced hash brown potatoes, such as Ore-Ida

1 tablespoon unsalted butter (reduce to ½ tablespoon for the bacon version), divided

1 red bell pepper, ½ inch diced (about 1 cup)

½ teaspoon kosher salt, plus a few pinches

¼ teaspoon ground black pepper

1 small bunch green onions, thinly sliced (about 1 cup)

12 large eggs

1 to 2 teaspoons hot sauce, to taste

2 ripe medium avocados

8 (8-inch) whole wheat flour tortillas or wraps

I find the idea of having a "morning routine" a little ridiculous, not because I don't like the idea, but because it would necessitate that I be sufficiently organized and punctual for said routine to take place. Most days, I'm slurping down a cup of coffee (or carrying the open mug straight into the car with me, because, *Where did I put that travel mug?*) and hastily grabbing whatever sustenance looks most portable. Thank goodness for the freezer breakfast burrito: it's here to meet you where you are. In the amount of time it takes you to find your shoes, one of these filling, tasty burritos can be hot and ready to nourish you, whether you take it to go or actually have a moment of peace to sit and savor it. This flexible recipe can be made with just about any combo of veggies, cheese, and protein. The base version, along with three of my favorite variations, have your back.

1. For the Base Recipe: Place the potatoes in a microwave-safe bowl. Cover and microwave on high for 1 minute. Stir and check if the potatoes are thawed. If not, continue heating in 30- to 45-second bursts until they're no longer frozen in the center.

2. In a large nonstick skillet, heat ½ tablespoon of the butter over medium heat. Add the potatoes, red bell pepper, salt, and black pepper.

3. Cook the potato mixture for 5 minutes, stirring occasionally, until the bell pepper has begun to soften. Stir in the green onions and continue cooking until they soften slightly, 2 to 3 minutes more. Remove

from the heat and transfer the mixture to a plate. With a slightly damp paper towel, carefully wipe the skillet clean.

4. In a large bowl, whisk together the eggs with the hot sauce. Return the skillet to medium heat and add the remaining ½ tablespoon butter. Once the butter has melted, swirl to coat the pan and pour in the eggs.

5. Scramble the eggs gently, using a rubber spatula to push the edges of the eggs toward the center as they set. When the eggs are almost cooked but still look wet and somewhat underdone, remove

recipe and ingredients continue

Variation 1:
For bacon spinach, add

8 slices thick-cut bacon, cut into bite-size pieces (about 8 ounces)

3 cups baby spinach (about 3 ounces)

2 cups shredded sharp cheddar cheese (about 8 ounces)

Variation 2:
For veggie pesto, add

2 cups finely chopped broccoli (about 5 ounces or 1 small crown)

3 tablespoons Creamy Basil Pesto from *The Well Plated Cookbook* (page 100) or your favorite store-bought pesto

2 cups shredded provolone, Havarti, or mozzarella cheese, or crumbled goat cheese (about 8 ounces)

Variation 3:
For denver special, add

1 cup ½-inch-diced cooked ham or Canadian bacon (about 5 ounces)

1 green bell pepper, ½ inch diced (about 1 cup)

2 cups shredded pepper Jack or Monterey Jack cheese (about 8 ounces)

the skillet from the heat and sprinkle with a little additional salt. Continue to gently push the eggs around in the still-hot pan for 10 or so more seconds, allowing them to finish cooking. Stir in the sautéed vegetable mixture, breaking up the eggs as needed so everything is evenly distributed. If freezing the burritos, let the eggs cool to room temperature.

6. When you're ready to assemble, halve the avocados and slice each half into 8 thin slices (you'll have 16 slices per avocado).

7. Tear off a square of aluminum foil or parchment paper large enough to wrap around your burrito and place it on a work surface. Set a tortilla in the center. Scoop and arrange one-eighth of the egg mixture (⅔ to ¾ cup) down the center of the tortilla. Top with ¼ cup of the cheese from your variation of choice and 4 avocado slices. Sprinkle lightly with salt.

8. To roll, lift two opposite sides of the tortilla toward the center (the now-folded sides will be the burrito's ends). Starting with one of the free sides, gently but firmly roll the burrito up until it is sealed. It will be VERY full, but persevere and tuck in the filling as you go—you'll thank yourself later. Wrap the burrito in the foil or parchment paper and label with the flavor and date. Transfer to a ziptop bag. Repeat the process for the remaining burritos. Seal the bag, removing as much air as possible. Freeze for up to 3 months.

For the Bacon Spinach: Start by sautéing the bacon over medium-low heat until it is crisp and the fat has rendered, 8 to 10 minutes. Transfer to a large plate. Drain all but ½ tablespoon fat from the skillet and use it in place of the first ½ tablespoon butter in the base recipe. Proceed with the recipe as directed, adding the spinach with the green onions in step 3 and stirring until it wilts. Add the cooked bacon into the scrambled eggs in step 5.

For the Veggie Pesto: Sauté the broccoli with the other vegetables in step 2. Scramble the pesto with the eggs in step 5.

For the Denver Special: Sauté the ham and green bell pepper with the other vegetables in step 2.

To Reheat on the Stove:

Allow the burritos to thaw overnight in the refrigerator. Heat a nonstick skillet over medium heat. Unwrap the burrito, lightly coat the skillet with nonstick spray, and place the burrito in the skillet, seam side down. Cook for 5 minutes. Lightly coat the top of the burrito with nonstick spray, flip, and heat on the other side until the burrito is crisp and heated through, about 5 minutes more.

To Reheat in the Microwave:

Let the burrito thaw in the refrigerator overnight, then microwave on a paper towel–lined plate on high for 1 to 2 minutes, until heated through. Or, if the burrito is still frozen, place it on a paper towel–lined plate and microwave for 3 minutes on low to defrost, then microwave on high for 1 to 2 minutes until hot. Enjoy right away, or crisp in a skillet first.

market swaps

This burrito recipe is highly adaptable and is a great way to use up veggies on the verge of expiring. Along with the eggs, use up to 4 cups of any chopped vegetables and/or protein (the potatoes and red bell pepper in the base recipe total 2 cups, so you can use 2 additional cups of anything you like). Try cooked and crumbled breakfast sausage, shredded carrots or cabbage, diced leftover roasted vegetables, rinsed and drained white beans—whatever your heart (and tummy) desire.

baja breakfast bowls

ACTIVE TIME: **20 minutes**

TOTAL TIME: **20 minutes**

YIELD: **Serves 4**

8 large eggs

1 teaspoon kosher salt, divided, plus additional to taste

1 tablespoon extra-virgin olive oil

1 medium red bell pepper, ¼ inch diced (about 1 cup)

½ small red or yellow onion, ¼ inch diced (about ½ cup)

1 (15-ounce) can reduced-sodium black beans, rinsed and drained

⅓ cup prepared salsa, plus additional as needed and for serving

⅛ to ¼ teaspoon chipotle chile powder (optional)

1½ cups prepared brown rice (see How to Cook Brown Rice, page 138)

¼ cup water, plus additional as needed

½ cup shredded pepper Jack, Monterey Jack, or sharp cheddar cheese (about 2 ounces)

⅓ cup chopped fresh cilantro, plus additional for serving

2 ripe avocados, roughly mashed (see Pro Tips)

1½ teaspoons unsalted butter

Having a favorite local coffee shop is good for the soul. Mine is Colectivo. It's just a few blocks from our house and overlooks Lake Michigan, and if you stopped in at any point during the years I spent writing my cookbooks, you probably saw me at one of the tables by the window, hunkered down over some pages and eating one of these breakfast bowls. A tasty, Southwest-inspired blend of salsa-ed eggs, chipotle-scented black beans, fresh veggies, and rice, this savory and filling breakfast bowl is my go-to order (at least whenever I wasn't eating their famous cowboy cookies, page 303). This recipe is my re-creation. To keep the prep quick, use leftover cooked brown rice. This recipe yields four easy-to-reheat servings, so it's great for meal prep (and, of course, the soul).

1. In a medium bowl, whisk together the eggs and ¼ teaspoon of the salt. Let sit at least 5 minutes while you prepare the beans and rice (because of how the salt impacts the eggs' protein structure, allowing them to rest will give the eggs a creamier texture).

2. Heat the oil in a medium saucepan over medium-high heat. Add the bell pepper, onion, and remaining ¾ teaspoon salt. Let cook, stirring occasionally, until the bell peppers are crisp-tender, about 5 minutes.

3. Add the black beans, salsa, and chipotle chile powder (if using). Cook until the beans and salsa are heated through, 1 to 2 minutes, then with a large spoon or potato masher, lightly mash about half of the beans. Stir in the prepared rice and water. Reduce the heat to low. Let cook, stirring occasionally, until the rice is hot, 2 to 3 minutes. If at any point the mixture looks dry, add more salsa or water as needed. It should be moist but not watery. Stir in the cheese and cilantro. Remove from the heat and cover to keep warm.

4. Heat a medium nonstick skillet over medium heat. Add the butter. As soon as it is melted, swirl to coat the pan, reduce the heat to low, and add the rested eggs. As soon as the edges are barely beginning to set (this will happen almost immediately), use a rubber spatula to gently push the edges toward the center of the pan. Let cook, using the spatula to

recipe continues

gently and continually move the set eggs toward the center and to break up big clumps, until the eggs look about three-quarters done (they should still be too wet to eat). Remove from the heat and continue using the spatula to move them gently until they are cooked but still soft. This entire process will take 3 to 5 minutes.

5. To serve, pile the warm rice and bean mixture into a bowl, then top with a scoop of the eggs, a scoop of the mashed avocado, and a pinch of salt. Enjoy immediately with additional salsa and cilantro as desired.

pro tips

While I love a good fruity salsa, such as mango or peach, it will give the breakfast bowls an odd flavor. Stick with purely savory flavors.

To save a dish, mash the avocado on the side of your serving bowl or directly inside the avocado peel.

do ahead

For a meal-prep-maven breakfast, portion the bean and rice mixture into four separate containers and refrigerate. Warm your serving in the microwave and top with freshly scrambled eggs and mashed avocado. You can also reheat scrambled eggs if you don't mind them being somewhat dry, so feel free to make those in advance as well.

market swaps

In place of (or in addition to) the bell pepper, feel free to use sautéed spinach, shredded carrots, or finely chopped broccoli or cauliflower.

variations

Tex-Mex Twist: Use a green salsa or add 1 (4-ounce) can of diced green chiles, drained.

Baja Breakfast Over Easy: Top each serving with 2 soft-fried eggs instead of scrambled eggs.

croque madame casserole

ACTIVE TIME:
30 minutes

TOTAL TIME:
1 hour 45 minutes

YIELD:
Serves 6

1 baguette, cut into
½-inch-thick slices
(about 12 ounces)

1½ teaspoons unsalted
butter

8 ounces very thinly sliced
Black Forest deli ham
(see Pro Tip)

12 large eggs, divided

1¼ cups nonfat milk

½ cup nonfat plain Greek
yogurt

3 tablespoons Dijon
mustard

¼ teaspoon kosher salt

¼ teaspoon ground black
pepper, plus additional
for serving

¼ teaspoon ground
nutmeg

⅛ teaspoon ground
cayenne pepper (optional)

1 cup shredded Gruyère,
Emmental, or similar
nutty, melty cheese
(about 4 ounces)

2 tablespoons chopped
fresh chives, for serving

The croque madame, a staple on French café menus, is a knife-and-fork grilled ham and cheese sandwich situation with béchamel sauce and a runny egg on top. It tastes spectacular. One winter, Ben and I set up shop in the French Alps, and I cooked our meals in a tiny kitchen. The croque madame was on the menu at least three times a week, and neither of us ever grew weary of it. Croque madame's one (and let's say only) downfall is that, because the eggs need to be fried individually and served immediately, it's challenging to make for a crowd. This breakfast casserole is the answer. It transforms the layers of buttery bread, salty ham, and nutty, melty Gruyère into a savory French toast bake that will transport you to a mountain village in France. You can prep this the night before, and the eggs bake right on top at the end, so everyone can help themselves hassle-free, including you!

1. Dry out the baguette (if your baguette is at least 1 day old and already dry, you can skip this step): Place racks in the upper third and center of your oven and preheat to 400°F. Arrange the baguette slices in a single layer on a rimmed baking sheet. Toast on the upper rack for 4 to 5 minutes, until fairly dry to the touch. Set aside. Reduce the oven temperature to 325°F (or turn it off if you plan to bake the next day).

2. Rub the butter all over the inside of a 9 by 13-inch baking dish. Arrange the baguette slices in three long, straight rows across the pan, leaning them on each other slightly, like fallen dominoes; each slice will be at an angle and partially overlapping the slice before it. Adjust the slices so the whole dish is covered fairly evenly.

3. Tear the ham into small pieces and scatter it evenly, tucking some bits of it between bread slices and leaving other bits peeking out on top.

4. In a large bowl, whisk together 6 of the eggs, the milk, yogurt, mustard, salt, black pepper, nutmeg, and cayenne until well mixed. Pour evenly over the baguette slices and ham. Press down on the bread pieces lightly, then sprinkle with the Gruyère. Coat a piece of aluminum foil large enough to cover the pan with nonstick spray, then use it to cover the dish, placing it spray side down. Refrigerate for at least 30 minutes, or overnight.

5. When you're ready to bake, remove the casserole from the

recipe continues

refrigerator. Place a rack in the center of your oven and preheat to 325°F. Bake the casserole covered for 30 minutes, then remove it from the oven and increase the oven temperature to 400°F. Leave the dish out of the oven while it heats.

6. Once the oven reaches 400°F, uncover the casserole. With the back of a spoon, create six evenly spaced, shallow depressions for the eggs—it's important the depressions be shallow or the eggs will not cook evenly. Working one egg at a time, crack each into a small bowl, then pour it carefully into a depression (the whites might run outside the bounds of the depression, which is fine). Return the casserole to the oven and bake until the egg whites are barely set and the yolks are still soft, 11 to 13 minutes. The time will vary depending upon how you've shaped the depressions and how done you like your eggs.

7. Remove the casserole from the oven and top with chives and additional black pepper. Let rest a few minutes, then scoop and enjoy hot, ensuring each serving has a good amount of baguette, ham, and egg.

pro tip

Rather than purchasing prepackaged ham slices, ask the deli counter to shave it so that it is falling apart. It is easier to distribute throughout the casserole, and the texture is desirably delicate.

variation

Croque Signora: Give it an Italian spin and swap the ham for prosciutto. Garnish with thinly sliced fresh basil in place of chives.

smoked salmon frittata

ACTIVE TIME:

20 minutes

TOTAL TIME:

1 hour 10 minutes

YIELD:

Serves 6

10 large eggs

1 cup nonfat plain Greek yogurt

1 teaspoon dried basil

½ teaspoon kosher salt, plus additional to taste

½ teaspoon ground black pepper, plus additional to taste

6 ounces hot-smoked salmon, flaked

3 ounces goat cheese, crumbled (about ½ cup)

¼ cup chopped sun-dried tomatoes in oil, drained and patted dry

3 tablespoons chopped fresh dill

2 tablespoons unsalted butter

1 small bunch green onions, thinly sliced (about 1 cup), divided

Listen, you don't need to impress anyone—but for times when you want to anyway, make this Smoked Salmon Frittata. The rich silkiness of the salmon provides a pleasing counterpoint to pockets of creamy, melty goat cheese and fluffy eggs. Plus, *ooh la la*, smoked salmon! For best results, use hot-smoked salmon, which is thick, flakes easily, and provides intense, salty umami notes. In the package, it looks like a single cooked fillet. Cold-smoked salmon (such as lox) is soft and usually comes in thin slices. It tastes great on bagels, but the thicker, meatier texture and more robust flavor of hot-smoked salmon is best for this frittata, regardless of whether your aim is to impress.

1. Place a rack in the center of your oven and preheat to 350°F. In a very large bowl, whisk together the eggs, yogurt, basil, salt, and pepper until well combined. Add the salmon, goat cheese, sun-dried tomatoes, and dill. With a spatula, fold gently until the ingredients are evenly distributed. The mixture will be very thick.

2. In a 10-inch ovenproof skillet, melt the butter over medium-low heat. Reserve 2 tablespoons of the green onions, then add the rest to the pan. Let cook, stirring periodically, until softened, about 4 minutes.

3. Remove the pan from the heat. Carefully pour the egg mixture into the skillet. Sprinkle the reserved green onions on top. Immediately transfer the skillet to the oven and bake for 45 to 50 minutes, until the eggs are puffed and a thin, sharp knife inserted in the center of the frittata comes out clean. Let rest a few minutes, then slice and serve directly from the skillet. Season with additional salt and pepper to taste.

strawberry warrior smoothie

mint chipper smoothie
page 41

morning person coffee banana smoothie
page 40

strawberry warrior smoothie

ACTIVE TIME:
5 minutes

TOTAL TIME:
5 minutes

YIELD:
1 large or 2 small smoothies (about 16 ounces total)

1 cup unsweetened almond milk or milk of choice

½ cup fresh banana slices, or swap frozen and reduce or omit the ice

¾ cup frozen strawberries

¼ cup frozen raspberries

1 tablespoon creamy almond butter

½ to 1 scoop vanilla protein powder, or an additional 1 tablespoon almond butter

¼ teaspoon ground cinnamon

¼ teaspoon pure vanilla extract

Ice, as needed

In the ultimate move to avoid the Wisconsin winter, a few years ago, Ben and I packed up half of our kitchen and our dog, Teddy, and drove twenty-seven hours to Scottsdale, Arizona, where we worked remotely. During our stay, I spent (er, invested?) a tidy sum on smoothies. One I especially adored was called the "Strawberry Warrior Smoothie." Not only did it taste extra fresh, but it also made me feel like a life-conquering champ every time I sipped it. No daily to-do list stood a chance against my surging, smoothie-fueled ambition. The smoothie shop used goji berries, but I find that tart raspberries are a delightful substitute that puts this cup of triumph right up there with the original's glory.

1. In a high-speed blender, place the ingredients in the order listed: the almond milk, banana, strawberries, raspberries, almond butter, protein powder, cinnamon, and vanilla. Blend until smooth.

2. To thicken the smoothie, add a small handful of ice and blend. Continue to add ice a few cubes at a time until your desired consistency is reached.

pro tips

Don't skip the almond butter. Its healthy fats give this smoothie staying power. Of course, you can feel free to swap any nut butter you prefer. Peanut butter will give it a PB&J twist; cashew butter will lend a more neutral flavor.

If you do not have a high-speed blender, add the frozen fruit gradually to help it blend more smoothly.

do ahead

Smoothies can generally be refrigerated for up to 1 day. Store them in an airtight container (the less air in the container, the better), such as a mason jar. Stir before sipping.

morning person coffee banana smoothie

ACTIVE TIME:
5 minutes

TOTAL TIME:
5 minutes

YIELD: **1 smoothie (about 12 ounces)**

1 large banana, cut into chunks and frozen (about ¾ cup)

½ cup brewed coffee, cold or at room temperature

1 tablespoon creamy peanut butter or almond butter

1 tablespoon pure maple syrup

½ cup nonfat vanilla Greek yogurt

1½ teaspoons unsweetened cocoa powder

½ to 1 scoop chocolate protein powder (optional)

Ice, as needed

Whenever I have a smoothie for breakfast, I find myself double-fisting: smoothie in one hand, coffee in the other (and this isn't brunch, but if it were, I'd have to squeeze a Bloody Mary in there somewhere). This coffee banana smoothie delivers two crucial sipping essentials in one! Leftover cooled coffee makes the liquid base of this thick, creamy, dreamy smoothie and gives it the caffeine boost we often need in the a.m. If you love iced coffee, chocolate milkshakes, and the combo of bananas and peanut butter, this smoothie gives your one hand the efficiency of two! *Cue fist bump.*

1. In a high-speed blender, place the ingredients in the order listed: the banana, coffee, peanut butter, maple syrup, yogurt, cocoa powder, and protein powder (if using). Blend until smooth.

2. To thicken the smoothie, add a small handful of ice and blend. Continue to add ice a few cubes at a time until your desired consistency is reached. Sip and feel the energy!

pro tips

Cocoa powder is STRONG. If you'd like your smoothie more chocolaty, add it very slowly (½ teaspoon at a time) and taste as you go. You may want to add more maple syrup, as cocoa can be bitter.

If you do not have a high-speed blender, add the banana pieces gradually to help them blend more smoothly.

do ahead

Make extra coffee the day before, then refrigerate it for your smoothie the next day.

mint chipper smoothie

ACTIVE TIME:
5 minutes

TOTAL TIME:
5 minutes

YIELD:
1 large or 2 small smoothies (about 16 ounces total)

1 cup firmly packed fresh spinach leaves (about 1 ounce)

1 medium banana, cut into slices and frozen (a generous ½ cup)

¾ cup unsweetened vanilla almond milk or milk of choice

½ medium avocado (see Pro Tips)

½ to 1 scoop vanilla protein powder, or 1 tablespoon almond butter plus ½ teaspoon pure vanilla extract

⅛ teaspoon pure peppermint extract, plus additional to taste

Ice, as needed

1 to 3 teaspoons honey or pure maple syrup (optional)

2 teaspoons mini chocolate chips or cacao nibs

When I was growing up, Shamrock Shake release day at McDonald's was a sacred holiday. You'd find our minivan at the front of the drive-through line, straws poised to mark the festive occasion. A few years ago, I treated myself to one only to discover that (GASP!) *it wasn't that good* (and certainly wasn't worth the tummy ache afterward). This copycat version is creamy, fresh, and made with feel-good ingredients. Don't let the avocado throw you—its taste is nearly imperceptible, and its healthy fats make the smoothie filling. And the chocolate chips? We just did McD's one better.

1. In a high-speed blender, place the following ingredients in the order listed: spinach, banana, almond milk, avocado, protein powder, and peppermint extract. Blend until smooth.

2. To thicken the smoothie, add a small handful of ice and blend. Continue to add ice a few cubes at a time until your desired consistency is reached.

3. Taste the smoothie and adjust: If you'd like the smoothie sweeter, add 1 to 3 teaspoons honey. If you'd like it more minty, add 1 to 2 more drops peppermint extract (be careful—it is *very* potent!). Once you are happy with the flavor, add the chocolate chips, then blend briefly so that the chips break down but you can still see bits of chocolate in the smoothie. Enjoy immediately.

pro tips

The taste of the avocado is very slight, but if you'd like to make it vanish, reduce the amount to ¼ medium avocado.

If you do not have a high-speed blender, add the banana pieces gradually to help them blend more smoothly.

overnight waffles, 4 ways

ACTIVE TIME:

30 minutes

TOTAL TIME:

8 hours 30 minutes

YIELD:

8 Belgian-style waffles

For classic waffles

2¼ cups milk or buttermilk (see Pro Tips)

4 tablespoons (½ stick) unsalted butter, cut into a few pieces

½ cup warm water (110° to 115°F)

1½ tablespoons pure maple syrup or honey

1 package active dry yeast (2¼ teaspoons)

1 teaspoon pure vanilla extract

1 teaspoon kosher salt

2½ cups white whole wheat flour, or a 50-50 blend of regular whole wheat flour and all-purpose flour

2 large eggs

¼ teaspoon baking soda

Nonstick spray or melted butter, for cooking

For serving: softened butter, warm maple syrup, or any of the topping ideas on page 45

On a proverbial desert island where I had to choose between eating pancakes or waffles for the rest of my life, I'd pick waffles every time. Yet, until I discovered the magic of overnight yeasted waffles, I rarely made them. Why? I am too lazy to separate eggs in the morning. Beating egg whites into peaks then gently folding them into the batter is the secret to a fluffy waffle interior. As it turns out, stirring a little active dry yeast into the batter and allowing it to rest overnight achieves a similar effect with far less effort. Better yet, when you wake up, the waffle batter is ready and waiting. Enjoy the classic version of this recipe in all its simple, golden glory, or mix it up with the variations and toppings suggested. No sunscreen required.

1. The night before, prepare the Classic Waffles Base: Place the milk and butter in a small saucepan. Heat over medium-low until the butter has melted. Remove from the heat and let cool until the mixture feels warm but not hot to the touch (110° to 115°F).

2. In a large bowl (leave lots of room in the bowl—the batter will expand considerably), combine the warm water, maple syrup, and yeast. Let sit for 5 minutes to bloom. The yeast should look foamy (if it does not, your yeast did not activate and the waffles won't rise properly—it may be expired, or your water was too hot or too cold; try again with new yeast).

3. Whisk in the warm milk and butter mixture, the vanilla, and salt. Then, whisk in the flour until smoothly combined. Cover the bowl and refrigerate overnight (or let proof at room temperature until doubled in size, 2 to 3 hours).

4. When ready to cook the waffles, preheat your waffle iron. Remove the batter from the refrigerator, if needed. In a small bowl, whisk together the eggs and baking soda. Add to the waffle batter and whisk until the batter recombines to a fairly even consistency (it will have separated somewhat during resting). To keep the cooked waffles warm between batches and crisp them up a bit further, preheat your oven to 200°F.

recipe and ingredients continue

For cinnamon butter pecan, add per waffle

1½ tablespoons finely chopped pecans

To serve: Mix 4 tablespoons (½ stick) softened butter, 1 tablespoon powdered sugar, 1 tablespoon honey, and ½ teaspoon ground cinnamon

For baked-in bacon, add per waffle

1 slice center-cut uncooked bacon, cut in half crosswise (do not use thick-cut bacon, as it will not crisp)

For blueberry crunch, add per waffle

Small handful fresh or frozen blueberries (if frozen, thaw and pat dry)

Small handful Ridiculously Addictive Maple Quinoa Granola (*The Well Plated Cookbook*, page 26) or your favorite store-bought granola

5. Lightly coat the waffle iron with nonstick spray or brush with melted butter. Add just enough batter to cover most of the griddle (about ½ cup).

6. For Classic Waffles: Close and cook according to the waffle iron's directions until the waffle is crisp and deep brown, 5 to 6 minutes. Serve immediately, or place on top of a wire rack set on top of a baking sheet and keep warm in the oven. Enjoy hot, with all your favorite toppings.

For the Variations: Immediately after adding the batter to the iron, sprinkle your desired toppings over the top of the batter, then close the waffle iron (for the bacon, lay the pieces parallel to one another, spacing them evenly). Cook as directed.

help! i'm scared of yeast

Fear not, young grasshopper. Think of yeast as any other ingredient. Two things are important: one, that your yeast is not expired, and two, that your liquid is the correct temperature (very warm bath water—110° to 115°F; go ahead and use an instant-read thermometer for peace of mind). This recipe builds in a safety net step by giving you a checkpoint to make sure the yeast blooms (aka is going to do its job). When you see it bloom, you know you're good to go.

pro tips

These waffles are fantastic with milk or buttermilk, so use whichever you have on hand. If using buttermilk, they may take a little longer to rise at room temperature.

This recipe calls for active dry yeast. Note that if you use instant yeast instead, blooming isn't necessary, though you may go ahead and do so to confirm it activates properly. Refer to your package directions for further activation instructions.

freezing the cooked waffles

Let the waffles cool completely on a wire rack (do not set them directly on a plate or the steam will make them soggy). Lay the waffles flat in a ziptop bag, separating layers with wax paper or parchment paper. Seal, squeezing out as much air as possible. If you are freezing a larger batch or need to consolidate them more tightly in the freezer, freeze the waffles flat on a baking sheet first, then transfer them to an airtight ziptop bag. Freeze for up to 3 months.

reheating the frozen waffles

Reheat the waffles directly from frozen in a toaster or toaster oven on low (break frozen sections apart as needed so they fit) or in the microwave (recrisp it in the toaster or oven after warming through), or wrap the waffle loosely in foil and reheat in a regular oven at 425°F, until the waffle is warmed through and it reaches your desired crispness. The amount of time will vary based on your waffle thickness; plan on 5 to 8 minutes in the oven.

10 tasty sweet and savory waffle toppings

1. **Funky Monkey:** Peanut Butter Drizzle (page 59), banana slices, mini chocolate chips

2. **Parfait:** Almond butter, vanilla Greek yogurt, sliced fresh fruit, granola

3. **Cinnamon Toast:** Combine ¼ cup granulated sugar with 1 teaspoon cinnamon. Butter the waffle generously, then with a small spoon, sprinkle the cinnamon sugar over the top.

4. **Blueberry Ginger Sauce** (page 63)

5. **Hazelnut Dream:** Chocolate hazelnut spread, sliced bananas or strawberries, chopped toasted hazelnuts

6. **Warm Cinnamon Sautéed Apples** (*The Well Plated Cookbook*, page 56)

7. **Sweet and Savory:** Crumbled goat cheese, cooked and crumbled bacon, cracked black pepper, drizzle of honey

8. **Southern Special:** Popcorn Chicken (page 238), maple syrup

9. **The Millennial:** Smashed avocado, everything bagel seasoning or red pepper flakes, flaky salt

10. **Breakfast Supreme:** Shredded cheddar cheese; poached, fried, or scrambled egg; salsa

oatmeal anything breakfast bars

ACTIVE TIME:
15 minutes

TOTAL TIME:
40 minutes

YIELD:
One 8 by 8-inch pan (8 to 10 bars)

⅔ cup assorted mix-ins of choice: chopped walnuts or pecans, dried cranberries, and/or chopped dried cherries

6 tablespoons unsalted butter

¼ cup packed light brown sugar

¼ cup pure maple syrup

¼ cup unsweetened applesauce

1 large egg, at room temperature

1 teaspoon pure vanilla extract

½ cup plus 2 tablespoons old-fashioned oats

½ cup white whole wheat flour, or a 50-50 blend of regular whole wheat flour and all-purpose flour

½ teaspoon baking soda

½ teaspoon kosher salt

⅓ cup dark chocolate chips or chopped dark chocolate (55% to 72% chocolate)

I see your half-empty bag of nuts, and I raise you my quarter bags of dried fruit and pumpkin seeds. Let's make Oatmeal Anything Breakfast Bars! A cross between an oatmeal bake and a breakfast cookie, these sweet breakfast treats are ideal for using up the odd bits of nuts, seeds, baking chips, and dried fruit you have lurking in your pantry. My one nonnegotiable is chocolate chips. Future you says thank you.

1. Place a rack in the center of your oven and preheat to 350°F. If using nuts as a mix-in, spread them on a rimmed baking sheet and bake until fragrant and toasted, about 8 minutes, stirring once or twice partway through. Transfer from the baking sheet to a plate. Line an 8 by 8-inch baking pan with parchment paper, leaving some overhang on opposite sides like handles. Coat with nonstick spray.

2. In a large microwave-safe bowl, melt the butter in the microwave on medium power (or set the bowl over a pan of simmering water and melt on the stove). Whisk in the brown sugar, maple syrup, and applesauce. Then, whisk in the egg and vanilla.

3. In a medium bowl, whisk together the oats, flour, baking soda, and salt. Add to the bowl with the wet ingredients, then with a rubber spatula or wooden spoon, fold gently to combine, stopping as soon as the flour disappears. Do not overmix.

4. Fold in the toasted nuts (if using), any other mix-ins, and the chocolate chips, just until combined. Scrape the batter into the prepared pan, then smooth the top.

5. Bake the bars for 24 to 26 minutes, until deep golden brown on top and a toothpick inserted in the center comes out with moist crumbs but no wet batter clinging to it. Let cool completely in the pan, then lift the bars onto a cutting board using the parchment overhang. Slice into bars of desired size.

pro tip

To keep your parchment paper from slipping around as you add the batter, secure it to the edges of the pan with office supply binder clips. Remove the clips prior to baking.

chocolate chip cherry bread

ACTIVE TIME:

30 minutes

TOTAL TIME:

1 hour 30 minutes

YIELD:

**One 9 by 5-inch loaf
(about 10 slices)**

½ cup granulated sugar

2 large eggs, at room temperature

¾ cup plus 2 tablespoons nonfat plain Greek yogurt, at room temperature

¼ cup honey

¼ cup canola oil, or melted and cooled coconut oil

1 teaspoon pure vanilla extract

¼ teaspoon pure almond extract

½ teaspoon kosher salt

1¼ cups white whole wheat flour, or a 50-50 blend of regular whole wheat flour and all-purpose flour

1½ teaspoons baking powder

¼ teaspoon baking soda

1¼ cups roughly chopped fresh or frozen sweet or tart cherries, divided (if frozen, thaw and pat dry)

⅓ cup plus 1 tablespoon dark chocolate chips (55% to 72% chocolate), divided

Door County, Wisconsin, a string of tiny picturesque beach towns hugging the state's upper peninsula (think Cape Cod but on the Great Lakes), is one of my favorite places on earth. There's no better time to visit than July, when the cherries are in peak season. I load up the car with boxes of these precious red jewels, and whichever ones aren't eaten by the end of the three-hour drive home, I bake into Chocolate Chip Cherry Bread. Studded with cherries and melty dark chocolate you'll have no choice but to lick off your fingers, this quick bread boasts a devastatingly moist crumb and a subtle note of almond, and it comes together in exactly one bowl. No need to wait for cherry season—you can use frozen cherries with great results.

1. Place a rack in the center of your oven and preheat to 350°F. Coat a 9 by 5-inch loaf pan with nonstick spray, then line with parchment paper so that the paper overhangs the two longest sides. Coat with nonstick spray once more.

2. In a large bowl, briskly whisk the sugar and eggs until the eggs look pale and foamy, about 1 minute. Whisk in the yogurt, honey, oil, vanilla extract, almond extract, and salt until the mixture is smoothly combined.

3. Sprinkle the flour, baking powder, and baking soda over the top. With a rubber spatula, stir gently to combine, stopping as soon as the flour disappears. The batter will be thick. Gently fold in 1 cup of the cherries and ⅓ cup of the chocolate chips

(reserve the remaining cherries and chips for sprinkling on top).

4. Pour the batter into the prepared loaf pan and smooth the top. Scatter the remaining ¼ cup cherries and 1 tablespoon chocolate chips over the top.

5. Bake for 50 to 55 minutes, until the bread is dark golden on top and at the edges (don't worry if it looks pretty dark; it's not burned—that's caramelized honey) and a toothpick inserted in the center of the loaf comes out clean. The loaf will not rise much. When fully baked, the center of the bread will register 200°F on an instant-read thermometer. Place the pan on a wire rack and let the bread cool in the pan for 15 minutes. With the parchment overhang, gently lift the loaf onto the rack, using a

recipe continues

butter knife to loosen the edges of the bread as needed. Resist the urge to slice immediately and let cool completely (it's worth it for the best texture!). Store leftovers in the refrigerator for 3 days.

market swaps

Use this bread to celebrate whatever fruit is in season. Instead of cherries, use diced ripe peaches, pears, strawberries . . . you name it! Feel free to adjust the spices to taste and swap out the dark chocolate. For example, if using a fall fruit such as pears, add a pinch of cinnamon. For peaches, ginger is lovely. Blueberries with white chocolate chips sounds divine. What I'm saying is, you have a lot of reasons to bake this bread.

aloha muffins

ACTIVE TIME:

30 minutes

TOTAL TIME:

1 hour

YIELD:

12 muffins

For the Muffins

⅓ cup coconut oil or canola oil

2 (8-ounce) cans crushed pineapple in 100% juice

1 cup all-purpose flour

¾ cup white whole wheat flour or regular whole wheat flour

1½ teaspoons baking powder

½ teaspoon baking soda

1½ teaspoons ground cinnamon

½ teaspoon ground allspice

½ teaspoon kosher salt

2 cups shredded unpeeled zucchini (about 1 medium)

¾ cup sweetened flake coconut

2 large eggs, at room temperature

⅓ cup packed light brown sugar

2 teaspoons pure vanilla extract

When I told Maggie, my recipe-testing sidekick through both of my books (she deserves sainthood), that we were going to make aloha muffins, she posed a highly reasonable question: "What's an aloha muffin?" I had little idea beyond the name. I wanted them to taste like a tropical vacation—tender bites of sunshine you could bake into reality anytime you pleased—but still be wholesome enough to land on the breakfast side of the thin line that divides muffins and cake. These sweet pineapple, zucchini, and coconut muffins with a touch of Caribbean-inspired allspice live up to their name. Let them whisk you away to paradise!

1. Place a rack in the center of your oven and preheat to 350°F. Coat a standard 12-cup muffin pan with nonstick spray.

2. In a medium, microwave-safe bowl, melt the coconut oil in the microwave at medium power (alternatively, you can melt it in a heatproof bowl set over a pan of simmering water). Set aside and let cool to room temperature (if using canola oil, no need to heat). Drain the pineapple, reserving 2 tablespoons of the juice for the glaze. Add the drained pineapple to the bowl with the oil.

3. In a separate large bowl, whisk together the all-purpose flour, white whole wheat flour, baking powder, baking soda, cinnamon, allspice, and salt. Thoroughly squeeze the shredded zucchini with a paper towel to remove as much excess water as possible, then add it to

the bowl. Add the coconut, then gently fold just until everything is evenly incorporated.

4. To the bowl with the pineapple and oil, add the eggs, brown sugar, and vanilla. Whisk until smoothly combined. If the coconut oil solidifies, gently warm the bowl in the microwave in 10-second bursts until it melts.

5. Make a well in the center of the dry ingredients, then pour the wet ingredients into it. With a spatula or wooden spoon, stir gently, folding the ingredients together just until combined and the flour disappears. The batter will be thick and shaggy.

6. Scoop the batter evenly among the prepared muffin cups (the cups will be quite full). Bake for 23 to 26 minutes, until a toothpick inserted in the center

recipe and ingredients continue

For the Glaze and Topping

¾ cup powdered sugar

2 tablespoons pineapple juice (from the cans above)

½ teaspoon pure vanilla extract

⅓ cup sweetened flake coconut

of a muffin comes out clean. Remove the muffins from the oven and place the pan on a wire rack. Let cool for 5 minutes in the pan, then use a fork or butter knife to carefully lift the muffins out of the pan and place them on the rack to cool completely (removing the muffins promptly after 5 minutes keeps them from becoming soggy).

7. Meanwhile, make the glaze and topping: In a small bowl, whisk together the powdered sugar, reserved pineapple juice, and vanilla. Place the coconut in an even layer in a small, dry skillet and heat over medium-low heat. Continually stir and fold over the coconut in the pan so it cooks evenly, until the coconut is a light, toasty brown and your kitchen smells amazing, 3 to 5 minutes. Transfer the coconut immediately to a plate. Note the total time to toast the coconut will vary depending upon the sugar content of the coconut, as well as your pan and stove. Watch the pan carefully to prevent burning.

8. Once the muffins have cooled, dip the tops into the glaze to lightly coat, letting the excess drip away, then immediately sprinkle with toasted coconut. Let the glaze set for a few minutes, then enjoy.

pro tip

These muffins are super moist, so they are best stored in the refrigerator. You can also store them at room temperature in an airtight container lined with a paper towel for 1 to 2 days.

do ahead

For quick grab-and-go breakfasts, wrap and freeze the muffins individually. Pull one or two out of the freezer the night before and place in the refrigerator, then in the morning, a fresh, homemade breakfast awaits.

next level

Piña Colada Muffins: Add 2 tablespoons coconut rum and 1 teaspoon rum extract to the batter. Make the glaze with coconut rum instead of pineapple juice.

Macadamia Dreams: Fold ⅓ cup chopped toasted macadamia nuts into the batter with the coconut.

cranny apple oatmeal muffins

ACTIVE TIME:
25 minutes

TOTAL TIME:
50 minutes

YIELD:
12 muffins

⅔ cup unsweetened applesauce

⅓ cup honey

¼ cup packed light or dark brown sugar

2 large eggs

⅓ cup canola oil or very light olive oil

2 teaspoons pure vanilla extract

1¼ cups old-fashioned oats

1¼ cups white whole wheat flour or regular whole wheat flour

½ teaspoon baking soda

¼ teaspoon baking powder

1 teaspoon ground cinnamon

¾ teaspoon kosher salt

1 small sweet-crisp apple, such as Honeycrisp or Pink Lady, ¼ inch diced (about ¾ cup; peeling is optional)

¾ cup fresh or frozen cranberries (no need to thaw), or ½ cup dried cranberries

2 tablespoons turbinado, demerara, or similar coarse sugar, divided

I have a penchant for—forgive me, but there is no other way to say this—old-person breakfast cereals: Grape-Nuts, bran flakes, Cream of Wheat, and above all, oatmeal. Here, oats meet their highest calling in the form of homey, old-fashioned apple oatmeal muffins that have an endearing, doting "grandma" quality to them. With tart bursts of cranberries, a kiss of cinnamon, and wholesome ingredients, these moist, tender muffins are truly timeless.

1. Place a rack in the center of your oven and preheat to 350°F. Lightly coat a standard 12-cup muffin pan with nonstick spray.

2. In a large bowl, whisk together the applesauce, honey, brown sugar, eggs, oil, and vanilla until evenly combined.

3. In a separate medium bowl, whisk together the oats, flour, baking soda, baking powder, cinnamon, and salt. Fold in the diced apples.

4. Add the dry ingredients to the wet ingredients and stir just until combined. Gently fold in the cranberries.

5. Scoop the batter evenly among the prepared muffin cups, filling each almost to the top. Sprinkle the turbinado sugar over the top (use about ½ teaspoon sugar per muffin). Bake for 22 to 24 minutes, until a toothpick inserted into the center of a muffin comes out clean. Place the pan on a wire rack. Let cool for 5 minutes in the pan, then use a fork or butter knife to carefully lift the muffins out of the pan and place them on the rack. Let cool completely . . . or for as long as you can stand the suspense.

pro tip

These moist little muffins will last at room temperature for 2 days and a bit longer in the refrigerator. Line the bottom of your storage container with a paper towel to absorb excess moisture.

cinnamon swirl
pumpkin banana bread

ACTIVE TIME:

30 minutes

TOTAL TIME:

2 hours

YIELD:

One 8½ by 4½-inch loaf (about 10 slices)

For the Pumpkin Banana Bread

2 large very ripe bananas, enough to yield 1 cup mashed

4 tablespoons (½ stick) unsalted butter, melted and cooled

¼ cup granulated sugar

⅓ cup honey

1 cup pure pumpkin puree (not pumpkin pie filling)

2 tablespoons nonfat plain Greek yogurt

2 large eggs, at room temperature

2 teaspoons pure vanilla extract

1 teaspoon ground cinnamon

¼ teaspoon ground nutmeg

⅛ teaspoon ground cloves

1 teaspoon baking soda

¼ teaspoon baking powder

½ teaspoon kosher salt

1½ cups white whole wheat flour, or a 50-50 blend of regular whole wheat flour and all-purpose flour

Here to relieve us of the near-impossible task of narrowing our breakfast baking ambitions to just one treat when there are so many tantalizing options is a marvelous one-bowl mashup: pumpkin banana bread! Mashed bananas add sweetness and fruitiness, pumpkin and its accompanying spice brigade make it taste cozy and snug, and the ribbon of cinnamon and sugar through the middle is reason enough to double the recipe. This is one of those breads you sneak slices of every time you walk through the kitchen. If you can resist sampling right away, this bread tastes even better after being refrigerated overnight, when the flavors have had time to get friendly.

1. Place a rack in the center of your oven and preheat to 325°F. Lightly coat an 8½ by 4½-inch loaf pan with nonstick spray.

2. Make the batter: In the bowl of a stand mixer fitted with the paddle attachment or in a large bowl with a hand mixer, mash the bananas (the mixer makes this quick and easy). Check the amount of mashed banana and adjust so that you have 1 cup in the bowl (save any extra for a smoothie; if you are a little bit short, top off the cup with additional pumpkin puree or Greek yogurt). Add the butter and sugar and beat on medium speed until smoothly combined. Beat in the honey, pumpkin, yogurt, eggs, and vanilla.

3. Sprinkle the cinnamon, nutmeg, cloves, baking soda, baking powder, and salt as

evenly as you can over the top. Sprinkle on the flour. With a rubber spatula or wooden spoon, stir gently to combine, just until the flour disappears.

4. Make the swirl: In a small bowl, stir together the sugar and cinnamon.

5. Scrape half of the batter into the prepared pan and spread into an even layer. Reserve 1½ tablespoons of the cinnamon-sugar mixture for the top, then sprinkle the rest evenly over the batter. With a small spoon, dollop the remaining batter over the top, then spread into an even layer. Sprinkle on the reserved cinnamon sugar.

6. Create the swirl: With a knife, start at one short

recipe and ingredients continue

For the Cinnamon Swirl

⅓ cup granulated sugar

2 teaspoons ground cinnamon

end of the pan and drag the knife through the batter in a continuous back-and-forth S motion. Be sure the knife goes nearly to the bottom of the pan; don't overswirl or you will mix the layers too much—five or six curves should do it. Go for it, then let it be.

7. Bake the bread for 30 minutes, then loosely tent the pan with foil. Continue baking for 30 to 40 additional minutes (1 hour to 1 hour 10 minutes total), until a toothpick inserted in the center comes out clean (the bread should register 195° to 205°F on an instant-read thermometer). Place the pan on a wire rack and let cool completely in the pan before unmolding and slicing. Devour!

pro tips

If you can handle the torture, after the loaf cools, refrigerate it for at least 1 hour before slicing. The banana flavor will come through a bit more, and resting makes the loaf extra moist and springy.

This bread recipe works well when doubled. For the pumpkin, use the full 15-ounce can. It will be a scant 1 cup of pumpkin puree per loaf, but the recipe will turn out fine.

Store leftovers in the refrigerator for up to 5 days or freeze for up to 3 months. I like to cut the cooled bread into slices, then wrap and freeze them individually for grab-and-go breakfasts. Do not store this bread at room temperature, as it will soften too much.

speed it up

Swap the cinnamon, nutmeg, and cloves in the batter for 1½ teaspoons pumpkin pie spice.

variation

Frosted Cinnamon Swirl Bread: In a small bowl, whisk together ⅔ cup powdered sugar, 1 tablespoon milk of choice, and ½ teaspoon pure vanilla extract until smooth. Adjust the consistency by adding more powdered sugar 1 tablespoon at a time or more milk 1 teaspoon at a time, until the glaze is thick but pourable. Drizzle over the top of the cooled bread.

banana crunch pancakes with peanut butter drizzle

ACTIVE TIME:
35 minutes

TOTAL TIME:
35 minutes

YIELD:
Eight 5-inch pancakes (serves 3 to 4)

For the Pancakes

¾ cup nonfat milk or milk of choice

1 teaspoon white vinegar, apple cider vinegar, or lemon juice

¾ cup white whole wheat flour, or a 50-50 blend of regular whole wheat flour and all-purpose flour

¼ cup old-fashioned oats

1 tablespoon baking powder

½ teaspoon ground cinnamon

¼ teaspoon kosher salt

3 to 4 ripe medium bananas

2 large eggs

2 tablespoons pure maple syrup or honey

2 tablespoons canola oil, or melted, cooled unsalted butter or coconut oil

Some of my best childhood memories are of spending occasional weekends in Kansas City with my Cool Aunt Roxanne. In addition to having a refrigerator stocked with flavored sodas and a swimming pool (heaven!), she always took us out for breakfast at a neighborhood café and ordered a stack of banana crunch pancakes to share with the table. A handful of granola in the batter gave them pleasing bits of texture to contrast the melt-in-your-mouth, buttery pancake. Banana slices, warm and lightly caramelized from the skillet, sealed the deal. I'm sharing this recipe (with the personal addition of a peanut-butter drizzle) in memory of my aunt. I now love to make these for my nieces, and I hope I can be as cool an aunt in their eyes as Aunt Roxanne was in mine.

1. If you'd like to keep the pancakes warm between batches, place a rack in the center of your oven and preheat to 200°F. Set a wire rack on top of a baking sheet, then place it in the oven. In a liquid measuring cup with a spout, combine the milk and vinegar. Let sit for 5 minutes (this clabbers the milk and creates a homemade "buttermilk"; if you have buttermilk on hand, feel free to use it here instead).

2. In a large bowl, whisk together the flour, oats, baking powder, cinnamon, and salt.

3. In a medium bowl, mash the ripest of the bananas (you should have a scant ½ cup once mashed—double-check if you aren't sure). Slice the remaining

bananas into thin (about ⅛-inch) coins and keep near the stove.

4. Into the mashed banana, whisk the eggs, maple syrup, and oil. Whisk in the milk until well combined. Make a well in the center of the dry ingredients, then carefully pour in the wet ingredients. With a spatula or wooden spoon, stir very gently to combine, stopping as soon as the dry bits of flour disappear. The batter will look lumpy. Gently stir in the granola and pecans—don't overmix! Let the batter rest 10 minutes while you prepare the peanut butter drizzle and preheat the skillet.

5. Make the peanut butter drizzle: In a small saucepan, warm the peanut butter, maple

recipe and ingredients continue

⅓ cup prepared granola, plus additional for serving (suggested: Ridiculously Addictive Maple Quinoa Granola from *The Well Plated Cookbook*, page 26)

3 tablespoons chopped pecans, sliced almonds, or additional granola

Butter or oil, for cooking the pancakes

For the Peanut Butter Drizzle

¼ cup creamy peanut butter

3 tablespoons pure maple syrup or honey

1 tablespoon unsalted butter

2 tablespoons nonfat milk or milk of choice, plus additional as needed

syrup, and butter over medium heat. As soon as it starts to bubble at the edges, remove from the heat and whisk in the milk until smooth. If the mixture is thicker than you would like, whisk in a little more milk until it reaches your desired consistency.

6. To cook the pancakes, heat a cast-iron skillet, nonstick skillet, or electric griddle over medium-low heat, until warmed enough for a drop of water to dance on the surface. If using anything other than a nonstick surface, add a little oil or butter to the pan to prevent the pancakes from sticking (most nonstick surfaces won't need oiling, but you can use it if you like). With a measuring cup, scoop the pancake batter by ⅓ cupfuls into the skillet, leaving 1 to 2 inches between each pancake for expansion. Immediately arrange 4 to 5 banana slices per pancake on top of the batter.

7. Let the pancakes cook on the first side until the edges look matte and dry and small bubbles appear on the top, 3 to 4 minutes. Carefully flip and cook until golden on the other side, 1 to 2 minutes more. Repeat with the rest of the batter, adjusting the heat and adding more butter or oil as needed so that the pancakes cook through and turn golden on the outside but do not burn or stick.

8. Serve the pancakes immediately or transfer them to the baking sheet in the oven to keep warm while you prepare the remaining batches. Rewarm the peanut butter drizzle with a little extra milk whisked in to thin it out as needed (the sauce will have thickened somewhat). Serve the pancakes hot, topped with the peanut butter drizzle, the remaining banana slices, and an extra sprinkle of granola.

do ahead

Make a double batch of these beauties, then keep the extras on hand in the freezer. Lay the pancakes in a single layer on a parchment-lined baking sheet, then place in the freezer. Once the pancakes are frozen, transfer them to a ziptop bag and store for up to 2 months. (Do not put unfrozen pancakes in a ziptop bag without first freezing them flat or they will turn into a frozen blob.) To reheat, lightly defrost the pancakes for about 30 seconds in the microwave, then pop them into the toaster for a lightly crisp exterior, or recrisp in a nonstick skillet.

lemon poppy seed pancakes with blueberry ginger sauce

ACTIVE TIME:
35 minutes

TOTAL TIME:
35 minutes

YIELD:
Sixteen 4-inch pancakes (serves 4 to 6)

For the Pancakes

2 tablespoons unsalted butter

1 cup white whole wheat flour or regular whole wheat flour

1 cup all-purpose flour

3 tablespoons granulated sugar

2 teaspoons baking powder

½ teaspoon baking soda

½ teaspoon kosher salt

2 cups low-fat buttermilk (see Pro Tip)

2 large eggs

¼ cup nonfat plain Greek yogurt

1 tablespoon poppy seeds

1 teaspoon pure vanilla extract

2 medium lemons

Nonstick spray, canola oil, or butter, for cooking

Every time I go out for brunch at Café at the Plaza, a gem of a neighborhood diner, I tell myself I am going to order something other than the lemon poppy seed pancakes with blueberry ginger syrup . . . and then I proceed to order, well, you know. They are not to be resisted! This recipe is my homage, made over with a few nutritious swaps like whole wheat flour and Greek yogurt. In place of syrup, I opt for a chunky, whole-blueberry sauce with the same gingery spice. It's a surprising and scrumptious contrast to the bright, lemony cloud of pancakes underneath.

1. In a small microwave-safe bowl, melt the butter in the microwave on medium power (alternatively, you can melt it in a small saucepan on the stove). Set aside to cool.

2. In a medium bowl, whisk together the white whole wheat flour, all-purpose flour, sugar, baking powder, baking soda, and salt. To a second medium bowl, add the buttermilk, eggs, yogurt, poppy seeds, vanilla, and cooled melted butter. Zest the lemons directly over the bowl, then halve one of the lemons and squeeze in 2 tablespoons juice. Whisk until well combined.

3. Make a well in the center of the dry ingredients, then pour in the wet ingredients, scraping the wet ingredient bowl with a rubber spatula to catch all the poppy seeds. With a spatula or wooden spoon, stir very gently until just combined (the batter will look quite lumpy and may even have a few stray specks of flour). Do not overmix. Let rest for at least 10 minutes or refrigerate overnight.

4. Make the blueberry ginger sauce: In a small saucepan over medium-high heat, stir together the blueberries, water, maple syrup, lemon juice, and ginger. Bring to a rapid simmer. Continue to simmer (the sauce will be very foamy), stirring every few minutes, until the blueberries have softened and collapsed and the sauce has thickened, 5 to 10 minutes. Remove from the heat and stir in the vanilla. Set aside to cool while you cook the pancakes. The sauce will continue to thicken as it rests.

recipe and ingredients continue

For the Blueberry Ginger Sauce

2 cups fresh or frozen blueberries (no need to thaw)

¼ cup water

¼ cup pure maple syrup

1 tablespoon freshly squeezed lemon juice (from the lemons above)

1 tablespoon grated fresh ginger (from about a 1-inch piece)

1 teaspoon pure vanilla extract

5. To keep the pancakes warm between batches, place a rack in the center of your oven and preheat to 200°F. Set a wire rack on top of a baking sheet, then place it in the oven. To cook the pancakes, heat a cast-iron skillet, nonstick skillet, or electric griddle over medium heat, until warmed enough for a drop of water to dance on the surface. Brush the surface lightly with oil, coat with nonstick spray, or add a little butter and let it melt (if you have a nonstick surface, you may not need any coating).

6. With a measuring cup, scoop the batter by ¼ cupfuls onto the heated surface, leaving 2 inches around the pancakes for them to expand. Cook on the first side until the edges look matte and set and the bubbles that form on the surface begin to break, about 5 minutes. Flip and cook on the second side until golden brown and the pancakes are cooked through, about 2 minutes more. Repeat with the remaining batter, adjusting the heat as needed so the pancakes cook through and turn golden on the outside but do not burn or stick. Serve immediately, topped with the blueberry ginger sauce, or transfer them to the baking sheet in the oven to keep warm while you prepare the remaining batches.

pro tip

While I am all for streamlining ingredients and avoiding an extra purchase whenever possible, actual buttermilk is critical in this recipe. While the milk plus lemon juice or vinegar trick (also called "clabbered milk") can work acceptably in some recipes, here you truly do need the real deal to make buttery and complex, not-too-thin pancakes. Buttermilk can last for weeks (and weeks) in the refrigerator, so go ahead and purchase a carton. These pancakes are worth it (and you can use the extra to make Banana Crunch Pancakes, page 59, too)!

speed it up

Grating or mincing fresh ginger is one of the more tedious kitchen tasks. Save time by purchasing fresh ginger paste in a tube. It's usually sold near the fresh herbs in most grocery stores. It can also be purchased in small frozen cubes that you can add directly to the sauce.

do ahead

Make the blueberry ginger sauce up to 3 days ahead. Rewarm gently on the stove with a little water to thin it out as needed. The pancake batter can be made the night before, then covered and kept in the refrigerator.

variations

World's Best Buttermilk Pancakes: Omit the lemon zest and poppy seeds. You now have the perfect pancake recipe.

Cinnamon Chocolate Chip Pancakes: Omit the lemon and poppy seeds; add 2 teaspoons cinnamon to the dry ingredients. Gently fold in 1 cup dark chocolate chips after combining the wet and dry ingredients.

Lemon Raspberry Pancakes: Omit the poppy seeds; gently fold 1 cup fresh or frozen raspberries into the batter (if using frozen, no need to thaw them).

Double Lemon Pancakes: Instead of using the blueberry ginger sauce, drizzle your pancakes with a quick lemon glaze. To make the glaze, whisk together the zest of 1 lemon, ¼ cup freshly squeezed lemon juice, and 1 cup plus 2 tablespoons powdered sugar until smooth. Add more powdered sugar or a little milk as needed to reach your desired consistency.

spicy tomato
and olive oil
burrata page 89

appetizers
munching
with friends

Whether you called neighbors over to your patio for an impromptu gathering because it's a beautiful day and you bought rosé (YOLO!), you're hosting a planned event, or you invited friends over for dinner that is (*oops!*) two hours behind schedule and everyone is starving, appetizers are a great idea. After all, who doesn't want to eat delicious food before more delicious food?

As a ~~notoriously ever-running-behind~~ spontaneous hostess, I packed this chapter full of my favorite kind of appetizers: the ones you can whip up on a moment's notice but that still feel elevated. Every one of these recipes contains a wow factor—whether it's an unusual flavor combination (Baked Brie with Balsamic Jalapeño Strawberries, page 70), moment of texture (Hot Honey Pistachio Ricotta Toasts, page 80), or simple showcasing of phenomenal ingredients (Spicy Tomato and Olive Oil Burrata, page 89). All hit the mark and exactly none of them are complicated. Those recipes that do take a little more time (Puff Pastry Cubano Bites, page 85) can be made 100 percent in advance.

And of course, what would a fabulous collection of appetizers be without a cocktail (or three) to wash them down? (Check out the Clarke House Cocktails, page 75.)

I can hear you now: *Oh, this old thing? It was easy!* Share these bites as everyone hangs, relaxes, and converses more freely. **Every day.**

baked brie with balsamic jalapeño strawberries

ACTIVE TIME:
15 minutes

TOTAL TIME:
30 minutes

YIELD:
Serves 8

1 cup diced strawberries (about ½ pint)

1 small jalapeño, seeded and finely chopped (about 1½ tablespoons)

3 tablespoons chopped fresh cilantro or basil, plus additional for serving

1 tablespoon honey

2 teaspoons balsamic vinegar

1 teaspoon kosher salt, plus additional to taste

¼ teaspoon ground black pepper, plus additional to taste

1 (8-ounce) wheel Brie cheese (never use low-fat Brie; you'll regret it)

2 tablespoons toasted sliced or slivered almonds

Crackers or toasted baguette slices, for serving (see Pro Tip)

do ahead

Make the strawberry mixture up to 1 day in advance and keep refrigerated.

This unlikely combination hails from Scottsdale, Arizona, where I first confirmed one of life's unassailable truths: if you go out for appetizers and cocktails, no matter how noble your intentions or how copious the leftovers in your refrigerator, you will, inevitably, end up staying for dinner. After tasting a restaurant's Brie and jalapeño bruschetta (and *fine*, a G&T or two), I knew we were staying for a full meal; if a restaurant could come up with something this creative and delicious, I needed to try more. This twist on baked Brie is creamy and indulgent to be sure (as any oozing wheel of cheese should be), but the juicy, punchy balsamic strawberries and subtle heat from the jalapeños give it a vibrancy and freshness that makes it appropriate at gatherings year-round, from summer picnics to holiday soirees. Go ahead, stay for dinner.

1. Place a rack in the center of your oven and preheat to 350°F. Line a baking sheet with parchment paper.

2. While the oven preheats, in a medium bowl, stir together the strawberries, jalapeño, cilantro, honey, vinegar, salt, and pepper. Let sit at least 15 minutes.

3. Place the Brie on the prepared baking sheet. Bake for 8 to 10 minutes, until the Brie is softened but not completely oozing. Transfer to a serving plate. Spoon the strawberry mixture over the top, along with some of the juices (you want the Brie to have a nice coating of the juice but not be drowning in it). Sprinkle with the almonds and garnish with a handful of additional fresh cilantro, salt, and pepper to taste.

pro tip

To toast baguette slices, preheat your oven to 400°F. Brush both sides of the slices lightly with olive oil, then place in a single layer on an ungreased rimmed baking sheet. Bake for 5 minutes, flip, then continue baking until lightly golden, 5 to 6 additional minutes. Let cool.

speed it up

No time to bake the Brie? Skip it! The strawberry mix is delicious spooned over room-temperature Brie too.

goat cheese log, 3 ways

ACTIVE TIME:
5 minutes

TOTAL TIME:
25 minutes

YIELD:
Serves 4 to 6

Variation 1: honey nut

1 (4-ounce) log goat cheese

⅓ cup raw pecans, walnuts, or pistachios

1 tablespoon honey

Flaky sea salt, such as Maldon or fleur de sel

Ground black pepper

Variation 2: cranberry cinnamon

1 (4-ounce) log goat cheese

¼ cup dried cranberries

¼ teaspoon ground cinnamon

⅛ teaspoon dried thyme

Variation 3: all the herbs

1 (4-ounce) log goat cheese

2 tablespoons minced mixed fresh, tender herbs, such as parsley, thyme, dill, chives, basil, or tarragon (I like chives mixed with 2 others), plus additional for the plate

For Serving

Crackers or toasted baguette slices (see Pro Tip, page 70)

Everyone needs an emergency appetizer—the one you always have the ingredients for, can make in your sleep, and that hardly needs a recipe. Fancied-up goat cheese is mine. Keep a log (or three—they last awhile) in your refrigerator, and with a little pantry creativity, you are no more than a few minutes away from landing a stellar appetizer on the plate. With its mildly tangy flavor and smooth, creamy texture, goat cheese lends itself well to both sweet and savory additions. Below are three of my go-tos. Use them as a starting point for your own delicious experimentation.

For All Versions: If time allows, place the goat cheese log in the freezer for 5 to 10 minutes (it is easier to roll when it is cold). Roll in your toppings of choice, pressing gently to adhere (see following instructions for each variation). Really coat all the outsides, including the ends of the log. Transfer to a serving plate. Let stand at room temperature for at least 20 minutes prior to serving.

For Honey Nut: Preheat your oven to 350°F and spread the nuts onto a baking sheet. Bake for 8 to 10 minutes, until they smell fragrant, super toasty, and delicious. Watch carefully! Nuts love to burn at the last moment. Chop as finely as possible, then spread them into an even layer on the cutting board. Roll the goat cheese in the nuts and transfer to a serving plate. Drizzle with the honey and sprinkle generously with flaky salt and pepper.

For Cranberry Cinnamon: Spread the cranberries on a cutting board. Sprinkle with the cinnamon and thyme, then very finely chop so that the cranberries are in small pieces and the cinnamon and thyme are incorporated throughout. Roll the goat cheese in the cranberry mixture, using your fingers to press it into the cheese as needed; this version is a little more hands-on. Transfer to the serving plate.

For All the Herbs: Use your fingers to toss the minced herbs together on the cutting board so you have an even mix. Roll the goat cheese in the herbs. If desired, garnish the serving plate with a sprinkle of additional herbs or whole herb sprigs.

recipe continues

speed it up

Honey Nut: Omit the nuts and drizzle a goat cheese log with honey (or hot honey if you have it!) and a pinch of flaky sea salt. Simple and perfect.

Cinnamon Cranberry: Mix ¼ cup whole cranberry sauce from a can with a few teaspoons of honey, a pinch of cinnamon, and orange zest to taste. Spoon over the goat cheese log.

All the Herbs: Replace the fresh herbs with 1½ tablespoons dried herbs de Provence.

leftover love

In the unlikely event you don't demolish the entire log of goat cheese, crumble the leftovers over your next salad for an instant upgrade.

10 no-cook cheese board ideas

Keep a few of these items on hand and you'll be ready to throw down a cheese board on demand.

1. Cured salami (this can last in your refrigerator pretty much indefinitely)

2. Marcona almonds (the rosemary sea salt ones from Trader Joe's are especially good)

3. Marinated artichokes

4. Truffle potato chips (decidedly excellent paired with the Clarke House Cocktails, page 75)

5. Kettle corn

6. Fancy tinned fish

7. Dark chocolate

8. Fig jam

9. Italian-style breadsticks

10. Parmesan, broken into shards (another lasts-forever refrigerator staple)

clarke house cocktails

Like any true home project, our backyard patio renovation wrapped up two months behind schedule. Since that's also the approximate length of patio season in Wisconsin, for the few remaining weeks we had left to use it, we went big, hosting friends for al fresco happy hours several nights a week. Guests were welcomed with a spread of easy appetizers (see Goat Cheese Log, 3 Ways, page 73) and the Chateau Clarke house cocktail menu: a list of cocktails I love to make and that (as it turns out) my friends *really* love to drink. Here are three of the greatest hits.

The 75 and gimlet both use simple syrup, so you have twice as many reasons to make it. They are ultra refreshing (and deceptively strong). For both cocktails I recommend a lighter, more cucumber-forward gin, such as Hendrick's, versus a more piney London dry gin like Tanqueray, which can overpower the basil.

The old fashioned, named for our dog, Teddy, swaps maple syrup for the sugar used in the usual recipe for a warm, slightly smoky twist. It will make you want to cozy up in front of a fire, one of Teddy's favorite pastimes.

erin's basil 75

ACTIVE TIME:
5 minutes

TOTAL TIME:
5 minutes

YIELD:
1 drink

8 fresh basil leaves, plus 1 large leaf for garnish

½ ounce freshly squeezed lemon juice

Ice

½ ounce Simple Syrup (page 76)

1½ ounces gin

2 to 3 ounces brut sparkling wine

1. In a cocktail shaker, place the 8 basil leaves and lemon juice. With a muddler or the handle of a wooden spoon, muddle the leaves very thoroughly to ensure the leaves release their oils. Fill the shaker with ice, then add the simple syrup and gin. Cover and shake vigorously for 20 seconds. Strain into a champagne flute. Top with sparkling wine.

2. To garnish, hold one hand near the top of the glass and with the other hand, smack the large basil leaf against it a few times so you are hitting the leaf right over the top of the glass (this releases the aromatics). Drop the leaf into the glass. *Santé!*

make a batch

Yields 8 drinks: In a pitcher, whisk together ½ cup freshly squeezed lemon juice, ½ cup simple syrup, and 1½ cups gin. Stir briskly to combine, cover, and refrigerate for up to 4 hours. For each drink, measure 2½ ounces into a cocktail shaker. Muddle with basil leaves and shake (most shakers will fit about 3 drinks' worth at a time). Strain into glasses, top with sparkling wine, and garnish as directed.

recipe continues

ben's basil gimlet

ACTIVE TIME:
5 minutes

TOTAL TIME:
5 minutes

YIELD:
1 drink

8 fresh basil leaves,
plus 1 large leaf for garnish

½ ounce freshly squeezed
lime juice

Ice

½ ounce Simple Syrup
(below)

2 ounces gin

1. In a cocktail shaker, place the 8 basil leaves and lime juice. With a muddler or the handle of a wooden spoon, muddle the leaves very thoroughly to ensure the leaves release their oils. Fill the shaker with ice, then add the simple syrup and gin. Cover and shake vigorously for 20 seconds. Strain into a coupe glass.

make a batch

Yields 8 drinks: In a pitcher, briskly whisk together ½ cup freshly squeezed lime juice, ½ cup simple syrup, and 2 cups gin. Stir briskly to combine, cover, and refrigerate for up to 4 hours. For each drink, measure 3 ounces into a cocktail shaker. Muddle with basil leaves and shake (most shakers will fit about 3 drinks' worth at a time). Strain into glasses and garnish as directed.

2. To garnish, hold one hand near the top of a coupe glass and with the other hand, smack the large basil leaf against it a few times so you are hitting the leaf right over the top of the glass (this releases the aromatics). Drop the leaf into the glass. *Salud!*

simple syrup

YIELD: ABOUT ½ CUP (ENOUGH FOR 8 DRINKS)

¼ cup granulated sugar   ¼ cup water

In a small saucepan (or large microwave-safe liquid measuring cup with a spout), combine the sugar and water. Bring to a simmer over medium-high heat (or microwave in 30-second bursts), whisking periodically, until the sugar dissolves. Remove from the heat, transfer to a heat-safe container, and chill.

forgot to make your simple syrup ahead?

I've been there. Whip it up quickly in the microwave, fill the cocktail shaker with ice, then pour ½ ounce of the (still-warm) syrup over it. The ice will chill it enough. From there, make your cocktail as directed.

pro tip

If you are making only 1 to 2 drinks and don't want to open an entire bottle of bubbly, purchase mini-bottles (187 ml), each of which contains enough sparkling wine for 2 drinks.

pro tip

Up your home cocktail game by filling coupe glasses with ice cubes just before you shake the drinks. When the drinks are ready to pour, dump out the ice, then strain the cocktails into the nicely chilled glasses.

teddy's old fashioned

ACTIVE TIME:
5 minutes

TOTAL TIME:
5 minutes

YIELD:
1 drink

2 ounces bourbon
(I like Bulleit, Basil Hayden,
or Four Roses)

1 teaspoon pure maple
syrup

3 to 4 dashes Angostura
bitters

Ice, preferably a giant
cocktail ice cube

Orange peel

Luxardo cherry (optional,
if you're feeling fancy)

1. In a rocks glass, stir together the bourbon, maple syrup, and bitters. If you have a fancy cocktail spoon, this is an excellent opportunity to show it off.

2. Add the giant cocktail ice cube or a small handful of ice cubes. Stir the drink gently in a circular motion until the drink is very chilled, about 20 seconds (this dilution is part of the process and smooths out the drink). Twist the orange peel directly over the glass to release the aromatics, then drop it in. Garnish with the cherry (if using). Sip slowly and immediately.

make a batch

Yields 8 drinks: Add a handful of ice to a pitcher. Top with 2 cups bourbon, 2 tablespoons plus 2 teaspoons pure maple syrup, and 24 dashes of bitters. Stir briskly to combine. Refrigerate for up to 4 hours. Stir again just before serving. Pour into glasses with fresh ice, garnish, and enjoy.

hot honey pistachio ricotta toast

ACTIVE TIME:
15 minutes

TOTAL TIME:
25 minutes

YIELD:
8 toasts

¼ cup honey

½ teaspoon red pepper flakes

4 slices crusty whole wheat sourdough bread

1 cup part-skim ricotta cheese

1 small lemon

¼ teaspoon kosher salt

¼ cup salted roasted pistachios, chopped

Flaky sea salt, such as Maldon or fleur del sel

One of the by-products of my profession is that friends (and strangers on the internet) often reach out because "I had this thing at a restaurant and it was so good and do you think you can re-create it?" One such instance involved a "life-changing" pizza with ricotta, hot honey, and pistachios. I became obsessed with the idea, and this dead-simple, super-scrumptious appetizer is the result. Instead of making pizza dough, which takes time to proof and bake, I use a toasty slice of good sourdough as the vehicle for the creamy, spicy, sweet, and crunchy topping. I can't wait for you to try this life-changing recipe (and reach out with your verdict too!).

1. In a small microwave-safe bowl or liquid measuring cup with a spout, place the honey and red pepper flakes (make sure your bowl has plenty of room for the honey to bubble). Microwave on high power until the honey is hot and a little thin, about 30 seconds depending upon your microwave. Stir and let cool to room temperature; this will take 10 to 15 minutes, but you can speed it along in the refrigerator.

2. Toast the bread: Place a rack in the upper third of your oven and preheat to 400°F. Place the bread slices on an ungreased baking sheet. Bake until lightly toasted, about 6 minutes, flipping the slices once halfway through. You also can toast them in a regular toaster or toaster oven. Cut the slices in half crosswise.

3. In a small bowl, place the ricotta. Zest half of the lemon directly over the bowl (about a scant ½ teaspoon) and add the kosher salt, then whisk together until combined (save the remaining lemon for another use).

4. To assemble, spread each piece of toast with a generous layer of ricotta. Place on a serving platter. With a spoon, drizzle the slices with the hot honey. Sprinkle with the pistachios and finish with a pinch of flaky salt. Enjoy while the bread is still warm or at room temperature.

baked "fried" olives with creamy buffalo dip

ACTIVE TIME:
20 minutes

TOTAL TIME:
40 minutes

YIELD:
**Serves 6
(about 30 olives)**

I go to the state fair for two reasons: cute baby animals and fried olives. Salty, briny, and crunchy with a spicy cream cheese center, fried olives are . . . is *exquisite* too fine a word for food on a stick? No matter, you'll be too busy devouring them to debate it. This version is my baked spin. Since individually stuffing olives and then freezing them so the filling doesn't ooze out while they bake is more of a project than I'm typically up for, I serve these crispy delights with a side of a creamy Buffalo dip that achieves a similar spicy sensation.

For the Olives

1 (12-ounce) jar cheese-stuffed olives (about 7 ounces drained)

¼ cup white whole wheat flour or all-purpose flour

1 large egg

1 tablespoon water

⅓ cup panko bread crumbs

⅓ cup Italian-seasoned bread crumbs (whole wheat if possible)

½ teaspoon Italian seasoning

Nonstick spray, for cooking

For the Creamy Buffalo Dip

½ cup nonfat plain Greek yogurt

2 to 3 teaspoons hot sauce, such as Frank's RedHot, plus additional to taste

⅛ teaspoon garlic powder

1. Place a rack in the upper third of your oven and preheat to 425°F. Drain the olives and use paper towels or a clean kitchen towel to dry them as completely as possible.

2. Set up your work station: Place the flour in a shallow bowl (a pie dish works well). In a separate shallow bowl, whisk the egg and water until well combined. In a third shallow bowl, combine the panko, Italian bread crumbs, and Italian seasoning. Arrange the bowls in a line (flour, eggs, bread crumbs). Line a large rimmed baking sheet with parchment paper.

3. Working about 8 olives at a time, roll the olives in the flour to coat. Shake off any excess, roll them in the beaten egg, and then place them in the bowl with the bread crumbs. Toss to coat the olives on all sides. Place the breaded olives on the prepared baking sheet. Repeat with the remaining olives.

4. Generously coat the top of the olives with nonstick spray. Bake for 10 minutes, then remove from the oven, shake the pan gently to roll the olives around a little so they brown evenly, and coat with nonstick spray once more. Return to the oven and continue baking until the olives are deep golden brown, about 10 additional minutes, shaking the pan again partway through (no need to add more spray). Remove from the oven and let cool for several minutes (the olives are HOT right out of the oven).

recipe continues

5. Meanwhile, make the creamy buffalo dip: In a small bowl, whisk together the yogurt, hot sauce, and garlic powder. Taste and adjust the heat and garlic as desired. Serve with the fried olives.

make this recipe in an air fryer

Bread the olives as directed and preheat your air fryer to 400°F. Generously coat the basket with nonstick spray and add a single layer of olives, spacing them so that they do not touch. Coat the top of the olives with nonstick spray. Air fry for 5 minutes, then remove the basket and use tongs to flip them over. Continue to air fry for 2 to 3 minutes more, until golden brown. Repeat with the remaining batches.

next level

Rather than purchase prestuffed olives, you can go all out and stuff them yourself with your cheese of choice. To make your life easier, purchase the largest pitted olives possible (look for colossal olives). If using a harder cheese, such as Manchego, cut it into small rectangular pieces, then tuck one piece inside each olive. For soft cheeses, such as goat cheese or pimento cheese, use your fingers (think of it as messy fun!), or place the cheese inside a piping bag or ziptop bag with the corner cut, and squeeze the cheese into each olive. Freeze for 20 minutes prior to baking.

puff pastry cubano bites

ACTIVE TIME:
30 minutes

TOTAL TIME:
1 hour 15 minutes

YIELD:
24 bites

2 sheets (one 17.3-ounce box) frozen puff pastry, thawed overnight in the refrigerator (I like Pepperidge Farm)

¼ cup Dijon mustard, divided

1¼ cups shredded Swiss cheese (about 5 ounces), divided

24 small pickle chips

6 ounces finely shaved Black Forest deli ham, divided

1 large egg, beaten with 1 tablespoon water to create an egg wash

Kosher salt, or flaky sea salt, such as Maldon or fleur de sel

You didn't buy this book for a recipe for pigs in a blanket (check your crescent roll can for that), so I'm going to give you something even better: Cubano Bites, which are very similar in spirit but pack far more flavor. Golden, buttery dough wrapped around the classic components of a Cubano sandwich—ham, pickle, cheese, and mustard—they are a fun, yummy surprise. You can make them well in advance, freeze, and then bake them on demand. Get ready for an upgraded pig-out!

1. Line a rimmed baking sheet with parchment paper. Put a second sheet of parchment paper on your work surface and unfold the first sheet of puff pastry onto it. With a rolling pin (a wine bottle works in a pinch), roll the pastry into a 10 by 11-inch rectangle; lightly flour the rolling pin as needed to keep the pastry from sticking. Use the paper to rotate the pastry so one of the shorter sides is nearest to you, if it's not already.

2. With a pastry brush, brush 2 tablespoons of the mustard over the top of the pastry, leaving a thin unbrushed border at the bottom and top edges (the two shorter sides) and spreading it all the way to the right and left edges (the longer sides). Sprinkle with half of the cheese, scattering it evenly over the mustard. Then add half of the ham, tearing it into smaller pieces as needed to cover the mustard evenly. Keep the top and bottom borders uncovered.

3. With a sharp chef's knife or pizza cutter, slice the pastry in half lengthwise then crosswise to create four quarters. Cut each quarter lengthwise into thirds so you have three long, thin strips per quarter (12 strips total). Each strip should be about 1½ inches wide by 5½ inches long, with the short sides of the strips facing you. Choose a pickle chip from your jar that's about 1 inch wide, shake off any excess pickle juice, and lay it in the center of each strip.

4. To form the rolls, fold the mustard-covered short end of each strip (the short ends running across the center that do not have a clean border) up and over the pickle. Then, fold the other end of the strip (the one with the border) over the top of the first, pressing lightly to seal. Transfer the rolls to the prepared baking sheet, seam side down. Repeat with the second sheet of pastry and

recipe continues

remaining mustard, cheese, ham, and pickles. You will have 24 rolls total. Refrigerate for at least 15 minutes, or cover and refrigerate for up to 1 day.

5. When you're ready to bake, place a rack in the center of your oven and preheat to 400°F. Remove the rolls from the refrigerator. Immediately brush them lightly with the egg wash and sprinkle with a pinch of salt. Bake the rolls for 16 to 18 minutes, until the pastry is brown and crisp, rotating the pan 180 degrees halfway through (you'll see a little liquid leak out; that's the juice from the pickles, no need to worry). Let the bites cool for at least 10 minutes, then transfer them to a serving plate. Serve warm or at room temperature.

do ahead

Assemble the bites as directed, but do not add the egg wash or salt. Place on a parchment paper–lined baking sheet in the freezer until hardened, then transfer to an airtight bag. Freeze for up to 1 month. Bake directly from frozen, topping with the egg wash and salt just before placing the bites in the oven. Add a few extra minutes to the cook time as needed.

You can also freeze fully baked and cooled bites, then reheat them directly from frozen on a parchment paper–lined baking sheet at 375°F.

spicy tomato and olive oil burrata

ACTIVE TIME:
20 minutes

TOTAL TIME:
20 minutes

YIELD:
Serves 6

1 (8-ounce) ball burrata cheese

¼ teaspoon kosher salt, plus an additional pinch

¼ cup extra-virgin olive oil

10 ounces 1-inch-diced peak-season tomatoes, or 1 pint cherry tomatoes, halved (about 10 ounces or 2 cups)

3 garlic cloves, thinly sliced

½ teaspoon red pepper flakes, plus additional to taste

3 green onions, thinly sliced (about ½ cup), divided

1 loaf ciabatta bread or baguette, cut into ½-inch slices and toasted (see Pro Tip, page 70)

My friends call this "The Dip," even though it's not so much a dip as permission to shovel copious quantities of luscious burrata cheese into your mouth. Burrata is a plump shell of mozzarella wrapped around a mixture of fresh cheese and cream, and while I can't confirm this with absolute certainty, I have good reason to believe it's what the angels are eating in heaven. Topped off with tomatoes sizzled in olive oil with a pinch of red pepper flakes for heat, it's become a signature every time I host a gathering, particularly in the summer when tomatoes are at their most tantalizing. If it's not peak tomato season, use cherry tomatoes, which have good flavor year-round. Alleluia!

1. Place the burrata in the center of a shallow serving dish. Sprinkle with a pinch of salt.

2. Heat the oil in a medium skillet over medium heat. Add the tomatoes, garlic, and red pepper flakes. Reserve 1 tablespoon of the green onions for serving, then add the rest to the skillet. Stir to combine the ingredients, then let cook, stirring every so often, until the tomatoes break down and the mixture thickens, 8 to 10 minutes. Stir in ¼ teaspoon salt.

3. Spoon the warm tomato mixture over the burrata and drizzle it with every drop of the delicious pan oil. Sprinkle with the reserved green onions and a pinch of salt to taste. Enjoy immediately for a warm/cold effect, or cover and refrigerate for up to 1 day. Let come to near room temperature prior to serving (no need to reheat; the topping also tastes yummy when cool). If you desire more spice, add a small pinch or two of red pepper flakes to taste.

next level

For a warm burrata appetizer, use an ovenproof serving dish. Just before serving, pop the tomato-topped burrata into a 350°F oven for 1 to 2 minutes, until the burrata is warmed but not completely melted.

elaine's mexicorn dip

ACTIVE TIME:
15 minutes

TOTAL TIME:
2 hours 15 minutes

YIELD:
Serves 8

1 cup low-fat (or full-fat) plain Greek yogurt (do not use nonfat)

¾ cup olive oil mayonnaise

2 teaspoons chili powder

2 teaspoons garlic powder

2 teaspoons ground cumin

3 (11-ounce) cans Mexican-style corn (sometimes called fiesta corn), drained

4 cups shredded sharp cheddar cheese (about 1 pound)

6 green onions, sliced (about 1 cup)

1 medium-large jalapeño, seeded and chopped (3 tablespoons to ¼ cup)

Tabasco, Cholula, or similar hot sauce (optional for serving)

For serving: Fritos Scoops, tortilla chips, carrot sticks, sliced bell peppers, or cherry tomatoes

This saves-the-day appetizer takes all of 5 minutes to stir together, and guests go bonkers for it. A slimmed-down version of Mexican street corn dip (elote dip), it's creamy, cheesy, and as spicy as you care to make it. I learned this recipe from my sister Elaine, who has perfected it over years of serving it at tailgates. As she (and anyone who eats it) will attest, while you can serve it with a variety of dippers like tortilla chips or veggies, the only true nonnegotiable is Fritos Scoops. Trust us. We've tested extensively.

1. In a large bowl, stir together the yogurt, mayonnaise, chili powder, garlic powder, and cumin.

2. Stir in the corn, cheese, green onions, and jalapeño. Refrigerate for at least 2 hours prior to serving. Sprinkle with hot sauce if desired and serve with Fritos Scoops and other dippers of choice.

do ahead

This dip can be refrigerated overnight, so feel free to make it a day in advance. If you want any to last until the party, hide it from everyone in your home, including yourself.

mom's house pepper jelly cream cheese dip

ACTIVE TIME:
10 minutes

TOTAL TIME:
10 minutes

YIELD:
Serves 12

1 (8-ounce) block reduced-fat cream cheese, or Neufchâtel cheese, at room temperature

¾ cup low-fat plain Greek yogurt, ricotta cheese, or sour cream (whichever you have around)

3 green onions, thinly sliced (about ½ cup), divided

1 (10-ounce) jar hot pepper jelly, divided

½ teaspoon kosher salt

¼ teaspoon garlic powder

Buttery round crackers, such as Ritz, for serving

Of all the things I learned from my mother, dumping a jar of hot pepper jelly over a block of softened cream cheese and then serving it with crackers as an emergency appetizer turned out to be one of the most useful. (Mom, I'm not sure if that's what you were going for, but I appreciate it!) This recipe zhuzhes it up by mixing part of the jelly into the cream cheese with simple seasonings, then topping it off with more jelly and a flourish of green onion. You will be asked to bring this to every gathering.

1. In a medium bowl, place the cream cheese, yogurt, half of the green onion, 3 tablespoons of the jelly, the salt, and garlic powder. With a spoon or fork, stir to combine. Transfer to a shallow serving dish and spread into an even layer.

2. Spoon the remaining jelly on top and smooth it into an even layer. Sprinkle with the remaining green onions. Enjoy immediately with crackers, or refrigerate until ready to serve (let stand at room temperature for at least 15 minutes prior to serving).

speed it up

Go old school and serve this Mom's original way: place a brick of cream cheese in its block-form glory on a serving plate and let it come to room temperature. Top with a generous amount of hot pepper jelly. Sprinkle with green onions to make it fancy. To serve, use a spreading knife to smear it liberally over crackers.

next level

Top the finished dip with 2 slices cooked and crumbled bacon.

salads
salads with substance

kale salad with apples, pomegranate, and wild rice page 107

I legitimately love salads. Not "love them because they are good for you" love them, or "love them because I ate chips for dinner last night" love them, or even "I want to eat a giant cookie and this salad will give me permission" love them. (You should eat the cookie regardless, by the way.) I love them because a good salad is genuinely delicious. Be it bright and bracing, creamy and salty, or even carby and/or cheesy, a proper salad is perfectly satisfying.

My kind of salad has heartiness, freshness, creaminess, and crunch. Whether it's a knife-and-fork situation (Chipotle Steak Salad, page 119), the lunch I want all week (Cult Kale Peanut Chicken Salad, page 105), or the potluck superstar (Rainbow Sesame Pasta Salad, page 110, and Big Bean Salad, page 113), a good salad is more than an obligatory afterthought. The ones in this chapter are what salads should be **every day**: real-deal, well-rounded dishes worth craving.

kind-of cobb salad page 101

roasted brussels sprouts caesar salad

ACTIVE TIME:
30 minutes

TOTAL TIME:
30 minutes

YIELD:
Serves 4

For the Salad

1 pound Brussels sprouts, stems trimmed, brown outer leaves removed, and halved

1 tablespoon extra-virgin olive oil

½ teaspoon kosher salt, plus additional to taste

¼ teaspoon ground black pepper, plus a few additional grinds for serving

1 large or 2 small heads romaine lettuce, chopped into 1-inch pieces (about 6 cups)

4 tablespoons freshly grated Parmesan cheese (about ¾ ounce), divided

For the Parmesan Croutons

2 slices whole wheat sandwich bread or sourdough bread

2 teaspoons extra-virgin olive oil

1 tablespoon freshly grated Parmesan cheese

⅛ teaspoon ground black pepper

Caesar is the gateway salad. Creamy, garlicky Parmesan dressing with croutons, more Parm, and minimal lettuce? Well if *that's* a salad, sign us all up! Unfortunately, restaurant Caesars often disappoint with wimpy romaine that drowns in excessive dressing, robbing it of freshness and crunch. Not this one! Roasted Brussels sprouts give the salad needed green heft and hold up well to the umami-rich dressing. Serve this salad immediately after the Brussels sprouts are out of the oven for a tremendously satisfying warm/cold effect. Let the salad gates open.

1. Place a rack in the center of your oven and preheat to 400°F. Put the Brussels sprouts on a rimmed baking sheet, along with any green leaves that have come loose (these get deliciously dark and crispy). Drizzle with the oil and sprinkle with the salt and pepper. Toss until the Brussels sprouts are evenly coated, then spread into a single layer. For even better crisping, flip the Brussels sprouts so that they are all cut side down. Bake for 20 to 30 minutes, until the Brussels sprouts are lightly charred and crisp on the outside and tender in the center. The outer leaves will be very dark. Watch carefully toward the end, as the cooking time will vary based on the size of your sprouts.

2. While the Brussels sprouts roast, make the croutons: Heat a large skillet over medium heat. Tear the bread into rough ½-inch to 1-inch pieces directly over the skillet, spreading them into an even layer. Drizzle with the oil, stir immediately, and spread back into an even layer. Cook, stirring often, until the bread cubes are golden and toasted, 3 to 5 minutes. Watch carefully and adjust the heat as needed to ensure they do not burn. Remove from the heat. Stir in the Parmesan and pepper.

3. Make the dressing: In the bowl of a food processor, place the yogurt, Parmesan, oil, lemon juice, anchovy paste, mustard, and garlic. Process until smooth, scraping down the bowl as needed.

4. To assemble the salad, place the romaine in a large serving bowl and drizzle with enough of the dressing to moisten it well. Top with 2 tablespoons of the Parmesan, half of the warm roasted Brussels sprouts, and

recipe and ingredients continue

For the Dressing

¾ cup nonfat plain Greek yogurt

½ cup freshly grated Parmesan cheese (about 1 ½ ounces)

¼ cup extra-virgin olive oil

3 tablespoons freshly squeezed lemon juice

1½ teaspoons anchovy paste, or 2 anchovy fillets

1½ teaspoons Dijon mustard

1 large garlic clove, roughly chopped

half of the croutons. Toss to coat, adding more dressing as desired—the croutons will soak up a fair amount, so you may need to add more than you do typically. Taste and add several grinds of pepper and salt if needed. Place the remaining roasted sprouts on top (do not toss) and sprinkle with the remaining 2 tablespoons Parmesan and remaining croutons. Enjoy immediately, with more dressing added to individual servings as desired.

speed it up

Use store-bought Caesar dressing (I like Greek yogurt–based dressings that are sold in the refrigerated section).

do ahead

The dressing can be refrigerated in an airtight container for up to 1 week. Before using, taste and refresh it with an extra squeeze of lemon juice and pinch of salt as needed.

This salad tastes excellent on day 2. Perk it back up with a squeeze of lemon juice.

variation

Caesar-Roasted Brussels Sprouts: Double the Brussels sprouts, then toss lightly with the dressing, Parmesan, and croutons (omit the romaine). Serve warm as a side.

kind-of cobb salad

ACTIVE TIME:
1 hour

TOTAL TIME:
1 hour 10 minutes

YIELD:
Serves 4 to 5

For the Salad

2 medium boneless, skinless chicken breasts (about 1¼ pounds)

¾ teaspoon kosher salt, divided, plus additional to taste

¼ teaspoon ground black pepper, plus additional to taste

⅓ cup raw pecan halves

2 small-medium sweet potatoes (about 1¼ pounds), scrubbed and ¾ inch diced

2 tablespoons extra-virgin olive oil, divided

1 tablespoon low-sodium soy sauce

1½ teaspoons pure maple syrup

1½ teaspoons smoked paprika

4 large eggs

1 cup cherry or grape tomatoes, or diced tomatoes of choice

1 medium avocado

The first time I tasted Cobb salad was at the age of twenty-two, when my boss at my first big-time corporate job took me out for a "get to know you" lunch. Business lunches stress me out because I am never sure what to order—it can't be too expensive (filet makes it look like I'm mooching), too messy (ribs and business suits do not mix), or too coma inducing (the Alfredo will put me to sleep at my desk). My strategic move? Wait to see what the boss orders. Thank goodness she picked Cobb salad, because I've been smitten with it since!

A traditional Cobb salad is made with bacon, hard-boiled eggs, blue cheese, diced chicken, and avocado. Greens are present, but they are not the point. I call this Kind-Of Cobb Salad because it keeps the decadent feel and contrasting creamy and cool ingredients of the original but has a few healthy tweaks, the most controversial of which is to replace the bacon with sweet potatoes roasted with maple syrup and smoked paprika. It sounds a little wild, but go with it. The velvety interiors and crispy exteriors of the sweet potatoes are such a fantastic addition, you'll wonder why the Cobb's creator didn't include them in the first place. This salad has several steps, but it yields a generous amount and makes an impressive presentation. It's ideal for bringing to a party or for enjoying as a casual lunch with friends and a glass of crisp white wine. Be your own boss.

1. Place racks in the upper and lower thirds of your oven and preheat to 400°F. Line a baking dish or baking sheet large enough to hold the chicken in a single layer with parchment paper or aluminum foil. Pat the chicken dry, then place in the baking dish and sprinkle all over with ½ teaspoon of the salt and the pepper. Let sit at room temperature for 20 minutes.

2. Toast the pecans: Spread the pecans onto an ungreased rimmed baking sheet. Place in the oven and bake for 8 to 10 minutes, until fragrant and toasted, stirring once halfway through. Roughly chop and set aside.

3. Roast the sweet potatoes: Line a large rimmed baking sheet with parchment paper or foil. Place the sweet potatoes in the center. Top with 1 tablespoon of the oil, the soy sauce, maple syrup, smoked paprika, and remaining ¼ teaspoon salt. Toss to coat evenly, then spread into a

recipe and ingredients continue

1 head romaine lettuce, roughly chopped into bite-size pieces (about 4 cups)

3 cups baby arugula (about 3 ounces)

2 ounces goat cheese, or blue cheese or feta cheese, crumbled (about ⅓ cup)

For the Dressing

¼ cup freshly squeezed lemon juice (from about 1 medium lemon)

3 tablespoons extra-virgin olive oil

1 tablespoon Dijon mustard

½ teaspoon kosher salt

¼ teaspoon ground black pepper

speed it up

Replace the baked chicken breasts with shredded store-bought rotisserie chicken. Or use your favorite method to cook chicken breasts from *The Well Plated Cookbook*, page 161.

single layer. Bake on either rack for 25 to 30 minutes, until the sweet potatoes are caramelized on the outside and tender on the inside, turning once halfway through. Set aside.

4. Hard-boil the eggs: Bring a medium pot of salted water to a gentle boil. With a slotted spoon, slowly lower the eggs into the boiling water. Adjust the heat to maintain a gentle, steady simmer. Let the eggs simmer at this low boil for 8 minutes for slightly jammy yolks (or up to 9 minutes for fully set yolks). In the meantime, prepare a large ice bath. Use the slotted spoon to carefully transfer the boiled eggs into the ice bath. With the back of a spoon, gently crack each shell, then return the eggs to the water (this makes the eggs easier to peel). Peel and halve or thinly slice.

5. Once the chicken has rested 20 minutes, drizzle the top of it with the remaining 1 tablespoon oil and rub to coat. Place in the oven with the sweet potatoes. Bake for 12 to 16 minutes, until the chicken reaches 155°F on an instant-read thermometer. Transfer to a cutting board and let rest uncovered for at least 5 minutes (the chicken's

pro tip

If you plan to enjoy this salad left over (or prefer your salad more well dressed as opposed to the light dress this recipe yields), make one and a half or two times the dressing so you have extra on hand.

temperature will continue to rise as it rests). Dice.

6. Make the dressing: In a small bowl or liquid measuring cup with a spout, whisk together the lemon juice, oil, mustard, salt, and pepper.

7. Shortly before serving, slice the cherry tomatoes in half. Cut the avocado into ¾-inch dice.

8. Assemble the salad: On a *very* large serving platter, place the romaine and arugula. Drizzle lightly with some of the dressing, then toss to moisten and combine the greens evenly. Sprinkle with a little salt and pepper. Arrange the diced chicken down the center in a straight line. In rows, line egg slices on one side and sweet potatoes on the other. Place the avocado next to the sweet potato and the tomatoes next to the eggs. Sprinkle the goat cheese and pecans all over the top. Spoon on a little more dressing. Enjoy immediately, with additional dressing as desired. (You also can skip the fancy presentation—toss everything together in a giant bowl and have at it.)

cult kale peanut chicken salad

ACTIVE TIME: **35 minutes**

TOTAL TIME: **35 minutes**

YIELD: **Serves 4 to 6**

For the Salad

1 large bunch curly kale
or 2 medium bunches
lacinato kale, stemmed
(about 8 ounces)

3 cups shredded savoy
cabbage (about ½ small
head)

¼ teaspoon kosher salt

¾ cup dry-roasted
peanuts, finely chopped

⅓ cup roughly chopped
fresh mint leaves

⅓ cup chopped fresh
cilantro

3 green onions, thinly
sliced (about ½ cup)

Shredded meat from
1 small rotisserie chicken
(about 3 cups; see
Pro Tips)

For the Dressing

¼ cup plus 1 tablespoon
extra-virgin olive oil

3 tablespoons rice vinegar

2 tablespoons creamy
peanut butter, natural or
regular

2 teaspoons toasted
sesame oil

2 teaspoons Dijon mustard

1 teaspoon honey

¼ teaspoon kosher salt

⅛ teaspoon ground
cayenne pepper

I realize that the terms "freak out" and "salad" don't typically appear in the same sentence, but that is exactly what I did when I tasted the salad that inspired this recipe at a small lunch spot in Aspen, Colorado. I ordered it and a Bloody Mary, with the assumption that the latter would be the highlight (mistake—I was outside Wisconsin, and other states just don't do Bloodies properly; see Bloody Mary Tomato Salad on page 114). The salad was a symphony of freshness from mint, crunchiness from roasted peanuts, brightness from a peanut dressing, and satisfaction from juicy pieces of chicken, all while still feeling nourishing thanks to a generous amount of tender, finely chopped kale. Weeks later, I found myself missing it, so I pulled up the restaurant's menu online, wondering if I could find recipes with similar ingredients.

It turns out this particular salad, called the Emerald Kale Salad, shows up on menus all over the United States at restaurants owned by the same group, and judging by the number of articles written about it, it has a cult following. As with many restaurant dishes, the original has five thousand ingredients, so I've streamlined it for us here. I am happy to report that it is just as obsessively good as the original.

1. Slice the kale into thin ribbons, then chop into bite-size pieces. You should have about 8 cups of tightly packed kale total. Place in a large bowl. Add the cabbage and sprinkle with the salt. Grab the kale and cabbage by large handfuls and gently squeeze and massage the pieces, working a few handfuls at a time, until the kale is softened and dark green in color. The massage is key for tender, yummy greens.

2. Make the dressing: In a small bowl or liquid measuring cup with a spout, stir together the olive oil, vinegar, peanut butter, sesame oil, mustard, honey, salt, and cayenne until smooth.

3. Pour enough of the dressing over the kale mixture to moisten it, then stir to combine. Add the peanuts, mint, cilantro, green onions, and chicken. Add additional dressing, stirring as you go, until the salad is moistened to your liking. Enjoy immediately or refrigerate for up to 4 hours prior to serving.

recipe continues

to shred cabbage

With a sharp chef's knife, cut the cabbage into four wedges by slicing it in half from the top of the head through the stem, then slicing each half through the stem once more. Cut out the core. Turn each resulting quarter piece sideways, and slice into super-thin (⅛-inch) strips.

pro tips

If you'd like to cook and shred your own chicken breasts for the salad (versus using a rotisserie chicken), place 3 medium boneless, skinless chicken breasts in a wide saucepan, and sprinkle with salt and pepper. Cover with 1 inch of cool water. Bring to a simmer over medium to medium-high heat. Allow to gently simmer until the chicken reaches 155° to 160°F on an instant-read thermometer, 10 to 12 minutes. Transfer to a cutting board or bowl and let rest for 5 minutes before shredding. For even more tips, see *The Well Plated Cookbook* (page 161).

Store leftovers in the refrigerator for 3 to 4 days (kale salad lasts well, even when the dressing is already on it). If desired, top the leftovers with an extra drizzle of olive oil and touch of rice vinegar to perk them back up.

If you know you'll be serving this salad over multiple days, or if you like extra dressing in general, make one and a half to two times the dressing and refrigerate it in a mason jar or similar container with a tight-fitting lid for up to 2 weeks. Shake again before using.

kale salad with apples, pomegranate, and wild rice

ACTIVE TIME:
45 minutes

TOTAL TIME:
45 minutes

YIELD:
Serves 4 to 6

For the Salad

1 cup wild rice or a wild rice blend

1 cup roughly chopped raw pecans

1 large bunch curly kale, stemmed (about 8 ounces)

¼ teaspoon kosher salt, plus additional to taste

2 medium sweet-crisp apples, such as Honeycrisp or Fuji, ½ inch diced (about 2 cups)

1 cup pomegranate arils

2 green onions, thinly sliced (about ⅓ cup)

4 ounces crumbled goat cheese or feta cheese (about ½ cup)

For the Dressing

⅓ cup extra-virgin olive oil

2 tablespoons unsulfured molasses (not blackstrap)

2 tablespoons apple cider vinegar

¾ teaspoon kosher salt

½ teaspoon ground black pepper

This stunner of a salad refuses to be an afterthought. Ruby-red pomegranate and verdant green kale make it look ultra festive, the earthiness of wild rice and apple feels at home in the winter months, and the salad has enough elegance and substance to hold its own in a holiday spread. It lasts well in the refrigerator, making it an ideal make-ahead option for parties and meal prep alike. When you need a big green salad for an occasion—be it a fancy dinner party or Tuesday lunch—this one always delights.

1. Prepare the rice according to the package instructions. Fluff and set aside.

2. Toast the pecans: Place a rack in the center of your oven and preheat to 350°F. Spread the pecans in a single layer on an ungreased rimmed baking sheet. Bake for 6 to 8 minutes, until toasted and fragrant. Keep an eye on them; nuts love to burn! Transfer the nuts to a bowl or plate and set aside.

3. While the rice cooks, make the dressing: In a small bowl or liquid measuring cup with a spout, whisk together the oil, molasses, vinegar, salt, and pepper.

4. Slice the kale into thin ribbons, then chop into bite-size pieces. You should have about 8 cups of tightly packed kale total. Place in a large bowl and sprinkle with the salt. Grab the kale by large handfuls and gently squeeze and massage it, working a few handfuls at a time, until the kale is softened and dark green in color. Don't shortcut this step; the more you massage, the more tender and tasty the kale will be.

5. Transfer the rice to the bowl with the kale. Pour two-thirds of the dressing over the top. Add the apple, pomegranate arils, green onions, goat cheese, and pecans. Toss to coat, adding more of the dressing as needed so that everything has a light coating (you'll use most, if not all of it). Taste and season with a pinch or two of additional salt as desired. Enjoy immediately or refrigerate for up to 4 hours prior to serving.

recipe continues

Kale salad is dressing thirsty, so chances are you'll be adding more to this salad than you'd expect. If you plan to enjoy some of the salad as leftovers (and you should—it can save for several days!), make extra dressing to serve with it.

speed it up

Buy pomegranate arils to save yourself the trouble of seeding the pomegranate.

Use steam-in-the-bag microwave rice.

market swap

Replace the pomegranate arils with ½ cup dried cranberries.

how to seed a pomegranate

Theories abound as to the best way to remove the seeds (aka arils) from a pomegranate, and I have tried them all. This is my favorite: Roll the pomegranate on your cutting board to loosen the seeds. Lay it on its side on the cutting board and slice it in half crosswise. Hold one half upside down over a large bowl. With the back of a wooden spoon, whack the outside of the pomegranate all over to knock out the seeds (be careful not to hit your fingers). If there are any seeds that are stuck in the pomegranate, gently pull the pomegranate apart to loosen them. Repeat with the second half.

rainbow sesame pasta salad

ACTIVE TIME: **40 minutes**

TOTAL TIME: **40 minutes**

YIELD: **Serves 10**

A colorful array of crunchy veggies, protein-packed edamame, and al dente pasta in a nutty sesame-soy dressing makes this recipe everything a pasta salad should be (fresh, vibrant, memorable) and nothing that it shouldn't (mayo slicked, mushy, a forgettable waste of plate space). It's a lively, welcome addition to any potluck, where it stands out from the usual bland, goopy, white-dressing-ed suspects. It yields a large amount, making it perfect for a crowd. If you are lucky enough to have leftovers, they make a yummy lunch, with the optional addition of diced chicken or crispy tofu providing a protein boost.

For the Pasta Salad

8 ounces whole wheat rotini pasta or another short shape, such as bow tie or penne

¼ cup white sesame seeds, or a mix of white and black

1 (10-ounce) bag julienne-cut (matchstick) carrots (about 2 cups)

2 medium red bell peppers, ½ inch diced (about 2 cups)

1 small head broccoli, finely chopped (about 2 cups)

1 small bunch green onions, thinly sliced (about 1 cup)

1 cup shelled edamame, thawed if frozen

⅔ cup chopped fresh cilantro

½ teaspoon kosher salt

For the Dressing

3 tablespoons low-sodium soy sauce

3 tablespoons rice vinegar

2 tablespoons sesame oil, toasted or untoasted

2 tablespoons extra-virgin olive oil

2 tablespoons pure maple syrup or honey

2 tablespoons minced fresh ginger (about a 2-inch piece)

¼ teaspoon red pepper flakes

1. Bring a large pot of salted water to a boil. Cook the pasta to al dente according to the package instructions. Drain in a large colander, then rinse with cool water to stop the cooking. Shake the colander to remove as much excess water as possible, then place it over a bowl or towel to drain further while you prepare the rest of the salad.

2. While the pasta is cooking, toast the sesame seeds: Place the sesame seeds in a small dry skillet and heat over medium heat, stirring very frequently with a spatula to move and turn the seeds, until the seeds are beginning to turn golden and smell fragrant, 2 to 3 minutes. Immediately transfer to a bowl to prevent burning.

3. Make the dressing: In a small bowl or liquid measuring cup with a spout, whisk together the soy sauce, vinegar, sesame oil, olive oil, maple syrup, ginger, and red pepper flakes until combined.

4. Shake the pasta in the colander once more to get rid of any remaining water, then transfer it to a large serving bowl. Pour on a little of the dressing and toss to lightly moisten the noodles. Add the carrots, bell peppers, broccoli, green onions, edamame, cilantro, salt, and toasted sesame seeds. Drizzle on more of the dressing and stir, adding additional dressing until you are happy with it. Everything should have a light coating but should not seem soggy. Taste and adjust the seasoning as desired (you may want a dash or two more of soy sauce or a pinch of kosher salt depending upon how salty yours is). Refrigerate until ready to serve. Enjoy cold or at room temperature.

do ahead

The day before, chop all the vegetables and make the dressing; store separately in the refrigerator. Up to 4 hours before serving, fully assemble the salad, holding back some of the dressing. Stir in the remaining dressing to freshen it up just before serving.

big bean salad

ACTIVE TIME:
30 minutes

TOTAL TIME:
1 hour 30 minutes

YIELD:
Serves 6 to 8

For the Salad

½ small red onion, very thinly sliced

8 ounces fresh green beans, trimmed and cut into 1-inch pieces (about 2½ cups)

1 (15-ounce) can reduced-sodium black beans, rinsed and drained

1 (15-ounce) can reduced-sodium light or dark red kidney beans, rinsed and drained

1 (15-ounce) can hominy, rinsed and drained

2 celery stalks, thinly sliced (about 1 cup)

1 medium red bell pepper, ½ inch diced (about 1 cup)

½ teaspoon kosher salt

½ cup finely chopped fresh cilantro

For the Dressing

¼ cup extra-virgin olive oil

¼ cup red wine vinegar

¾ teaspoon kosher salt

½ teaspoon ground cumin

¼ teaspoon smoked paprika

Here is your side for when you have a big gathering, aren't sure what people like, and realize you could use something on your plate other than potato chips. My friend Melissa always brings a bean salad to our summer parties at the lake, because the kids and grown-ups both like it, because it's nice to ingest a vegetable in the midst of all the snacking, and (I suspect) because she has two very rambunctious little boys and can pull it together with them running laps around her kitchen. I took it in a slightly Tex-Mex direction with the addition of hominy, which adds surprise pops of creaminess, and a bright cumin vinaigrette. It's refreshing, crunchy, and just right for a lazy afternoon of relaxing and grazing.

1. Place the onion in a small bowl and cover with cold water. Let it soak while you prepare the rest of the salad (this keeps the flavor but mellows the onion's harsh, lingering bite).

2. Bring a large pot of salted water to a boil. Add the green beans and blanch until the pieces are bright green and crisp-tender, 2 to 3 minutes. Drain in a colander and immediately rinse with very cold water to stop the cooking. Spread onto a clean kitchen towel and pat dry.

3. Make the dressing: In a medium bowl or a liquid measuring cup with a spout, whisk together the oil, vinegar, salt, cumin, and smoked paprika.

4. In a large serving bowl, place the black beans, kidney beans, hominy, celery, bell pepper, salt, cilantro, and blanched green beans. Drain the onion, pat dry, and add to the bowl. Drizzle on the dressing, then stir to combine. Taste and add more salt and/or vinegar to taste. If time allows, refrigerate for 1 hour. Give it a big stir just before serving. Enjoy cold or at room temperature.

market swaps

While I like the texture and color contrast of lightly chewy hominy and creamy red kidney beans, feel free to use a different bean variety. White beans, such as cannellini or great northern, and black-eyed peas all work well in this recipe.

Instead of celery, use a different crunchy veggie, such as thinly sliced fennel, finely chopped cauliflower, or seeded and thinly sliced English cucumber.

bloody mary tomato salad

ACTIVE TIME:
25 minutes

TOTAL TIME:
25 minutes

YIELD:
Serves 4 to 6

For the Dressing

2 tablespoons extra-virgin olive oil

1 tablespoon minced shallot (about ½ small)

1 tablespoon freshly squeezed lemon juice

1 teaspoon Dijon mustard

1 teaspoon Worcestershire sauce

1 teaspoon hot sauce, such as Frank's RedHot

½ teaspoon celery salt

⅛ teaspoon kosher salt

For the Salad

1½ pounds mixed tomatoes, cored and cut into ¼-inch-thick slices (use a pretty mix of heirloom varieties for the most dramatic presentation)

½ cup green olives, such as Castelvetrano, pitted and halved

¼ cup shredded sharp white or yellow cheddar cheese (about 1 ounce)

½ cup chopped celery leaves (see Pro Tips)

4 slices bacon, cooked and crumbled (see Pro Tips)

Here in Wisconsin, a Bloody Mary isn't only a brunch beverage—it's a full-on meal. We pride ourselves on the garnishes, loading 'em up with cubes of cheese, salami, and sticks of bacon (if you order a pitcher at one local restaurant, it comes topped with a fried chicken!). This salad is a proper Bloody Mary, deconstructed and turned into a presentation-worthy dish. Juicy tomatoes, sharp, creamy cheddar cheese (bonus points if it's from Wisconsin!), crunchy bacon, and a pinch of celery salt in the dressing make this juicy, salty, tangy salad one to remember.

1. Make the dressing: In a small bowl or liquid measuring cup with a spout, whisk together the oil, shallot, lemon juice, mustard, Worcestershire, hot sauce, celery salt, and kosher salt. Taste and adjust the seasoning as desired; if you'd like it spicier, add more hot sauce or a little celery salt. For a zippier dressing, add more mustard.

2. Arrange the tomatoes on a large, shallow serving platter. Scatter the olives over the top.

3. Spoon the dressing over the tomatoes and olives. Sprinkle with the cheddar, celery leaves, and bacon. Serve immediately or refrigerate for up to 1 hour.

pro tips

Use the leftover celery stalks to make Fancy P(ants) on a Log Celery Salad (page 123). Or instead of celery leaves, use 1 to 2 tablespoons of chopped fresh flat-leaf parsley or chives.

To cook bacon quickly and easily, bake it: Preheat your oven to 400°F. Line a large rimmed baking sheet with aluminum foil. Arrange the bacon strips on the sheet so they are not touching. Bake until crisp, 10 to 12 minutes for thinner bacon or 16 to 20 minutes for thicker bacon. Transfer to a paper towel–lined plate.

next level

For the ultimate Bloody Mary experience, add 1 to 2 teaspoons vodka to the salad dressing.

market swaps

I prefer white cheddar for its look on the platter, but if you already have sharp yellow cheddar on hand, it will taste just as delicious.

peach and crispy prosciutto panzanella

ACTIVE TIME:
40 minutes

TOTAL TIME:
1 hour

YIELD:
Serves 8

For the Dressing

½ cup extra-virgin olive oil

⅓ cup champagne vinegar, or ¼ cup white wine vinegar

2 teaspoons honey

½ teaspoon kosher salt, plus additional for serving

¼ teaspoon ground black pepper, plus additional for serving

1 medium shallot, minced (about ¼ cup)

For the Salad

1 small or ½ large sourdough boule, or similar artisan bread (about 8 ounces), cut into ¾-inch cubes (about 6 cups)

4 ounces thinly sliced prosciutto

3 ripe medium peaches, thinly sliced (about 18 ounces or 3 cups sliced)

2 medium tomatoes, cored and cut into 1-inch cubes (about 12 ounces or scant 2 cups)

1 pint cherry tomatoes, halved (about 10 ounces or 2 cups)

Panzanella, a Tuscan bread salad consisting of cubes of stale bread, tomatoes, and onion in copious amounts of fruity olive oil, is like many classic Italian dishes—no one 100 percent agrees on how to make it, but regardless of whose version you try, it's probably going to be delicious. Panzanella celebrates summer at its most exemplary, especially this version which includes one of the season's most precious gifts: fresh peaches. Pearls of mozzarella cheese provide moments of lushness and are a classic match with tomato. The prosciutto adds salty notes to complement the sweet peach. While you don't *have* to crisp the prosciutto in the oven, once you taste how this easy step concentrates its flavor and provides necessary crunch, you'll be very glad you did.

1. Place racks in the center and upper third of your oven and preheat to 400°F.

2. Make the dressing: In a small bowl or large liquid measuring cup with a spout, whisk together the oil, vinegar, honey, salt, and pepper. Stir in the shallot. Let sit while you prepare the rest of the salad.

3. Dry out the bread (if your bread is already left over and dry, you can skip this step): Arrange the bread cubes on a large rimmed baking sheet in a single layer. Bake on the upper rack for 5 to 6 minutes, until lightly toasted and fairly dry to the touch. Set aside.

4. Crisp the prosciutto: On a parchment paper–lined baking sheet, arrange the prosciutto slices in a single layer. Place on the center rack and cook for 5 to 6 minutes, until crisp. Set aside.

5. Assemble the salad: In a very large bowl, place the peaches, cubed tomatoes, cherry tomatoes, cucumber, mozzarella, basil, mint, and bread cubes. Pour two-thirds of the dressing over the salad and stir gently to coat. Everything should be nicely moistened with the dressing and the peaches' and tomatoes' own juices. If the bread seems dry, add more dressing as needed. Refrigerate for at least 20 minutes to allow the bread to soften and the flavors to marry.

recipe and ingredients continue

1 English (hothouse)
cucumber, unpeeled,
halved lengthwise, seeded,
and ½ inch sliced

1 (8-ounce) container
mozzarella pearls, drained

½ cup chopped fresh basil

¼ cup chopped fresh mint

Kosher salt and ground
black pepper

6. When ready to serve, give the salad a big stir and add a few good pinches of salt and pepper to taste. Crumble the crisped prosciutto over the top. Serve chilled or at room temperature.

speed it up

Skip crisping the prosciutto. Instead, cut it crosswise into thin strips and add to the salad prior to refrigerating it. You also can omit the prosciutto and season the final salad with a few pinches of additional salt as needed.

do ahead

Up to 3 days in advance, cube the bread. Store at room temperature in a ziptop bag. As long as the bread is dried out (most artisan loaves will be), you can skip toasting it in the oven.

Panzanella is best served within 2 hours of assembly as the bread will continue to soften, but it can be refrigerated for up to 4 hours.

next level

Swap the mozzarella pearls for 8 ounces of burrata cheese, torn into bite-size pieces. Mix some pieces into the salad and scatter some over the top.

market swaps

You can use a regular cucumber in place of the English cucumber. Peel it first, slice lengthwise, and use a small spoon to scrape out the seeds.

Feel free to use any mix of ripe stone fruits in place of all or some of the peaches. Nectarines, plums, and cherries would all be scrumptious additions.

To make this lean more toward a green salad, stir in a few handfuls of arugula at the end. Adding greens is also a great way to perk up leftovers.

chipotle steak salad with citrusy arugula, avocado, and tomatoes

ACTIVE TIME: **30 minutes**

TOTAL TIME: **1 hour**

YIELD: **Serves 4**

For the Steak

1½ pounds flank steak, or skirt steak or hanger steak

1 tablespoon paprika

1 tablespoon light or dark brown sugar

2 teaspoons chipotle chile powder

1 teaspoon ground cumin

1 teaspoon kosher salt

Zest of 1 small lime

For the Salad

4 cups arugula (about 4 ounces)

8 ounces tomatoes— cherry or grape are the best choice out of season

2 ripe medium avocados

1 small lime (reserved from above)

1 tablespoon extra-virgin olive oil

1 garlic clove, minced (about 1 teaspoon)

1 teaspoon honey

½ teaspoon kosher salt, plus a few pinches

½ cup crumbled feta cheese or queso fresco (about 2 ounces)

A go-to strategy when I'm trying to get my husband, Ben, to do something around the house is to start doing it myself, then wait for him to intervene (especially effective when I start putting holes in the wall or reaching for power tools). When we moved into our first home, grilling was new to us both, and I hoped he'd take over, so I walked outside with a lighter and tongs. I'm not sure if he grabbed both because he didn't trust me to light propane or because grilling made him feel manly, but either way, we eat a lot of this Chipotle Steak Salad when he's in charge, so I'm a happy girl. Set atop a bracing, peppery arugula salad and showered in creamy feta, it's the ideal meal for patio dining and attainable for grillers of all levels. No grill? No problem! You can broil the steak instead.

1. Prepare the steak: Remove the steak from the refrigerator and allow to come to room temperature for 20 minutes. In a small bowl, stir together the paprika, brown sugar, chipotle chile powder, cumin, and salt. Zest the lime right into the bowl, reserving the remaining lime. Pat the steak very dry, then rub the spice mixture all over it.

2. Prepare the salad: Place the arugula in a large bowl. Cut the tomatoes into a ½-inch dice (if using cherry or grape tomatoes, slice in half) and add them to the bowl. Cut the avocados into a ½-inch dice and add to the bowl.

3. Into the same bowl you used for the steak rub (or a small liquid measuring cup with a spout), juice the lime (you should have about 1½ tablespoons) and add the oil, garlic, honey, and ½ teaspoon salt. Whisk to combine and set aside.

4. Cook the steak: Heat a gas or charcoal grill over medium-high heat (425° to 450°F), or heat your oven's broiler. If using the broiler, line a large rimmed baking sheet with foil; if grilling, make sure the grates are very clean, then oil them. Grill or broil the steak until it

recipe continues

reaches 125°F on an instant-read thermometer, 2 to 4 minutes per side depending on its thickness. (This is for medium-rare, which is best for flank steak; if you like your steak more well done, cook it 1 to 2 minutes more, but note this cut of meat will be tough.) Transfer the steak to a cutting board, cover, and let rest for 10 minutes.

5. When ready to serve, pour enough of the dressing over the top of the arugula mixture to moisten it. Toss to coat and divide among the plates. Cut the steak across the grain into very thin slices. Arrange the steak slices on top of the salad and sprinkle lightly with a pinch of salt. Sprinkle with the feta, dividing it evenly among the plates. Enjoy while the steak is warm.

pro tip

If you'd like to keep some of the salad for leftovers, dress only the portion you will be serving right away; store the remaining salad and dressing separately in the refrigerator.

fancy p(ants) on a log celery salad

ACTIVE TIME:
30 minutes

TOTAL TIME:
35 minutes

YIELD:
Serves 4

For the Salad

10 long celery stalks with leaves

½ cup raw almonds

½ cup raisins or dried cranberries

For the Dressing

3 tablespoons freshly squeezed lemon juice

3 tablespoons creamy almond butter

1 tablespoon honey

1 teaspoon extra-virgin olive oil

½ teaspoon kosher salt, plus additional to taste

¼ teaspoon red pepper flakes, plus additional to taste

This salad is about more than nostalgic love of childhood snacks. It's about that extra bunch of celery you have in your refrigerator right now because you only needed two stalks of it to make a different recipe (like the Big Bean Salad, page 113). I wanted to come up with a legitimately delicious way to use celery other than chopping it up for a crudités plate, where it would inevitably be picked around anyway. This is celery for the sake of celery, living up to its true potential. Refreshing and crispy with a punchy almond-lemon dressing and bits of chewy raisins (or dried cranberries), this salad will give you new respect for the stalks going limp in your refrigerator. Don't skip the ice-bath—it is what wakes up the celery, giving it life and crunch.

1. Separate the leaves from the celery stalks. Lightly chop the leaves and reserve for serving. Cut the stems diagonally into ¼-inch-thick slices. Place the slices in a big bowl of ice water and let sit for 15 minutes (I promise it is worth it to make the celery taste extra fresh and crunchy). Drain, pat dry, and transfer to a large serving bowl.

2. Meanwhile, place a rack in the center of your oven and preheat to 350°F. On a rimmed baking sheet, spread the almonds into a single layer. Bake for 8 to 10 minutes, stirring once or twice, until the almonds are golden brown and smell toasty.

Transfer to a cutting board, roughly chop, and place in the bowl with the celery.

3. Make the dressing: In a small bowl or large liquid measuring cup with a spout, whisk together the lemon juice, almond butter, honey, oil, salt, and red pepper flakes.

4. To the bowl with the celery, add the raisins and chopped celery leaves. Spoon on enough dressing to moisten the salad, then toss to coat. Taste and add more dressing, salt, or red pepper flakes to taste. Enjoy immediately or refrigerate until ready to serve.

pro tip

This salad keeps well for 3 days in the refrigerator. Discard any liquid that has collected at the bottom and stir well before serving.

speed it up

While I love the extra crunch of the irregular shapes of chopped whole almonds, to save yourself a few minutes, use slivered or sliced almonds instead; toast as directed, checking them a minute or two early.

roasted cauliflower arugula salad with grapes

ACTIVE TIME: **20 minutes**

TOTAL TIME: **35 minutes**

YIELD: **Serves 4**

During the winter months, when in-season produce is scarce and you long for something green, let this salad be your respite. Grapes are one of the tastier fruits this time of year, and roasted cauliflower, with its tender, caramelized center and crisped edges, tastes yummy year-round. The ingredients here look simple, but they will surprise you. Crisp red grapes provide tart pops of freshness, cauliflower provides bulk, arugula is peppery and grounding, Parmesan lends nutty complexity, and toasted walnuts bring the crunch. Serve it as a hearty side, or add diced chicken, quinoa, and/or white beans to make it the main event.

For the Salad

1 medium head cauliflower (about 2½ pounds)

2 tablespoons extra-virgin olive oil

1 teaspoon kosher salt

¼ teaspoon ground black pepper

½ cup roughly chopped raw walnuts

5 ounces fresh arugula (about 5 cups)

2 cups seedless red grapes (about 12 ounces), halved

4 tablespoons finely grated Parmesan cheese (about ¾ ounce), divided

For the Dressing

2 tablespoons nonfat plain Greek yogurt

1 tablespoon extra-virgin olive oil

1 tablespoon apple cider vinegar

1 tablespoon freshly squeezed lemon juice

1 tablespoon Dijon mustard, plus additional to taste

1 tablespoon honey, plus additional to taste

½ teaspoon kosher salt

1. Place a rack in the upper third of your oven and preheat to 400°F. Cut the cauliflower into florets: Trim off the stem end, then cut it into four even wedges from the top down through the base. Trim away the hard inner core areas, then cut into 1-inch florets (you should have about 6 cups). Place on a large rimmed baking sheet and top with the oil, salt, and pepper. Toss to coat, then spread into a single layer. Roast for 25 to 30 minutes, tossing halfway through, until the cauliflower is dark and crispy in places and caramelized in the center.

2. Toast the walnuts: Place the nuts in a small dry skillet over medium-low heat. Cook, stirring frequently, until fragrant and starting to turn golden, 4 to 6 minutes (be careful—nuts can burn quickly). Alternatively, you can toast the nuts on an ungreased rimmed baking sheet in the oven with the cauliflower for 6 to 8 minutes, tossing once halfway.

3. Make the dressing: In a small bowl or liquid measuring cup with a spout, whisk together the yogurt, oil, vinegar, lemon juice, mustard, honey, and salt. Taste and adjust the seasoning as desired. It should be tart, sweet, and zingy. For a sweeter dressing, add more honey; for more zip, add more mustard.

4. Place the arugula in a large bowl and spoon a little of the dressing over the top. Toss to lightly moisten, then add the warm cauliflower, half each of the grapes and walnuts, and 2 tablespoons of the Parmesan. Toss to coat, adding a little more dressing if you like (add it very gradually, tossing after each addition—be careful not to overdress). Top with the remaining grapes, walnuts, and 2 tablespoons Parmesan. Serve immediately with the remaining dressing alongside.

pro tip:

For fast lunches, make a double or even triple batch of the cauliflower for leftovers. Quickly recrisp it in the toaster oven, then toss this salad together in minutes.

one-pot
rosemary
chicken
and potatoes

page 160

mains
meals you'll eat and repeat

Welcome to my happy place! It's also my stressful place and my inspired place. It's the place where, depending upon how my day went, I find myself thinking either "REALLY, we are doing this *again*?" or "Yay, we get to do this *again*! Same time tomorrow?"

"Always," replies the dinner bell. We'll always do this again tomorrow.

Whether it enlivens you with creative energy or fills you with dread, the prospect of preparing a meal isn't a static experience. Depending upon what else is going on in your life, the state of your refrigerator, and/or how many mouths you need to feed (not to mention said mouths' eating preferences), cooking can be a real drag. It can also be energizing, restoring, and (I believe) an act of love.

I'm in the business of equipping you with recipes that help you avoid the former and fill your life with the latter. After all, we all need to eat, so let's cut the stress, wash fewer dishes, and make it DELICIOUS. Whether you feel like cooking today or not, the recipes here offer a variety of tastes and prep times so you can find one to suit your needs and cravings.

We kick off with one-pan meals. They're ideal for when you're in a rush and needed dinner 10 minutes ago, but by no means are they afterthoughts. I'd just as soon as serve One-Pot Rosemary Chicken and Potatoes (page 160) at a dinner party as I would pull it together on a Tuesday for myself and Ben. Heads up: every now and then I'll ask you to use two sheet pans, but that's just so things caramelize properly. Everything will come together into one at the end, and you won't have to worry about a separate side.

From there, we have a cache of recipes for when you're in the mood for something especially comforting. If you're craving carby (Baked Ziti–Style Cauliflower, page 166), or creamy and cheesy (White Pizza Spaghetti Squash Boats, page 169), you'll find a dish to meet your appetite. You'll also find plenty of hearty mains and dinner-party-worthy dishes that are still simple enough for a weeknight. My hope is that if you're cooking Balsamic Berry Chicken Thighs (page 183) anyway, you won't think twice about asking your neighbor over to join you for an impromptu meal and conversation.

Last, we have a section that encompasses a little bit of everything, from classic comforts with a twist (Kale White Bean Pesto Pasta, page 199), to dishes inspired by my travels (don't miss Okonomiyaki, page 205), to meal-prep-style dishes you can make ahead and assemble on the fly (BBQ Chickpea Bowls, page 197). What these dishes have in common is that they are all meatless, but I promise they are so robustly flavored and hearty, you'll hardly notice. To be sure, I tested all of these on dedicated meat eaters and received warm rounds of approval.

And of course with every recipe, you'll find I've lightened things up a wherever possible but never ever at the expense of flavor. Don't Stacked Butternut Squash Black Bean Enchiladas (page 217) and Loaded Broccoli Potato Cheddar Chicken Skillet (page 159) sound *delicious*? They are! They also are filled with veggies, protein, and whole grains. You'll be too busy thinking about second helpings to notice they're "healthy," and that's the whole idea!

I want dinner to be your favorite time of day, to infuse energy into your cooking when you're less enthused, and to give you more time around the table **every day**.

....

one-pan plan

Sheet Pan Honey Orange Pistachio Salmon and Broccoli

Baked Tomatillo Fish and Zucchini

Takeout-Style Sheet Pan Shrimp and Veggies

Sheet Pan Shrimp Primavera

Sheet Pan Peanut-Roasted Squash and Tofu

Sheet Pan Crispy Honey Mustard Pork Chops and Sweet Potatoes

Sheet Pan French Onion Chicken and Brussels Sprouts

Sheet Pan Mediterranean Pork Tenderloin with Tahini Butter Sauce

Sweet Citrus Chicken and Rice

Loaded Broccoli Potato Cheddar Chicken Skillet

One-Pot Rosemary Chicken and Potatoes

mood = comfort food

Creamy Harvest Chicken Pasta

Baked Ziti–Style Cauliflower

White Pizza Spaghetti Squash Boats

Chili Pie

Green Goddess Chicken Thighs

Cheater's Cassoulet

Balsamic Berry Chicken Thighs

Crispy Chicken Schnitzel with Caramelized Cabbage

Roasted Pork Tenderloin with Brussels Sprouts, Grapes, and Maple Sauce

Slow Cooker Pork Tinga Tacos

veggie mains with ALL THE FLAVOR

Curried Ginger Tofu Bowls with Coconut Rice

BBQ Chickpea Bowls

Kale White Bean Pesto Pasta

Bam Bam Noodles

Okonomiyaki (Savory Japanese Cabbage Pancakes)

Lentil Kofta

Sweet Potato Samosa Pie

Sweet Potato Black Bean Quesadillas

Stacked Butternut Squash Black Bean Enchiladas

sheet pan honey orange pistachio salmon and broccoli

ACTIVE TIME:
20 minutes

TOTAL TIME:
40 minutes

YIELD:
Serves 4

½ cup roasted, salted pistachios, chopped

4 tablespoons extra-virgin olive oil, divided

1¼ teaspoons kosher salt, divided, plus additional for serving

1 medium orange

1 tablespoon honey

2 garlic cloves, minced (about 2 teaspoons)

1 teaspoon paprika

½ teaspoon ground cumin

½ teaspoon ground black pepper, divided

1 pound broccoli florets (about 8 cups or 2 medium crowns)

4 (6-ounce) skin-on salmon fillets

This recipe, which is one of my favorite sheet pan recipes of all time, started with baklava—or should I say it started with baklava intentions. Inspired by the half-used bag of pistachios in our pantry, I got the bright idea to make the iconic layered dessert, spent a delicious hour researching it (did you know baklava is the ancestor to strudel?), and then opened the freezer door to realize we did not, in fact, have phyllo dough. *WELL, LOOK AT THAT.* It's dinnertime, and those pistachios are not going to eat themselves.

Honey, orange, and pistachio—three flavors you'll find in baklava—also happen to be heavenly in savory preparations, as this succulent salmon testifies. The addition of paprika to the honey glaze gives it warmth and complexity, the pistachios add richness and crunch, and broccoli turns it into a complete meal. Go ahead and bookmark this page now.

1. Place a rack in the center of your oven and preheat to 425°F. Line a large rimmed baking sheet with parchment paper.

2. In a small bowl, add the pistachios, 1 tablespoon of the oil, and ¼ teaspoon of the salt. Zest the orange directly over the bowl, then stir to combine (reserve the rest of the orange).

3. In a separate small bowl, combine 1 tablespoon of the oil, the honey, garlic, paprika, cumin, ½ teaspoon of the salt, and ¼ teaspoon of the pepper.

4. Place the broccoli in the center of the prepared baking sheet. Drizzle with the remaining 2 tablespoons oil and sprinkle with the remaining ½ teaspoon salt and ¼ teaspoon pepper. Toss to coat (be sure the florets are well and evenly moistened so they do not burn), then spread into an even layer. Roast for 10 minutes.

5. With paper towels, pat the salmon dry. Remove the broccoli from the oven and toss with a spatula. Move the broccoli florets around to the outsides

recipe continues

of the pan, clearing a space in the center for the salmon. Place the salmon skin side down in the cleared space, ensuring the fillets do not touch.

6. Brush the salmon generously with the honey-spice mixture. It will be thick and sticky, but smush it on as evenly as you can. Top the salmon evenly with the pistachio mixture.

7. Return the pan to the oven and bake the salmon for 8 to 12 minutes, depending upon the thickness of your salmon, until it reaches 135°F on an instant-read thermometer inserted at the thickest part. It should look medium-rare to medium in the center and flake easily with a fork. Let rest for 3 minutes on the baking sheet.

8. Quarter the zested orange and squeeze the juice over the top of the salmon and broccoli. Season the salmon with a pinch of additional salt. Enjoy warm.

speed it up

No shame in the precut game! Purchase a bag of already chopped broccoli florets to make this recipe even more lightning fast.

baked tomatillo fish and zucchini

ACTIVE TIME:
35 minutes

TOTAL TIME:
45 minutes

YIELD:
Serves 4

2 medium zucchini
(about 1 pound)

1¾ teaspoons kosher salt,
divided

¼ cup water

¼ cup white vinegar

1 tablespoon granulated
sugar

1 medium jalapeño,
cut crosswise into
¹⁄₁₆-inch-thick rounds
(about ¼ cup)

2 tablespoons extra-virgin
olive oil

2 garlic cloves, minced
(about 2 teaspoons)

1 (11-ounce) can Mexican-
style corn (sometimes
called fiesta corn), drained

1 (14- to 16-ounce) jar
tomatillo salsa (salsa verde)

⅓ cup chopped fresh
cilantro, divided

4 (6-ounce) firm, flaky white
fish fillets, such as cod

Prepared brown rice,
for serving (see How to
Cook Brown Rice, page 138)

My early-twenties recipe repertoire was a case study in different ways to use a jar of salsa. Anytime a recipe fell flat—soup, eggs, frozen veggie burger, baked potato, you name it—my solution was a big scoop of the red stuff. Now that I'm older and wiser, I know to use the green stuff too. Made primarily with tomatillos and green chiles, salsa verde tastes spicy, vegetal, and complex. Here, it elevates a simple white fish like cod into a citrusy, spicy, and refreshing multifaceted event. It's ideal on a hot summer evening, when you want something filling but not too heavy and fresh corn is in its prime. At other times of the year, it's quite delicious with canned or frozen corn. Add as many jalapeños as you dare. Grow that repertoire.

1. Place a rack in the center of your oven and preheat to 400°F. Trim off the ends of your zucchini, then quarter them lengthwise so you have four long batons per zucchini. Cut the batons crosswise into ¼-inch pieces. Place the zucchini in a colander and toss with ½ teaspoon of the salt. Set the colander on a plate or towel and let stand for 10 minutes to draw out excess water.

2. In a small saucepan, combine the water, vinegar, sugar, and 1 teaspoon of the salt. Bring to a simmer, then stir to dissolve the sugar and salt. Remove from the heat and add the jalapeño slices. Let sit for at least 10 minutes to pickle.

3. Over the sink, shake out the excess water from the zucchini, then pat it dry. Heat the oil in a large, deep ovenproof skillet over medium-high heat. Once the oil is hot and shimmering, add the zucchini, spreading it into an even layer. Let cook undisturbed for 2 minutes, then stir and spread back into an even layer. Continue cooking, stirring every couple of minutes, until the zucchini is browned in places, about 6 minutes more. Stir in the garlic and corn. Let cook 1 minute more.

4. While the zucchini cooks, in a medium bowl, place the salsa and half of the cilantro. Drain the jalapeño slices, then finely

recipe continues

chop half of them and add them to the bowl with the salsa. Stir to combine (reserve the unchopped slices). Pour half of the salsa mixture into the skillet with the vegetables, stir, and let simmer for 2 minutes. Remove the skillet from the heat.

5. Pat the fish dry, then arrange it in the skillet on top of the vegetable mixture, spacing the fillets evenly. Sprinkle the fish with the remaining ¼ teaspoon salt. Spoon the remaining tomatillo mixture over and around the fish. Scatter the reserved jalapeño slices on top.

6. Transfer the skillet to the oven and bake the fish for 10 to 15 minutes, until it flakes easily with a fork, appears opaque in the center, and an instant-read thermometer inserted in the fillets registers 145°F. Sprinkle with the remaining cilantro. For each portion, scoop rice into a shallow bowl. Use a spoon to top with a portion of the fish and plenty of the saucy vegetables.

speed it up

Use drained jarred pickled jalapeños in place of the homemade ones in step 2.

Skip salting the zucchini; your resulting sauce will be more liquidy but will still taste yummy.

market swaps

Swap the zucchini for your in-season veggie(s) of choice. Try chopped asparagus or green beans, diced carrots, or a mix. Note that harder vegetables (like carrots) will need to sauté longer to become tender.

Use a different firm, flaky white fish instead of the cod, such as halibut, haddock, or mahi-mahi. Large or jumbo peeled, deveined shrimp (26/30 count; fresh or frozen and thawed) can also be substituted (note that they may finish baking several minutes early).

takeout-style sheet pan shrimp and veggies

ACTIVE TIME:
30 minutes

TOTAL TIME:
45 minutes

YIELD:
Serves 4

For the Shrimp and Vegetables

2 red bell peppers, cut into 1-inch pieces

2 cups sugar snap peas (about 8 ounces)

1 large yellow onion, cut into 1-inch pieces

2 tablespoons extra-virgin olive oil, divided

1 teaspoon ground ginger, divided

½ teaspoon kosher salt, divided

¼ teaspoon ground black pepper

1 pound large or jumbo shrimp (26/30 count), peeled and deveined, tails on or off (fresh or frozen and thawed) (see Pro Tips, p. 141)

Sliced green onions (optional), for serving

Prepared brown rice, for serving (see How to Cook Brown Rice, page 138)

My steamy love affair with Asian-inspired shrimp recipes dates back to my senior year of high school, when we were allowed to leave campus for a half-hour lunch. This gave me exactly enough time to hit up the Chinese takeout section of the nearest grocery store deli, inhale a carton of shrimp fried rice or noodles, and make it back for third-period French. These saucy sheet pan shrimp and veggies remind me of those worry-free lunches, but with a wholesome bend I didn't discover until after college. Everything cooks together on a sheet pan, including the sweet and savory soy–peanut butter stir-fry sauce. Serve this over cooked brown rice or whole grain soba or spaghetti noodles for a fast, nutritious meal you can savor slowly . . . or gobble up before the bell rings.

1. Place a rack in the center of your oven and preheat to 425°F. Line a large rimmed baking sheet that is at least 11 by 17 inches with parchment paper. Place the bell peppers, snap peas, and onion in the center. Drizzle with 1½ tablespoons of the oil and top with ½ teaspoon of the ginger, ¼ teaspoon of the salt, and the black pepper. Toss to combine, ensuring the vegetables are as evenly coated as possible. Spread into an even layer. The vegetables will touch and slightly overlap. Bake for 15 minutes.

2. Meanwhile, rinse the shrimp and pat dry. Place in a medium bowl and top with the remaining ½ tablespoon oil, ½ teaspoon ginger, and ¼ teaspoon salt. Toss to coat.

3. Make the sauce: To a medium saucepan, add the soy sauce, vinegar, honey, peanut butter, cornstarch, garlic, and red pepper flakes. Whisk briskly until combined. Bring to a simmer over high heat, whisking constantly. Let simmer, still whisking constantly, until the sauce has thickened to a peanut butter–like consistency, about 1 minute. Remove from the heat. Whisk in the water.

4. Once the vegetables have baked for 15 minutes, remove them from the oven and use a spatula to turn them so they roast evenly. Spread them back into an even layer. Return to the oven and continue baking for

recipe and ingredients continue

¼ cup low-sodium soy sauce

3 tablespoons rice vinegar

2 tablespoons honey

1 tablespoon creamy peanut butter

2 teaspoons cornstarch

2 garlic cloves, minced (about 2 teaspoons)

¼ teaspoon red pepper flakes

2 tablespoons water

10 to 15 more minutes, until they are tender and turning lightly crisp in places.

5. To the baking sheet with the roasted vegetables, add the shrimp and any spices or oils that collected in the bowl. Scrape the sauce over the top. With a large spoon, stir to coat the vegetables and shrimp evenly with the sauce, then spread into an even layer.

6. Return the pan to the oven and bake for 4 to 6 minutes, until the shrimp just turn pink and are no longer translucent. As soon as the shrimp are done, remove the pan from the oven to keep the shrimp from tasting dry. Sprinkle with green onions (if using) and enjoy immediately with rice.

how to cook brown rice

To cook brown rice, rinse your desired amount of rice (1 cup dry rice yields 3 cups cooked) in a mesh sieve. Drain and place in a medium saucepan with a pinch of kosher salt and twice the amount of water as rice. (For example, for 1 cup rice, add 2 cups water.) Bring to a boil, then cover and reduce the heat to low. Let simmer for 45 minutes, lowering the heat as needed so the rice does not boil over. Turn off the heat and let sit, covered, for 10 minutes. Fluff with a fork and serve.

sheet pan shrimp primavera

ACTIVE TIME:
45 minutes

TOTAL TIME:
45 minutes

YIELD:
Serves 4

1 medium red bell pepper, cut into ¼-inch strips

1 medium zucchini or yellow summer squash, ends trimmed, quartered lengthwise, and cut into ½-inch slices

1 small red onion, halved through the ends, then cut lengthwise into ¼-inch-thick slices

2 tablespoons extra-virgin olive oil, divided

2½ teaspoons Italian seasoning, divided

1¼ teaspoons kosher salt, divided

1 pound asparagus spears, tough ends trimmed, cut into 2-inch pieces

1 pound jumbo shrimp (26/30 count), peeled and deveined (see Pro Tip)

¼ teaspoon ground black pepper

1 small lemon

¼ cup finely grated Parmesan cheese (about 1 ounce)

¼ cup chopped fresh basil

When it comes to bright, happy, eat-the-rainbow meals, primavera (Italian for "spring") is a show-off. Primavera celebrates the return of fresh produce to the market stalls after a long, starch-heavy winter. I most look forward to it in March, when asparagus makes its glorious appearance, but it is wonderful well into the summer and early fall. Bell peppers, zucchini, yellow squash, broccoli, and even mushrooms can all find a home in this recipe. Use whatever you have in your garden or looks most tempting at the store. Make it *grandióso!*

1. Place racks in the upper and lower thirds of your oven and preheat to 400°F. Place the bell pepper, zucchini, and onion in the center of a large rimmed baking sheet. Drizzle with 1 tablespoon of the oil, 1 teaspoon of the Italian seasoning, and ½ teaspoon of the salt. Toss to coat, then spread into an even layer. Place on the lower rack (note what time you place the pan in the oven).

2. Meanwhile, place the asparagus on a second rimmed baking sheet. Drizzle with ½ tablespoon of the oil, ½ teaspoon of the Italian seasoning, and ¼ teaspoon of the salt. Toss to coat, then spread into an even layer. Place on the upper rack and bake along with the other vegetables. Continue baking until both pans of vegetables are nearly tender and beginning to brown, 25 to 30 minutes total for the peppers and 15 to 20 minutes for the

asparagus. Halfway through, use a spatula to turn the vegetables in both pans so they cook evenly. Spread into even layers again, then return the pans to the oven, switching their positions on the upper and lower racks.

3. While the vegetables cook, pat the shrimp very dry, then place in a bowl. Top with the remaining ½ tablespoon oil, 1 teaspoon Italian seasoning, ½ teaspoon salt, and the black pepper. Zest the lemon directly into the bowl. Toss to coat the shrimp. Cut the zested lemon into wedges and reserve for serving.

4. Once the vegetables have baked, consolidate all the vegetables onto a single baking sheet. Add the shrimp and any extra oil and seasonings that have collected in the bottom of the bowl over the top. With a

recipe continues

spatula, carefully toss the shrimp and vegetables together, then spread them back into an even layer.

5. Return the pan to the upper rack of the oven and bake for 4 to 6 minutes, until the shrimp just turn pink and are no longer translucent. Watch carefully so that the shrimp do not overcook. Remove the pan from the oven and squeeze the lemon wedges over the top. Sprinkle with the Parmesan and basil. Enjoy immediately.

pro tips

For the fastest possible prep, purchase deveined, easy-peel shrimp. Since fresh shrimp can be pricey, I typically purchase frozen shrimp, let them thaw overnight in the refrigerator, then rinse them under cool water before using them in the recipe.

To stretch the recipe for a larger (or hungrier) group, serve it with a side of cooked brown rice, quinoa, or pasta that's lightly coated with lemon juice, olive oil, garlic, and salt and pepper to taste.

tails on or off?

Whether to remove the tails from the shrimp prior to baking is up for debate. There is some thought that the tails keep the shrimp from drying out and that the tails look better on for presentation purposes. I find that as long as I watch the shrimp very carefully and remove them from the oven as soon as they are done, they taste perfectly juicy and moist. The choice between ideal presentation and avoiding picking tails off at the table is up to you and your mood!

market swaps

Feel free to swap the vegetables suggested in this recipe for any blend of vegetables you like. Make sure to plan accordingly, as some vegetables take longer to roast than others. Plan on at least 25 minutes for cubed root vegetables and cauliflower or broccoli, and 15 to 20 minutes for thinner "bendy" vegetables like green beans.

sheet pan peanut-roasted squash and tofu

ACTIVE TIME:
40 minutes

TOTAL TIME:
1 hour 15 minutes

YIELD:
Serves 3 to 4

1 (14- to 16-ounce) package extra-firm tofu

½ cup pure maple syrup

¼ cup rice vinegar

3 garlic cloves, minced (about 1 tablespoon)

3 tablespoons creamy peanut butter

2 tablespoons low-sodium soy sauce

1½ tablespoons minced fresh ginger (about a 1½-inch piece)

1½ tablespoons extra-virgin olive oil

¼ teaspoon kosher salt, plus additional to taste

2 medium limes, divided

1 tablespoon cornstarch

1 large or 2 small acorn squash (about 1½ pounds)

¼ cup chopped dry roasted peanuts, plus additional for serving

¼ cup chopped fresh cilantro, plus additional for serving

If you don't love tofu, I know for a fact you haven't tried this recipe yet. On its own, tofu is, well, rather terrible. But when baked in the oven until meaty and crispy and soaked in a sticky maple-peanut sauce, tofu tastes *fantastic*. To keep this an all-in-one meal situation, I pair the tofu with roasted winter squash. The squash's naturally caramelly flavor is pure yumminess with the maple glaze. You'll surprise everyone with this recipe, including yourself!

1. Place racks in the upper and lower thirds of your oven and preheat to 425°F. Line two large rimmed baking sheets with parchment paper. Drain the tofu, then with your hands, gently squeeze out as much water as you can without breaking or crushing the block. Cut the tofu into 1-inch cubes. Spread the cubes out on a double layer of paper towels. Place more paper towels on top, gently blot, and let rest with the towels in place.

2. In a medium bowl or large liquid measuring cup with a spout, place the maple syrup, vinegar, garlic, peanut butter, soy sauce, ginger, oil, and salt. Zest one lime directly over the bowl, then add its juice. Whisk until smooth.

3. Pat the tofu dry one last time, then transfer it to a large bowl. With light fingers, gently toss with the cornstarch to evenly coat, then pour about one-third of the sauce on top. With a large spoon, stir to coat the tofu evenly (don't worry if a few crumbles break off). Let sit while you prep the squash.

4. Halve the acorn squash lengthwise through the stem and scoop out the seeds. Lay the cut sides flat on a cutting board, then cut them crosswise into ½-inch-thick half-moon slices. Place the slices in the center of one of the prepared baking sheets. Pour half of the remaining sauce over the squash and toss to coat (some of the sauce will run off the squash). Spread the slices into an even layer.

recipe and ingredients continue

Prepared brown rice,
for serving (How to Cook
Brown Rice, page 138)

5. Toss the tofu pieces in the sauce once more, then arrange them in a single layer on the second baking sheet so the pieces are not touching; pour any sauce left behind in the tofu bowl over the top. (If you have some crumbles left at the bottom of the bowl, put them in a small pile on the baking sheet and roast as a makeshift tofu blob; it looks odd but will taste delicious.)

6. Place the tofu on one oven rack and the squash on the other. Roast for 15 minutes. Pull out the pans, flip the squash and tofu, and brush everything with some of the remaining sauce. Return the pans to the oven, switching their rack positions, and continue baking until the squash slices are fork-tender and the tofu is crispy and lightly dark—10 to 15 additional minutes for the squash and 15 to 20 additional minutes for the tofu.

7. Transfer the tofu to the baking sheet with the squash. The squash should still be quite warm, but if it has cooled more than you would like, return the baking sheet to the oven for 2 to 3 minutes to warm it through. Just before serving, sprinkle with the peanuts and cilantro. Quarter the remaining lime and squeeze the juice of two of the wedges over the top. Taste and add a pinch of salt if desired. Serve hot with rice, the remaining sauce for drizzling, and more cilantro, peanuts, and lime to taste.

pro tip

The beauty of acorn squash compared to some of its other winter squash peers is that once roasted, the skin is so thin and delicate that you can eat it. I love the texture, but if you find it off-putting, remove it from the slices after roasting.

market swaps

This recipe is delicious with any variety of winter squash. Use one with thin skin, such as delicata, and you won't need to peel it; or swap peeled, cubed butternut squash, adjusting the roasting time as needed.

sheet pan crispy honey mustard pork chops and sweet potatoes

ACTIVE TIME:
30 minutes

TOTAL TIME:
55 minutes

YIELD:
Serves 4

¼ cup plus 1 teaspoon kosher salt, divided

4 cups lukewarm water

4 center-cut pork chops (boneless or bone-in), ¾ to 1 inch thick, trimmed of excess fat

3 tablespoons extra-virgin olive oil, divided

1½ cups panko bread crumbs

1 tablespoon dried parsley

2 teaspoons garlic powder

1 teaspoon onion powder

¾ teaspoon ground black pepper, divided

2 pounds sweet potatoes (about 3 medium)

1 tablespoon honey

⅓ cup plus 6 tablespoons all-purpose flour, divided

2 large eggs

3 tablespoons Dijon mustard

Pork chops and I have a rough history, but thanks to some therapy in the form of honey-mustard glaze, bread crumbs, and an accurate meat thermometer, we're now on the best of dinner terms. The crust on these juicy chops is crusty and crunchy but not so thick that it becomes gummy or detracts from the savoriness of the pork. The trick is to whisk some flour into the beaten eggs to make the coating a bit more substantial, a tip I picked up from the fine folks at America's Test Kitchen. Tender sweet potatoes turn this into an all-in-one dinner overachiever in the best possible way.

1. Brine the pork chops (it's worth it!): Place ¼ cup of the salt in a large bowl, then add the water. Stir until most of the salt dissolves. Add the chops so that they are fully submerged. Set aside for 15 minutes while you prepare the bread crumbs and sweet potatoes (or refrigerate for up to 4 hours).

2. Place racks in the center and upper third of your oven and preheat to 425°F. In a large skillet over medium-high heat, heat 1 tablespoon of the oil. Add the panko, parsley, garlic powder, onion powder, ½ teaspoon of the salt and ¼ teaspoon of the pepper. Cook, stirring very frequently, until the crumbs are golden and toasted, about 3 minutes. Set aside to cool.

3. Line a rimmed baking sheet with parchment paper or aluminum foil. Scrub the sweet potatoes (no need to peel), trim off the ends, and cut them into pieces that are roughly 1 inch in size. Place in the center of the baking sheet. Top with the remaining 2 tablespoons oil, the honey, ¼ teaspoon of the pepper, and the remaining ½ teaspoon salt. Toss to coat, then spread into a single layer. Turn the cubes so that their widest, flattest sides are touching the baking sheet. Roast on the center rack for 25 to 30 minutes, until tender and caramelized, tossing once halfway through.

4. Set up your dredging stations: In a wide, shallow dish (a pie dish works well), whisk

recipe continues

together ⅓ cup of the flour and the remaining ¼ teaspoon pepper. In a second shallow dish, whisk the eggs and mustard until well blended. Add the remaining 6 tablespoons flour to the egg mixture and whisk until only pebble-sized lumps remain. Place the bread crumbs in a third shallow dish.

5. Set an ovenproof rack on top of a second rimmed baking sheet and coat it generously with nonstick spray. Once the pork has brined for at least 15 minutes, remove it from the brine, rinse under cool water, and pat very dry.

6. Working one pork chop at a time, dredge it in the flour and then the egg mixture, letting the excess drip off (it will be a fairly thick coating). Coat both sides of the pork with bread crumbs, patting gently as needed to help the crumbs adhere. Transfer to the prepared baking rack. Repeat with the remaining pork.

7. If the sweet potatoes aren't finished roasting, move them to the upper rack until they are ready. Place the pork chops on the center rack. Bake for 15 to 22 minutes, depending upon the thickness of your chops, until they reach 140°F on an instant-read thermometer; check right at the 15-minute mark to gauge their progress.

8. Remove the chops from the oven and let rest on the rack for 5 minutes. If the sweet potatoes have cooled out of the oven, turn off the oven, then place them inside to rewarm as the pork rests. Enjoy hot, with a pinch of additional salt to taste.

do ahead

Toast the bread crumbs up to 2 days in advance. Store in an airtight container at room temperature.

You can prepare the chops up to the point of baking, then freeze for up to 1 month in an airtight ziptop bag. Bake directly from frozen at 425°F for 35 to 40 minutes.

sheet pan french onion chicken and brussels sprouts

ACTIVE TIME:
40 minutes

TOTAL TIME:
1 hour 20 minutes

YIELD:
Serves 4

2 medium yellow onions, halved through the ends, then cut lengthwise into ¼-inch-thick slices

1 pound Brussels sprouts, stems trimmed, brown outer leaves removed, and halved

12 garlic cloves, peeled and left whole (see Pro Tip)

3 tablespoons extra-virgin olive oil, divided

2 tablespoons Dijon mustard, divided

2½ teaspoons kosher salt, divided

6 ounces good-quality whole-grain sourdough bread, cut into 1½-inch cubes (about 2½ heaping cups)

2 tablespoons unsalted butter

4 bone-in, skin-on chicken thighs (2½ to 3½ pounds, depending on size)

½ teaspoon ground black pepper

The first time I tried French onion soup was at an old-timey café at lunch with my Grammy. I took one look at the hunk of golden, cheese-smothered bread at the table beside me and decided that if that counted as a meal, I wanted IN. I still savor a decadent bowl of French onion soup every now and then, but what I've come to adore as a regular occurrence is giving recipes the "French onion treatment": adding caramelized onions, hunks of toasty bread, and melty, nutty cheese. Here, the French onion trifecta elevates juicy pieces of bone-in chicken and fiber-rich Brussels sprouts into a sheet pan superstar. In addition to being a wholesome, comforting dinner, this spin on French onion has a distinct advantage over the original. Rather than caramelizing on the stove for forty-five minutes or more, the onions roast right on the sheet pan unattended, leaving you free to go about your tasks (like, ahem, pouring yourself a nice glass of French wine).

1. Place racks in the upper and lower thirds of your oven and preheat to 400°F. For easy cleanup, line two large rimmed baking sheets with aluminum foil or parchment paper.

2. In a large bowl, place the onions, Brussels sprouts, and garlic. In a small, heatproof bowl or large liquid measuring cup with a spout, whisk together 2 tablespoons of the oil, 1 tablespoon of the mustard, and 1 teaspoon of the salt. Pour over the vegetables. Toss to coat as evenly as possible, then spread into an even layer on the first baking sheet. Place on the upper rack and bake for 10 minutes.

3. Place the bread cubes into the now-empty bowl you used for the veggies (no need to wipe it clean). In the same bowl you used to whisk the olive oil, melt the butter in the microwave at medium power (alternatively, you can melt it in a heatproof bowl set over a pan of simmering water), then whisk in the remaining 1 tablespoon oil, remaining 1 tablespoon mustard, and ½ teaspoon of the salt. Pour over the bread cubes and toss to coat. Spread onto the second baking sheet.

recipe and ingredients continue

1 cup shredded Gruyère cheese, or Swiss, Emmental, or similar Alpine-style melty, nutty cheese (about 4 ounces)

1½ tablespoons chopped fresh thyme

4. With paper towels, pat the chicken very dry. Nestle the chicken thighs between the bread cubes, skin side up. Sprinkle the chicken with the pepper and remaining 1 teaspoon salt.

5. Remove the baking sheet with the Brussels sprouts and onions from the oven, toss the vegetables, and spread them back into an even layer. Return the pan to the oven on the lower rack. Place the chicken on the upper rack. Bake for 15 minutes, then remove both pans from the oven. Carefully toss the bread cubes and toss the vegetables once more. Return the pans to the same oven racks.

6. Continue baking the Brussels sprouts and onions until the vegetables are caramelized and tender and the chicken until it reaches an internal temperature of 160°F at the thickest part, 10 to 15 minutes more, depending on the size of your chicken. If some of the chicken pieces finish earlier than others, transfer the done pieces to a plate, then return the pan to the oven and continue baking until the remaining chicken is cooked through. If you'd like the bread cubes crispier, once the chicken is removed, pop them back into the oven until your desired texture is reached.

7. Transfer the chicken to the baking sheet with the Brussels sprouts and onions, tossing the Brussels sprouts and onions a little if they are cooking unevenly. Turn the oven to broil.

8. Broil the chicken and vegetables on the upper rack for about 3 minutes, until further crisped (watch closely!). Scoop the bread cubes and any juices that have collected on the pan onto the baking sheet with the chicken so that everything is cozy. Sprinkle the bread and veggies with the Gruyère and the whole pan with the thyme. Serve hot with big scoops of the croutons and the roasted veggies and garlic.

pro tip

To quickly and easily peel garlic cloves, lay each clove flat on a cutting board. Lay the side of a chef's knife on top so it covers the clove. Carefully but firmly hit your fist on the side of the knife over the clove to loosen the skin. Peel it away.

using chicken breasts instead of thighs

Prefer white meat? Swap all or a portion of the thighs for bone-in, skin-on chicken breasts. Prior to cooking, with a very sharp, sturdy chef's knife, cut the breasts in half crosswise (that's through the shorter side if you think of the breast from left to right and top to bottom), placing the knife on top of the breast and cutting down through the bone, carefully but firmly wiggling the knife as needed. For each breast, you should be left with two pieces of chicken that are roughly similar in size. The breast halves will cook in roughly the same amount of time as the thighs.

sheet pan mediterranean pork tenderloin with tahini butter sauce

ACTIVE TIME:
30 minutes

TOTAL TIME:
1 hour

YIELD:
Serves 3 to 4

For the Pork and Vegetables

1 pork tenderloin
(1¼ to 1¾ pounds)

3 tablespoons extra-virgin olive oil

3 garlic cloves, minced
(about 1 tablespoon)

2 teaspoons kosher salt

1 teaspoon dried thyme

1 teaspoon dried oregano

½ teaspoon ground cumin

¼ teaspoon ground black pepper

⅛ teaspoon red pepper flakes

1 medium lemon

2 large red, yellow, or orange bell peppers

1 medium red onion

Chopped fresh flat-leaf parsley (optional for serving)

No cuisine makes me lose my composure quite like Mediterranean food. Surround me with colorful vegetables, fresh herbs, and pots of tahini and hummus, then drizzle everything with olive oil, and I'm a happy girl. This sheet pan supper is inspired by souvlaki, a Greek dish made of skewered grilled meat and veggies. It's juicy, slightly smoky, citrusy, and ideal for dousing in yummy sauces. I'm especially partial to the tahini butter sauce below. After my friend Taylor tasted it, she exclaimed, "That sauce is now an integral part of my identity. I need it on everything!" Serve this with Spiced Rice and Lentils with Caramelized Onions (page 289) or warm pita bread.

1. With paper towels, pat the pork dry. With a sharp knife, cut away and discard the silverskin (tough membrane) from the pork. Transfer the pork to a large bowl or ziptop bag.

2. In a small bowl or liquid measuring cup with a spout, whisk together the oil, garlic, salt, thyme, oregano, cumin, black pepper, and red pepper flakes. Zest the lemon directly into the bowl, then add its juice. Stir to combine, then pour half of the mixture over the pork. Turn to coat (if using a bag, seal it completely first). Marinate at room temperature for 30 minutes, or cover and refrigerate for up to 12 hours. Let come to room temperature

prior to cooking. Reserve the remaining marinade for the vegetables.

3. While the pork marinates, cut the bell peppers into ¾-inch pieces and the onion into ½-inch chunks.

4. When you're ready to cook, place a rack in the center of your oven and preheat to 400°F. Line a large rimmed baking sheet with parchment paper or aluminum foil. Place the peppers and onion in the center, then pour the reserved marinade over the top. Toss to coat, then spread the vegetables into a single layer. Roast the vegetables for

recipe and ingredients continue

For the Tahini Butter Sauce

¼ cup tahini

2 tablespoons unsalted butter

⅛ teaspoon kosher salt

12 minutes, turning them once halfway through.

5. Remove the pan from the oven. Toss the vegetables once more, then move them toward the edges of the pan to clear a narrow space down the center for the pork. Remove the pork from the marinade and place it in the cleared center of the sheet. Return the pan to the oven and continue to cook for 22 to 28 minutes, until the pork is cooked through. The pork should register 135° to 140°F on an instant-read thermometer inserted in the thickest part (do not overcook or the pork will be dry).

6. Transfer the pork to a cutting board, cover, and let rest for 10 minutes. If you'd like the vegetables crispier, spread them back into a single layer and return them to the oven. To rewarm the vegetables prior to serving, a few minutes before the pork finishes resting, turn off the oven and place the baking sheet inside.

7. While the pork rests, prepare the tahini butter sauce: Place the tahini, butter, and salt in a small saucepan over low heat. Whisk until the butter is melted and the sauce is smoothly combined. It should be thin enough to easily drizzle.

8. Once the pork has rested, cut it crosswise into ½-inch-thick slices; the center pieces will be pink (but perfectly cooked through!) and the end pieces will be well done. Serve warm with the vegetables, a drizzle of the tahini butter sauce, and a sprinkle of fresh parsley (if using).

sweet citrus chicken and rice

ACTIVE TIME:
1 hour

TOTAL TIME:
2 hours 15 minutes

YIELD:
Serves 6

1½ pounds boneless, skinless chicken thighs

1¾ teaspoons kosher salt, divided

1 teaspoon garlic powder

1 teaspoon smoked paprika

2 tablespoons extra-virgin olive oil, divided

2 tablespoons honey

4 medium carrots, scrubbed and ½ inch diced (about 2 cups)

2 red, orange, or yellow bell peppers, ½ inch diced (about 2 cups)

1 green bell pepper, ½ inch diced (about 1 cup)

1 small yellow onion, ¼ inch diced (about 1 cup)

1 medium jalapeño, seeded and finely chopped (about 2 tablespoons)

3 garlic cloves, minced (about 1 tablespoon)

½ teaspoon dried thyme

¼ teaspoon ground cayenne pepper (optional)

2 tablespoons tomato paste

The cardinal rule of hosting a dinner party is to never cook something you haven't made before. Thus, in my infinite wisdom, I try out a new recipe pretty much anytime someone comes over for a meal. Such was the case with an early iteration of this Sweet Citrus Chicken and Rice. In addition to being forty-five minutes late, it set off the smoke alarm. Fortunately, everyone loved it so much, no one minded the wait—or the temporary background noise. With light, bright notes of zippy lime, the caramelly complexity of almost-burnt honey, and plenty of filling protein and nutrients thanks to juicy chicken and colorful veggies, this is a refreshing all-in-one meal you can proudly serve to friends or save for a weeknight ahead.

1. Cut the chicken into 1-inch cubes. In a medium bowl, stir together 1 teaspoon of the salt, the garlic powder, and smoked paprika. Add the chicken, stirring to coat the pieces evenly with the spices.

2. Heat 1 tablespoon of the oil in a Dutch oven or similar large, heavy-bottomed pot over medium-high heat. When the oil is hot and shimmering, add the chicken and honey. Cook, stirring constantly, until the chicken pieces are a nice golden brown on all sides, about 4 minutes; the chicken does not need to be cooked through.

3. Reduce the heat to medium-low. Add the remaining 1 tablespoon oil, the carrots, red bell peppers, green bell pepper, onion, jalapeño, and ½ teaspoon

of the salt. Partially cover the pot and let the veggies sweat until softened, 10 to 15 minutes. Lift the lid periodically to stir, allowing the moisture from the lid to drip back down into the pot as you do. Stir in the garlic, thyme, and cayenne (if using). Cook, stirring constantly, until the garlic is very fragrant, about 1 minute.

4. Add the tomato paste and Worcestershire sauce. Cook and stir for 30 seconds. Stir in the rice, coating it with the spices. Carefully pour in the coconut milk and water, then add the remaining ¼ teaspoon salt. Stir, using a wooden spoon or sturdy spatula to scrape up any browned bits stuck to the bottom of the pan. Increase the heat to

recipe and ingredients continue

1 tablespoon
Worcestershire sauce

1 cup brown rice

1 (13.5-ounce) can light
coconut milk

1 cup water, plus additional
as needed

1 cup frozen peas, no need
to thaw

2 tablespoons unsalted
butter, cut into a few pieces

Juice of 2 small limes
(about 3 tablespoons)

1 small bunch green
onions, thinly sliced
(about 1 cup), divided

high and bring the liquid to a
boil.

5. Reduce the heat to low, cover
the pot, and let simmer gently
for 30 minutes. Remove the lid,
stir, and let simmer uncovered
until the rice is tender but still
has a little bit of chew and most
of the liquid has cooked away,
20 to 30 minutes more. Stir the
pot periodically to prevent the
rice from sticking. Adjust the

heat as needed so that the liquid
simmers steadily but does not
boil aggressively. If at any point
the rice looks dry, add additional
water as needed. Stir in the peas,
butter, lime juice, and three-
quarters of the green onions.
Cover again, turn off the heat,
and let stand for 15 minutes to
allow the rice to absorb more of
the liquid. Stir, sprinkle with the
remaining green onions, and
enjoy hot.

loaded broccoli potato cheddar chicken skillet

ACTIVE TIME:
45 minutes

TOTAL TIME:
45 minutes

YIELD:
Serves 4

If you are looking for a new dinner to add to your greatest hits list (and I think we could all do with more recipes that every member of our household embraces with enthusiasm), this easy, cheesy dinner is it. Two of the most kid-friendly veggies—potatoes and broccoli—make it subtly nutritious, chicken adds lean protein, and cheddar and bacon will convince even the most reluctant eaters.

6 slices thick-cut bacon, cut crosswise into ½-inch strips (about 6 ounces)

1 pound Yukon Gold potatoes (about 2 medium), peeled and ¼ inch diced

1 pound ground chicken

1 small yellow onion, ½ inch diced (about 1 cup)

1 small head broccoli, chopped into tiny florets (about 2 cups)

1 tablespoon Worcestershire sauce

1 teaspoon garlic powder

½ teaspoon kosher salt

¼ teaspoon ground black pepper

3 green onions, thinly sliced (about ½ cup), divided

½ cup grated sharp cheddar cheese (about 2 ounces)

⅓ cup grated pepper Jack cheese, or Monterey Jack or additional cheddar (about 1½ ounces)

1. Heat a large cast-iron skillet or similar heavy-bottomed, ovenproof skillet over medium-low heat. Add the bacon and cook, stirring occasionally, until crisp and brown and the fat has rendered, about 8 minutes. With a slotted spoon, transfer the bacon to a paper towel–lined plate. Discard all but 2 tablespoons of the drippings from the pan.

2. Increase the skillet heat to medium. Add the potatoes. Cook, stirring often, until the potatoes are turning golden and becoming tender (they should still be too firm to eat), about 6 minutes.

3. Add the chicken, yellow onion, broccoli, Worcestershire, garlic powder, salt, and pepper. Cook, breaking up the chicken, until the potatoes and onions are tender and the meat is fully cooked through, about 6 minutes more.

4. Stir in half of the green onions. Taste and adjust the salt and pepper as desired. Sprinkle the cheddar and pepper Jack over the top. Place on the upper third rack of your oven, then turn the oven to broil. Broil until the cheese is melted, 2 to 3 minutes (watch carefully to ensure it does not burn). Remove from the oven and immediately sprinkle with the reserved bacon and remaining green onions. Let rest a few minutes, then serve.

speed it up

Skip the bacon and sauté the potatoes in 2 tablespoons canola oil instead of the bacon drippings.

one-pot rosemary chicken and potatoes

ACTIVE TIME:
35 minutes

TOTAL TIME:
1 hour

YIELD:
Serves 4

2¼ to 2½ pounds bone-in, skin-on split chicken breasts (2 very large breasts or 3 to 4 smaller breasts)

1½ teaspoons kosher salt, divided

½ teaspoon ground black pepper, divided

3 tablespoons extra-virgin olive oil, divided

1½ pounds baby red potatoes, scrubbed with skins on

4 sprigs fresh rosemary

6 garlic cloves, minced (about 2 tablespoons)

¼ cup freshly squeezed lemon juice (from about 1 medium lemon)

¼ teaspoon red pepper flakes

Anyone who thinks their tastes are too refined for a baked chicken and potatoes dish clearly hasn't tried this fantastic recipe. The ingredients don't look complex on paper, but when potatoes and chicken are browned just so, then enlivened with fresh lemon, woodsy rosemary, and zesty garlic, you have a home run of a dinner that manages to feel down to earth and elevated at the same time. While I'm all for making easy swaps where possible, for this recipe, fresh rosemary is essential—it makes the dish. You'll find yourself cooking this recipe as often for healthy weeknight meals as for your best company.

1. Position your oven racks such that a Dutch oven or similar large pot can bake in the center. Preheat to 425°F. If your chicken breasts are large (14 ounces or more), with a very sharp, sturdy chef's knife, cut them in half crosswise (that's through the shorter side if you think of the breast from left to right and top to bottom), placing the knife on top of the breast and cutting down through the bone, carefully but firmly wiggling the knife as needed. For each breast, you should be left with two pieces of chicken that are roughly similar in size. Sprinkle the top (skin side) of the chicken breasts with 1 teaspoon of the salt and ¼ teaspoon of the black pepper.

2. In a Dutch oven or similar large, heavy-bottomed,

ovenproof pot with a tight-fitting lid, heat 2 tablespoons of the oil over medium-high heat. Once the oil is very hot but not yet smoking, place the chicken skin side down in a single layer in the pot. It's OK if the chicken touches a little at the sides, but do not overlap the pieces or the skin will not brown properly. Cover and let the chicken cook until the skin is deep golden brown, 5 to 8 minutes, disturbing it as little as possible. If some of the pieces brown more quickly than others, transfer them to a plate, then let the remaining breasts continue cooking until golden.

3. While the chicken cooks, cut the potatoes into halves (if your potatoes are small) or quarters (if they are larger). The pieces

recipe continues

should be roughly 1½ inches in size.

4. Remove the browned chicken pieces from the pot. To the pot, add the remaining 1 tablespoon oil (no need to wipe the pot in between). Add the potatoes and remaining ½ teaspoon salt and ¼ teaspoon pepper. Stir to coat the potatoes with the oil and seasoning, then cover and let cook until the potatoes are golden on the outside, 8 to 10 minutes, stirring occasionally so that they brown evenly.

5. While the potatoes cook, strip the rosemary leaves from the stems. Discard the stems and finely chop the leaves. (You should have about 2 tablespoons.) In a small bowl or large measuring cup with a spout, whisk together the chopped rosemary, minced garlic, lemon juice, and red pepper flakes.

6. Uncover the pot. Arrange the chicken pieces skin side up on top of the potatoes and drizzle with any juices that have collected on the plate. Pour the lemon juice mixture over the top.

7. Transfer the pot to the oven and roast, uncovered, until the chicken reaches an internal temperature of 160°F at the thickest part, 20 minutes for smaller pieces and up to 35 minutes for larger pieces. If some pieces cook more quickly than others, transfer the cooked pieces to a clean plate and cover to keep them warm, then return the pot to the oven and continue baking until all the chicken is cooked through. Let rest 5 minutes. Serve warm, seasoned with additional salt and pepper as desired.

next level

If you're a lemon lover, squeeze a few lemon wedges over the top of the baked chicken prior to serving for an extra burst of fresh citrus.

leftover love

Refrigerate leftovers for up to 3 days. Since chicken can easily dry out when reheated, I like to shred mine and serve it at room temperature or chilled over salad.

Crisp up leftover potatoes in a 400°F oven: Arrange the potatoes on a baking sheet, lightly drizzle with a bit of olive oil, and toss to coat. Spread into a single layer and bake for 5 to 8 minutes, until hot.

creamy harvest chicken pasta

ACTIVE TIME:
50 minutes

TOTAL TIME:
50 minutes

YIELD:
Serves 6 to 8

1 pound Brussels sprouts, stems trimmed, brown outer leaves removed

1 tablespoon extra-virgin olive oil

12 ounces cooked apple chicken sausage, halved lengthwise and cut into ¼-inch-thick half-moon slices

2 tablespoons unsalted butter

1 small yellow onion, ¼ inch diced (about 1 cup)

2 garlic cloves, minced (about 2 teaspoons)

2½ teaspoons kosher salt, divided

1 teaspoon dried rubbed sage

¼ teaspoon ground nutmeg

¼ teaspoon ground black pepper

1 small butternut squash, cut into ½-inch pieces (about 1¼ pounds, or 3½ cups cubes)

1 pound whole wheat rotini, fusilli, or similar short, twisty pasta

If your favorite autumn ingredients jumped into a single skillet together, this nourishing, cozy one-pot pasta would emerge on the other side. The brilliance of this recipe lies in boiling the squash until it's tender, then stirring it into sauce so a portion breaks down and makes the sauce rich and velvety, no heavy cream required. On a cool fall evening, there are few better recipes.

1. Fill a medium-to-large pot (large enough to boil the squash and pasta together) with water. Bring to a boil over high heat.

2. While you wait for the water to boil, using a sharp chef's knife or mandoline, carefully cut the Brussels sprouts lengthwise into very thin slices (¼ inch or less).

3. Heat the oil in a Dutch oven or similar large, heavy-bottomed pot over medium-high heat. Add the sausage and cook, stirring from time to time, until browned on all sides, about 4 minutes. Transfer to a plate.

4. In the now-empty pot, melt the butter over medium heat. Add the onion and cook, stirring often, until it softens and begins to brown, about 5 minutes. Add the Brussels sprouts and cook, stirring often, until brighter green in color but barely wilted, about 3 minutes. Add the garlic, ½ teaspoon of the salt, the sage, nutmeg, and black pepper.

Cook, stirring constantly, for 30 seconds. Stir in the sausage, then remove from the heat.

5. Once the water comes to a boil, season with the remaining 2 teaspoons salt and add the squash. Let boil for 8 minutes, then add the pasta. Continue boiling until the pasta is al dente and the squash is very tender and on the verge of falling apart, about 8 minutes more. Reserve 1½ cups of the pasta water (don't forget!), then drain the pasta and squash.

6. Return the cooked pasta and squash to the now-empty pasta pot and add 1 cup of the reserved pasta water. Heat over medium heat, stirring vigorously until the squash breaks down a bit, 1 to 2 minutes. Some of the squash will mash into the pasta, while other pieces will remain fairly intact. Transfer to the pot with the Brussels sprouts.

recipe and ingredients continue

½ cup finely grated Parmesan cheese (about 2 ounces), plus additional for serving

½ teaspoon red pepper flakes

1 teaspoon apple cider vinegar

7. Add the Parmesan, red pepper flakes, and vinegar. Stir to combine, adding the remaining pasta water as needed to loosen the pasta. It should look silky and creamy. Taste and adjust the seasoning as desired—depending upon your pasta water, you may want an extra pinch or two of salt. Enjoy hot, with a generous sprinkle of additional Parmesan.

make it meatless

We love this pasta with an apple chicken sausage to keep with the fall vibes, but it's also super satisfying as a meatless main. Enjoy it as is (just omit the meat), or for a protein boost, stir in a 15-ounce can of rinsed and drained white beans, such as cannellini or great northern.

speed it up

Skip slicing the Brussels and use a 12- to 16-ounce bag of shredded or shaved Brussels sprouts instead.

Use store-bought cubed fresh butternut squash.

baked ziti-style cauliflower

ACTIVE TIME:
1 hour

TOTAL TIME:
1 hour 40 minutes

YIELD:
Serves 8

2 small heads cauliflower, chopped into florets (about 4½ cups)

3 tablespoons extra-virgin olive oil, divided

2 teaspoons Italian seasoning, divided

1¼ teaspoons kosher salt, divided

4 ounces whole wheat ziti, or penne, fusilli, rotini, or similar sturdy, tube-shaped pasta (about 1 heaping cup dried pasta)

1 pound 90% lean ground beef

1 medium yellow onion, ½ inch diced (about 1½ cups)

¼ teaspoon ground black pepper

3 garlic cloves, minced (about 1 tablespoon)

½ teaspoon red pepper flakes

1 (24-ounce) jar prepared tomato-based pasta sauce

⅓ cup chopped fresh basil, plus additional for serving

If a red-checkered-tablecloth Italian joint and a hip California restaurant got together, they'd serve this cauliflower baked ziti. It has all the cheesy glory and essential carb comfort of classic baked ziti, but a portion of the noodles is replaced with roasted cauliflower florets. It's profoundly satisfying in the most old-school way, but the tender, caramelized bites of cauliflower give it a new-school levity you'll welcome when you want your dinner to make you feel full and happy, without sending you express into a food coma. Since this recipe uses whole grains and the cauliflower provides a generous serving of veg, if I'm in a hurry, I serve it as an all-in-one meal for myself and Ben. If hosting friends, I like to add a quick side of Every Night Roasted Vegetables (*The Well Plated Cookbook*, page 262) or Roasted Brussels Sprouts Caesar Salad (page 99).

1. Place racks in the upper and lower thirds of your oven and preheat to 425°F. Coat a 9 by 13-inch casserole dish with nonstick spray.

2. Divide the cauliflower between two large rimmed baking sheets. Drizzle the florets on each sheet with 1 tablespoon of the oil, then sprinkle each with 1 teaspoon of the Italian seasoning and ¼ teaspoon of the salt. Toss to coat, then spread into an even layer. Bake on the upper and lower racks for 20 minutes. Remove the pans from the oven, then use a spatula to turn the cauliflower so it roasts evenly. Spread back into a single layer, switch the pans' positions on the upper and lower racks, and continue baking

until the cauliflower is tender in the center and caramelized at the edges, 10 to 15 minutes more. Reduce the oven temperature to 375°F.

3. Meanwhile, bring a large pot of salted water to a boil (it will look too large for the pasta, but you'll use it again to stir everything together later). Cook the pasta until just shy of al dente, according to the package instructions; it will continue cooking while the ziti bakes, so make sure it still is a little too chewy to eat. Drain, then return to the pot.

4. In a large skillet, heat the remaining 1 tablespoon oil

recipe and ingredients continue

1 (15-ounce) container
part-skim ricotta cheese
(about 2 cups)

2 cups shredded part-skim
mozzarella cheese
(about 8 ounces)

over medium-high heat. Add
the beef, onion, black pepper,
and remaining ¾ teaspoon salt.
Cook, breaking apart the meat,
until it is browned and cooked
through, 6 to 8 minutes. Stir in
the garlic and red pepper flakes.
Cook for 1 minute more.

5. Add the browned beef to
the pot with the drained pasta.
Add the pasta sauce, basil,
and roasted cauliflower. Stir
to evenly combine. Transfer
half of the pasta mixture to the
prepared dish.

6. Dollop half of the ricotta over
the top of the pasta and sprinkle
with 1 cup of the mozzarella.
Repeat with the remaining pasta,
ricotta, and mozzarella.

7. Place the ziti dish on a
rimmed baking sheet to catch
any drips. Carefully transfer
it to the lower oven rack. Bake
uncovered for 25 to 30 minutes,
until the mozzarella is melty
and the casserole is hot and
bubbly. Transfer to the upper
rack and broil for 1 to 2 minutes
to brown the cheese. Sprinkle
with additional chopped basil.
Let cool for at least 10 minutes
before serving.

pro tip

When reheating pasta, first add a splash of water or chicken broth
to your serving to keep the noodles from drying out.

make it meatless

Swap the beef for one (15-ounce) can of rinsed and drained white
beans, such as cannellini or great northern, or your favorite ground
meat alternative.

market swaps

Swap up to half of the cauliflower with other mixed roasted veggies.
Eggplant, red pepper, and zucchini would be scrumptious for
summer. Brussels sprouts and butternut squash are an ideal fall
combo.

white pizza spaghetti squash boats

ACTIVE TIME:
35 minutes

TOTAL TIME:
1 hour 30 minutes

YIELD:
Serves 4 to 6

For the Spaghetti Squash

2 medium spaghetti squash (about 2 pounds each)

2 teaspoons extra-virgin olive oil

½ teaspoon kosher salt

A few pinches ground black pepper

3 tablespoons water

For the Filling

2½ teaspoons extra-virgin olive oil, divided

1 pound ground Italian turkey or chicken sausage, removed from its casing if needed

5 ounces baby arugula (about 5 cups)

5 ounces baby spinach (about 5 cups)

2 garlic cloves, minced (about 2 teaspoons)

1 teaspoon dried thyme

¼ teaspoon kosher salt

¼ teaspoon ground black pepper

A picky eater during my elementary school years, I entered nightly negotiations with my mother over how much of my dinner I had to finish prior to being allowed dessert. Spaghetti squash was one of the rare vegetables I would agree to eat in full, provided she topped it with the agreed-upon quantities of brown sugar, cinnamon, and maple syrup. We ate so much spaghetti squash, I didn't electively cook it for myself until I was in my thirties.

Eventually, stuffed spaghetti squash boats like these reconnected me with the produce love of my youth. As if to bring my relationship with spaghetti squash full circle, this recipe is a play on a different childhood favorite that my mother never needed to convince me to inhale with gusto: white pizza. Mozzarella, goat cheese, and Greek yogurt act as the creamy pizza "sauce," arugula brings a peppery kick, and sautéed sausage makes it ultra filling. Both childhood Erin and grown-up Erin approve.

1. Bake the squash: Place a rack in the center of your oven and preheat to 400°F. Line a large rimmed baking sheet with parchment paper. With a very sharp chef's knife, cut off the ends of the squash so you have a flat surface on each side. Stand the squash up on its wide, flat end and carefully slice it in half from top to bottom. With a spoon, scoop out the seeds and discard. Arrange the squash cut side up on the prepared baking sheet. Drizzle the cut sides of the squash with ½ teaspoon of the oil each and sprinkle each with ⅛ teaspoon of the salt and a small pinch of black pepper.

Rub the oil, salt, and pepper over the insides of the squash. Flip the squash so it's cut side down and add the water to the pan around the squash. Bake for 40 to 50 minutes, until the outsides give easily when pressed and the insides of the squash are tender. Remove the squash from the oven, carefully flip cut side up, and let rest until cool enough to handle.

2. Move a rack to the upper third of the oven if needed. Turn the oven to broil. Fluff and loosen the insides of the squash

recipe and ingredients continue

¼ teaspoon red pepper flakes, plus additional to taste

4 ounces goat cheese, crumbled (about ¾ cup)

½ cup nonfat plain Greek yogurt

1 cup shredded part-skim mozzarella cheese, provolone cheese, or a blend (about 4 ounces), divided

pro tip

Baked, unstuffed spaghetti squash halves can be refrigerated for up to 5 days, so feel free to roast them a few days in advance.

make it meatless

Follow the recipe as directed, omitting the sausage and additional 1½ teaspoons olive oil needed to brown it. Sprinkle the finished squash with toasted pine nuts.

next level

For an additional layer of flavor, swap the mozzarella for its rich, mildly nutty cousin fontina.

with a fork to create spaghetti squash "strands." Set aside.

3. While the squash cools, prepare the filling: Heat 1½ teaspoons of the oil in a very large nonstick skillet over medium heat. Add the sausage and cook, breaking apart the meat, until it is browned and cooked through, about 5 minutes. With a slotted spoon, transfer the sausage to a plate and set aside.

4. With a paper towel, carefully wipe the skillet clean and return it to medium heat. Add the remaining 1 teaspoon oil. Once hot, add the arugula, spinach, garlic, thyme, salt, black pepper, and red pepper flakes. Cook until the greens wilt, 30 seconds to 1 minute.

market swaps

Not a fan of goat cheese? While I adore its creamy flavor here, you can try swapping feta (reduce the amount of salt in the filling a bit since feta is salty) or omit it entirely and stir in extra mozzarella or provolone cheese instead.

For a milder flavor, the arugula can be swapped for the same amount of spinach without any changes to the recipe.

Swap the spinach and arugula for a heartier green such as Swiss chard or kale. Because chard and kale are slower cooking, you'll need to increase their sauté time in step 4, adding a bit of water if they begin to stick to the skillet. Once the greens are tender, proceed with the recipe as directed.

5. To the skillet, add the fluffed squash strands, sausage, goat cheese, yogurt, and ½ cup of the mozzarella. Stir to combine, using a fork to gently break apart and distribute the squash, sausage, and greens as needed. You'll have a few pockets of cheese throughout, which will be delicious. Taste and adjust the seasoning as desired. Depending upon the saltiness of your goat cheese, you may want a pinch or two of additional salt.

6. Scoop the filling into the squash halves, distributing it equally among each. Sprinkle the remaining ½ cup mozzarella over the top. Return to the oven and broil for 4 to 6 minutes, until the cheese is melted and turning golden. Watch it very carefully in the last few minutes so the squash does not burn. Remove from the oven. Enjoy hot.

chili pie

ACTIVE TIME:
45 minutes

TOTAL TIME:
1 hour

YIELD:
Serves 4 to 6

For the Filling and Serving

1 tablespoon extra-virgin olive oil

1 medium yellow onion, ¼ inch diced (about 1½ cups)

1 green bell pepper, ¼ inch diced (about 1 cup)

1 red bell pepper, ¼ inch diced (about 1 cup)

1 teaspoon kosher salt

½ teaspoon garlic powder

¼ teaspoon ground black pepper

1 pound ground turkey

1 tablespoon chili powder

½ teaspoon ground cumin

⅛ teaspoon ground cinnamon

1 (15-ounce) can reduced-sodium black beans, or dark or light red kidney beans, rinsed and drained

1 (15-ounce) can reduced-sodium pinto beans, rinsed and drained

1 (8-ounce) can tomato sauce

My sister Elizabeth at one point had four girls under the age of six (including identical twins!), so when she says a recipe is a kid-approved keeper, you know her word is gold. Chili pie—a thick, saucy, and meaty mixture baked under a golden cornbread topping—is one of her family's favorite dinners, and now it's one of ours too. The spices here are mild enough to appeal to tender palates, though you can certainly up the heat if you wish. The cornbread batter will look thin as you are spreading it over the chili, but don't worry. It puffs up just enough and forms a golden, lightly crisp top crust that's ideal for your family to sink their spoons down into to scoop the hearty chili below.

1. Place a rack in the center of your oven and preheat to 425°F. Coat a deep 9-inch pie dish or deep 8 by 8-inch or 9 by 9-inch baking dish with nonstick spray. In a medium microwave-safe bowl, melt the butter for the cornbread topping in the microwave. Set aside to cool to room temperature.

2. Make the filling: Heat the oil in a large skillet or Dutch oven over medium-high heat. Add the onion, green bell pepper, red bell pepper, salt, garlic powder, and black pepper. Sauté until the onion is beginning to soften, about 5 minutes, then add the turkey, chili powder, cumin, and cinnamon. Cook, breaking apart the meat, until the turkey is browned and cooked through, 8 to 10 minutes.

3. Add the black beans, pinto beans, and tomato sauce. Fill up the tomato sauce can with 8 ounces water, then pour it into the skillet. Bring to a simmer and cook, stirring occasionally, for 8 minutes. The mixture will thicken and reduce a little—it should be similar in consistency to a sloppy joe filling.

4. Meanwhile, make the cornbread topping: In a medium bowl, whisk together the cornmeal, flour, baking powder, and salt. To the bowl with the melted butter, add the egg, milk, and honey, then whisk to combine. Add the dry ingredients to the wet ingredients and fold gently to combine, stopping as soon as the dry ingredients disappear. Fold in the cheese.

recipe and ingredients continue

For serving: chopped fresh cilantro, diced avocado, and plain Greek yogurt (or sour cream)

For the Cornbread Topping

4 tablespoons (½ stick) unsalted butter

¾ cup yellow cornmeal

1 tablespoon white whole wheat flour or all-purpose flour

1½ teaspoons baking powder

¼ teaspoon kosher salt

1 large egg, at room temperature

⅓ cup reduced-fat milk, at room temperature

1 tablespoon honey

½ cup shredded pepper Jack cheese (about 2 ounces) or sharp cheddar cheese

5. Once the filling has simmered, transfer it to the prepared dish and spread into an even layer. With a spoon, dollop the cornbread batter over the filling. With the back of the spoon or an offset spatula, spread the batter into a thin, even layer, extending it as near to the edges as you can. It will seem like too little batter, but it will thicken up as it bakes.

6. Place the dish on a large rimmed baking sheet to catch any drips. Bake until the cornbread is nicely golden brown and cooked through, 12 to 15 minutes. Let rest a few minutes. To serve, use a big spoon to scoop down through the cornbread topping into the filling beneath, ensuring each serving has a portion of both. Top with cilantro, avocado, and Greek yogurt as desired.

green goddess chicken thighs

ACTIVE TIME:
30 minutes

TOTAL TIME:
1 hour 20 minutes

YIELD:
Serves 4

2 pounds boneless, skinless chicken thighs

¾ cup nonfat plain Greek yogurt

3 tablespoons extra-virgin olive oil

2 cups lightly packed, roughly chopped mixed tender fresh herbs (basil, parsley, dill, tarragon, cilantro . . . whatever is in your garden!)

½ cup roughly chopped fresh chives

2 garlic cloves, peeled

1 tablespoon Worcestershire sauce

1 teaspoon kosher salt

½ teaspoon ground black pepper

1 medium lemon

My commitment to having an herb garden is so strong, I once lost my apartment security deposit for drilling a plant light into the wall so I could grow herbs throughout the Minnesota winter. Surely if the landlord had tasted my fresh, herbaceous creations, like these saucy, green goddess–dressed chicken thighs, he would have forgiven me. "Green goddess" is a term used for a creamy sauce made with heaps of fresh herbs, lemon, and garlic. It tastes like a night on a summer patio or a stroll through the farmers market. This dish is the ideal meal for when you want something that's filling but still feels light and bright. I like to serve this beside a bed of brown rice or couscous that's drizzled with even more of the goddess sauce so I have yet another way to lap it up.

1. Pat the chicken dry with paper towels. With the tines of a fork, poke the smooth sides of the thighs a few times to create holes, then transfer them to a large bowl or ziptop bag.

2. In the bowl of a food processor, place the yogurt, oil, tender herbs, chives, garlic, Worcestershire, salt, and pepper. Zest the lemon directly into the bowl, then add the juice, being careful not to get any lemon seeds into the processor (you should have about ¼ cup juice). Puree until smooth, scraping down the sides of the bowl a few times as needed. Taste and adjust the seasoning as desired. It should be bright, zippy, and herby.

3. Transfer half of the marinade from the food processor to a small serving bowl, then add the rest to the chicken. With a large spoon, stir to coat the thighs (or seal the bag, removing as much air as possible, and squish the bag around until the chicken is evenly coated). Let marinate at room temperature for 30 minutes, or refrigerate for up to 12 hours; if refrigerating, allow to sit at room temperature for 30 minutes prior to cooking. Cover and refrigerate the reserved marinade until ready to serve.

4. When ready to cook the chicken, place a rack in the center of your oven and preheat to 425°F. Coat a 9 by 13-inch baking dish with nonstick spray.

recipe continues

Remove the thighs from the marinade, letting the excess drip away. Arrange in a single layer in the dish, tucking the loose side portion of each thigh underneath. It's OK for the thighs to touch at the sides, but they should not overlap. Bake for 18 to 20 minutes, until the chicken registers between 155° and 160°F on an instant-read thermometer. Transfer to a plate (discard any liquid that collects in the dish), cover, and let rest for 5 minutes. Serve warm with the reserved green goddess marinade on the side.

speed it up

To cook the chicken thighs even more quickly (or to avoid turning on your oven), grill them: Let the chicken come to room temperature, then preheat your grill to medium/medium-high (375° to 400°F). Clean and oil the grates. Place the chicken thighs on the grill presentation (smooth) side down, shaking off any excess marinade first. Cover the grill and let cook for 4 to 5 minutes on the first side, then flip. The chicken should lift off the grill relatively easily; if it is sticking, allow it to cook another minute or two, then try again. Cook on the other side for 4 to 6 minutes more, until it registers 155° to 160°F. Let rest and serve as directed.

next level

For ultimate umami, swap the Worcestershire sauce for 2 anchovy fillets or 1 teaspoon anchovy paste.

cheater's cassoulet

ACTIVE TIME:
1 hour

TOTAL TIME:
6 hours

YIELD:
Serves 6 to 8

For the Confit Chicken Thighs

3 pounds bone-in, skin-on chicken thighs (6 to 8, depending upon their size)

1 tablespoon kosher salt

1 tablespoon apple cider vinegar or white vinegar

1 teaspoon dried thyme

½ teaspoon ground allspice

4 large garlic cloves, minced (about 4 teaspoons)

2 tablespoons extra-virgin olive oil

For the Cassoulet

12 to 14 ounces smoked mild turkey sausage, such as kielbasa

4 tablespoons extra-virgin olive oil, divided, plus additional as needed

3 medium carrots, scrubbed and ½ inch diced (about 1½ cups)

1 large yellow onion, ½ inch diced (about 2 cups)

Cassoulet—a classic southern French country casserole of slow-simmered pork, confit meat (usually duck), white beans, and sausage—is notoriously time intensive. You need to start days in advance, the steps are numerous, and no one in France seems to be able to agree on the "real" recipe. So obviously I had to cook it.

After two days, three emergency trips to the grocery store, a crash course in how to confit duck legs, and many "pardon my French" moments later, I set the bubbling cassoulet down on the table and told my friends to enjoy, because *no way* was I ever going to put myself through that again. Then, we all took a bite—and I knew I most definitely was going to cook cassoulet again.

Since spending days on dinner doesn't fit with real life 99.9 percent of the time, I created this shortcut version you can pull off in a reasonable amount of time. It still takes a few hours, so it's more of a special occasion situation, but most of that time is unattended. In place of duck, this cassoulet uses chicken thighs that are cooked gently in olive oil until they become meltingly tender, and the dry white beans are replaced with canned beans for simplicity (and because I never can seem to remember to soak them the night before). This cassoulet might not be *authentique*, but it certainly is delicious. Enjoy this as a truly stick-to-your ribs meal on a cold evening with warm company.

1. The day before or morning you plan to make the cassoulet, marinate the chicken thighs: With paper towels, pat the chicken thighs dry, then transfer them to a 9 by 9-inch or similarly sized baking dish. You want the thighs to fit together very snugly with no extra room in the dish. With the tines of a fork, poke holes all over the thighs. In a small bowl, stir together the salt, vinegar, thyme, allspice, and garlic.

Rub all over the outsides of the chicken, turning the thighs to coat them. Adjust the thighs as needed so they are skin side up. Cover and refrigerate for at least 4 hours or up to 1 day.

2. Bake the thighs: Uncover the pan and drizzle with the oil. Place on the center rack in a cold oven. Turn the oven to 300°F. Bake for 1 hour to 1 hour

recipe and ingredients continue

4 sprigs fresh thyme, tied into a bundle with kitchen twine, plus 2 teaspoons chopped, divided

1 teaspoon smoked paprika

¾ teaspoon kosher salt

½ teaspoon ground black pepper

3 garlic cloves, minced (about 1 tablespoon)

2 tablespoons tomato paste

1½ cups low-sodium chicken broth, plus additional as needed

2 (15-ounce) cans reduced-sodium white beans, such as great northern or cannellini, rinsed and drained

1 cup panko bread crumbs

15 minutes, until the thighs pierce easily with a paring knife and register at least 170°F on an instant-read thermometer (see Pro Tip). Transfer to a plate. Discard the juices in the pan.

3. Make the cassoulet: Preheat the oven to 375°F. Coat a 9 by 13-inch or similarly sized baking dish with nonstick spray.

4. Cut the sausage diagonally into ½-inch-thick slices. Add 2 tablespoons of the oil to a Dutch oven or similar large, heavy-bottomed pot. Heat over medium-high heat until the oil is sizzling. Add the sausage pieces and cook, stirring occasionally, until browned on all sides, about 4 minutes. Remove the sausage to a plate and set aside.

5. Reduce the heat to low. Add the carrots, onion, and thyme bundle. Cook, stirring occasionally, until the vegetables are softened and turning golden brown, 10 to 15 minutes. (Don't shortcut this step! It builds important flavor.) If at any point the pot looks dry, drizzle in more oil as needed.

6. Stir in the smoked paprika, salt, pepper, garlic, and tomato paste and cook, stirring constantly, for 30 seconds.

7. Pour in the chicken broth and stir, using a wooden spoon to scrape up any bits stuck to

the bottom of the pot. Stir in the beans. Let simmer until the liquid is reduced by one-third, 3 to 4 minutes. Remove the thyme bundle. With a wooden spoon or potato masher, mash a portion of the beans so the mixture in the pot is a little thicker but you have plenty of intact beans remaining.

8. Peel away and discard the chicken skin. Shred the chicken into bite-size pieces, then add the meat to the pot. Add the sausage and stir to combine. The mixture should be a tiny bit liquidy; if it's not, add more broth or water as needed. Transfer to the prepared baking dish and spread into an even layer.

9. In a small bowl, stir together the panko and the remaining 2 tablespoons oil. Sprinkle evenly over the top of the cassoulet.

10. Bake the cassoulet for about 20 minutes, until the filling is hot and bubbly and the topping is beginning to take on some color. Switch the oven to broil. Broil the cassoulet for 3 to 4 minutes, until the bread crumbs are toasted (watch closely to ensure they do not burn). Sprinkle with the 2 teaspoons chopped thyme. Let cool for at least 5 minutes, then serve with a great big spoon.

pro tip

Chicken thighs are forgiving, particularly when bathed in olive oil. Don't worry if yours get a little above 170°F; they'll still be melt-in-your-mouth tender. Note that if they were previously frozen, when you cut into them you may see red juices. This happens as a result of the freezing process; it does not mean your chicken is undercooked. When determining meat doneness, go by the temperature on your thermometer.

do ahead

Assemble the cassoulet up to 1 day in advance. Bake from refrigerated, adding 10 or so minutes to the cooking time. Some traditionalists say cassoulet is better the next day, so feel free to take their advice. Fully bake it the day before, then rewarm it in the oven at 350°F with a splash of chicken broth to make sure it stays nice and saucy.

next level

Make Your Own Fresh Bread Crumbs: Tear two slices of crusty bread into chunks and pulse them in a food processor until they form fine crumbs. Use in place of the panko.

balsamic berry chicken thighs

ACTIVE TIME:
35 minutes

TOTAL TIME:
55 minutes

YIELD:
Serves 3 to 4

2¼ pounds bone-in, skin-on chicken thighs (4 to 6 thighs)

2½ teaspoons kosher salt, divided

1 teaspoon ground black pepper, divided

1 tablespoon extra-virgin olive oil

1 small yellow onion, ¼ inch diced (about 1 cup)

2 tablespoons minced fresh ginger (about a 2-inch piece)

10 ounces frozen mixed berries, or a combination of fresh blueberries, blackberries, and strawberries (about 2 cups)

⅓ cup balsamic vinegar

¼ cup honey

¼ cup chopped fresh basil

Cooked brown or wild rice, for serving (see How to Cook Brown Rice, page 138)

Among habits I have zero intention to break is overbuying berries every single summer. Since I don't have a family of fruit bats to feed, it's all hands on deck to make sure our surplus doesn't go to waste. In addition to desserts (especially Blueberry Cornmeal Crisp, page 309), I love using berries in surprising savory applications like these sweet and tangy chicken thighs. This recipe is elegant enough for company but simple enough for a Tuesday night. Serve it with a big side of roasted vegetables, along with brown rice or a hunk of crusty bread for sopping up the berry sauce.

1. Remove the chicken from the refrigerator and let it come to room temperature. Place a rack in the upper third of your oven and preheat to 400°F. Pat the chicken very dry and season all over with 2 teaspoons of the salt and ½ teaspoon of the pepper.

2. Heat the oil in a large cast-iron skillet or similar heavy-bottomed ovenproof pan over medium-high heat. Once the oil is hot, add the chicken skin side down and sear for 4 minutes without disturbing. Continue cooking, rearranging the pieces occasionally so that the skin browns evenly, until the skin is deep golden brown, 6 to 8 minutes more. Transfer to a plate, skin side up (no need to sear the other side).

3. Reduce the heat to medium. Add the onion and remaining ½ teaspoon salt and ½ teaspoon pepper. Cook until the onion is beginning to soften and brown, about 4 minutes.

4. Stir in the ginger and cook for 30 seconds. Stir in the berries. Cook until they soften, about 5 minutes for frozen berries, breaking up any large pieces of fruit, such as whole strawberries. Add the vinegar and honey. Let simmer, stirring occasionally, until it reduces by roughly a third, about 5 minutes more.

5. Add the chicken back to the skillet skin side up, along with any juices that have collected on the plate. Transfer to the oven and bake for 12 to 15 minutes, until the chicken registers 160°F on an instant-read thermometer. If some of the pieces finish earlier than others, transfer them to a plate, then return the skillet to the oven to finish cooking the remaining chicken. If desired, broil to crisp the skin further, about 1 minute (watch carefully!). Let rest for 5 minutes. Sprinkle with basil. Serve with rice, with the sauce spooned liberally over the top.

crispy chicken schnitzel with caramelized cabbage

ACTIVE TIME: 1 hour

TOTAL TIME: 1 hour

YIELD: Serves 4

For the Cabbage

1 small head savoy cabbage or green cabbage

4 tablespoons extra-virgin olive oil, divided

1 tablespoon honey

1 teaspoon kosher salt

¼ teaspoon ground black pepper

For the Chicken

2 medium boneless, skinless chicken breasts (about 1¼ pounds; see Pro Tip)

1 teaspoon kosher salt, plus a few additional pinches

¾ cup white whole wheat flour or all-purpose flour

2 large eggs

1½ cups panko bread crumbs

⅛ teaspoon ground cayenne pepper

4 tablespoons canola oil, divided, plus additional as needed

4 tablespoons (½ stick) unsalted butter, divided

1 small lemon, cut into wedges

With a heritage that is a potpourri of western European, I lean into whichever lineage is most relevant to the holiday at hand, which means that come Oktoberfest, I take tremendous pride in my Germanic roots. In addition to frequenting Milwaukee's many beer gardens (all in the name of doing my ancestors proud, of course!), I cook up this crispy-outside, juicy-inside chicken schnitzel. This is simple comfort food at its best. To round out the meal, pop a pan of humble cabbage into the oven. What emerges is lightly charred, caramelized, and so delicious, you might forget it's a vegetable.

1. Prepare the cabbage: Place a rack in the center of your oven and preheat to 450°F. Cut the cabbage into eight wedges: First, cut it in half lengthwise through the stem. Then lay each half flat on the cutting board and slice in half lengthwise. Finally, halve each quarter lengthwise. For easy cleanup, line a large rimmed baking sheet with parchment paper. Arrange the cabbage in a single layer on top and brush with 2 tablespoons of the olive oil. Flip the cabbage over.

2. In a small bowl, whisk together the remaining 2 tablespoons olive oil and the honey. Brush liberally over the tops and sides of the cabbage, then drizzle any remaining over the top. Sprinkle with the salt and pepper. Roast the cabbage

for 20 minutes, then flip with a spatula and continue roasting until the cabbage is tender and the edges are dark brown, 15 to 20 minutes more. Don't worry if some of the edge pieces are super dark; they're the yummiest parts. Remove from the oven and reduce the oven temperature to 250°F.

3. Meanwhile, prepare the chicken: Split each chicken breast in half horizontally to create two thin cutlets. As you cut, carefully lay your hand on top and feel to make sure you are splitting it fairly evenly. Working one at a time, place a cutlet in a large ziptop bag or cover with plastic wrap. With a meat mallet, rolling pin, or the base of a skillet, lightly pound out the

recipe continues

chicken until it is *super* thin—about ⅛ inch. Proceed slowly and gently to ensure you do not tear the meat. Repeat with the remaining cutlets. Season the pounded chicken all over with 1 teaspoon of the salt.

4. Set up your dredging stations: In a wide, shallow dish (a pie dish works well), place the flour. Beat the eggs in a second shallow dish, then combine the bread crumbs and cayenne in a third. With tongs, grab one end of a chicken cutlet and dip the cutlet in the flour, then the eggs, then the bread crumbs, coating both sides and shaking off any excess as you go. Dip just one cutlet at a time and handle the meat as little as possible to keep it tender. Transfer to a clean plate and repeat with the remaining cutlets. Place a wire rack on top of a baking sheet and keep it near the stove. Return the cabbage to the oven to keep it warm.

5. In a large skillet, heat 1 tablespoon of the canola oil over medium heat. Once the oil is hot, add 1 tablespoon of the butter to the skillet and swirl it to melt. Working away from yourself, carefully lower two cutlets into the skillet, ensuring that they have some space between them (if the pan is crowded, cook them one at a time or they will be more dense). Cook on the first side until golden, about 3 minutes, then add another 1 tablespoon of the oil and 1 tablespoon of the butter. Flip and cook on the other side until it is golden brown, 1 to 2 minutes more. Transfer to the prepared baking sheet, sprinkle with a pinch of additional salt, and place in the oven to keep warm.

6. Add another 1 tablespoon of the oil and 1 tablespoon of the butter to the skillet. Repeat with the remaining cutlets, adding the remaining 1 tablespoon oil and 1 tablespoon butter just before flipping. Serve with the caramelized cabbage and lemon wedges. Squeeze the lemon all over the chicken and cabbage, and season with additional salt to taste.

pro tip

To make chicken breasts easier to split into cutlets, place them in the freezer for 10 to 15 minutes prior to cutting.

roasted pork tenderloin with brussels sprouts, grapes, and maple sauce

ACTIVE TIME:
30 minutes

TOTAL TIME:
45 minutes

YIELD:
Serves 3

⅔ cup whole wheat couscous

1 pork tenderloin (about 1¼ pounds)

2½ cups red or green seedless grapes (about 1 pound)

1 pound Brussels sprouts, stems trimmed, brown outer leaves removed, and halved

3 tablespoons extra-virgin olive oil, divided

1½ teaspoons kosher salt, divided

½ teaspoon ground black pepper, divided

1 cup low-sodium chicken broth

2 tablespoons balsamic vinegar

3 tablespoons pure maple syrup

2 teaspoons chopped fresh thyme

Scenario: It's time for something more exciting than chicken, but you're not feeling beef, someone else at the table won't touch fish, and you need dinner less than an hour from now. HELLO, PORK TENDERLOIN. This too-often-overlooked cut cooks in a flash, is lean and tender, and feels a little more special than your standard piece of poultry. Roasted alongside savory Brussels sprouts and red grapes—which collapse and intensify into robust, juicy morsels when baked—this stellar one-pan meal manages to be effortless and extraordinary at the same time. Serve it with simple steamed couscous or Kale Salad with Apples, Pomegranate, and Wild Rice (page 107) for a fabulous fall-feels dinner.

1. Cook the couscous according to the package instructions. Set aside.

2. Remove the pork from the refrigerator and let it stand at room temperature. Place racks in the upper third and center of your oven and preheat to 450°F. In the center of a large rimmed baking sheet, place the grapes and Brussels sprouts. Drizzle with 2 tablespoons of the oil, ½ teaspoon of the salt, and ¼ teaspoon of the pepper. Toss to coat, then spread the Brussels sprouts and grapes into an even layer, flipping the Brussels sprouts cut sides down. Bake on the upper rack for 18 to 22 minutes, until the grapes

soften and the Brussels sprouts crisp.

3. Meanwhile, pat the pork very dry with paper towels. With a sharp knife, cut away and discard the silverskin (tough membrane) from the pork, then cut the tenderloin in half crosswise so you have two shorter pieces. Season all over with the remaining 1 teaspoon salt and ¼ teaspoon pepper.

4. In a large, ovenproof skillet, heat the remaining 1 tablespoon oil over medium-high heat. Once the oil is hot but not yet smoking, swirl the pan to coat. Add the pork and cook, turning

recipe continues

occasionally, until it is nicely browned on all sides, about 4 minutes.

5. Transfer the skillet to the oven's center rack. Bake the pork for 8 to 12 minutes, until it reaches 140°F on an instant-read thermometer inserted at the thickest part. Transfer the pork to a cutting board, cover, and let rest while you finish the recipe. If one of the pieces finishes earlier than the other, remove it first, then continue baking the other piece.

6. Heat the skillet you used to cook the pork over medium-high heat. Carefully pour in the broth and vinegar. With a wooden spoon, scrape the skillet to loosen any browned bits. Let simmer rapidly, stirring occasionally, until the liquid is reduced by approximately half, about 4 minutes. Stir in the maple syrup. Let simmer 30 seconds more, stirring constantly. Remove from the heat.

7. To serve, slice the pork into 1-inch medallions. Sprinkle the thyme all over the pork, grapes, and Brussels sprouts. Serve the pork hot with a scoop of the roasted grapes and Brussels sprouts, side of couscous, and maple sauce spooned over everything.

market swaps

Swap the couscous for brown rice, quinoa, or cauliflower rice.

slow cooker pork tinga tacos

ACTIVE TIME:
20 minutes

TOTAL TIME:
**5 hours 30 minutes
(on high); 8 hours
30 minutes (on low)**

YIELD:
Serves 8 to 10

3 to 3½ pounds bone-in pork shoulder roast or pork butt

2 teaspoons kosher salt

1 teaspoon ground black pepper

2 tablespoons extra-virgin olive oil

1 (14.5-ounce) can fire-roasted diced tomatoes in their juices

6 garlic cloves, minced (about 2 tablespoons)

3 to 4 canned chipotle chiles in adobo (individual chiles, not whole cans!), thinly sliced (3 to 4 tablespoons)

1 to 3 teaspoons adobo sauce from the can of chipotles (optional for spicier pork)

1 tablespoon Worcestershire sauce

1 large yellow onion, cut lengthwise into ½-inch slices

2 teaspoons dried oregano

"Tinga" describes a dish popular throughout Mexico of fall-apart-tender shredded meat (chicken is traditional) in a tomato, onion, and chipotle sauce. From tacos to nachos to straight out of the pot with a fork, I have yet to find a wrong way to enjoy it. This slow-cooker rendition gives pork shoulder, one of the best meats for low-and-slow cooking, the tinga treatment. It's breathtaking how a relatively short list of ingredients can transform into a dish this intensely smoky, saucy, and straight-up restaurant worthy. Cook it every time you're hosting a party, want incredible leftovers, or just don't feel like paying much attention to your dinner while it cooks.

1. Season the pork all over with the salt and pepper. Heat the oil in a cast-iron or similar heavy-bottomed skillet or a Dutch oven over medium-high heat. Once the oil is hot but not yet smoking, add the pork. Brown the meat on all sides until the pork has a nice crust, about 10 minutes. Turn it every few minutes and do not disturb it more often than needed to ensure it browns properly.

2. While the pork browns, in a 5- or 6-quart slow cooker, stir together the tomatoes, garlic, chipotle chiles, adobo sauce, Worcestershire, onion, and oregano. Place the pork on top and spoon some of the tomato mixture over the top. Cover and cook on high for 5 to 6 hours or low for 8 to 10 hours, until the pork is fall-apart tender. Transfer the pork to a large bowl, leaving the cooking liquid in the slow cooker.

3. Shred the pork with two forks. With a slotted spoon, scoop the tomatoes, chipotles, and onion slices out of the slow cooker and place them on top of the pork. Stir to combine. The pork should be very juicy. If you'd like it even juicier, add a few spoonfuls of the remaining cooking liquid until you are happy with it. Taste and adjust the seasoning as desired (at this point, I usually add another pinch or two of salt). If you'd like the pork spicier, add more of the cooking liquid or some additional adobo sauce from the can of chipotle peppers (start 1 teaspoon at a time—it's powerful!).

recipe and ingredients continue

For serving: corn or flour tortillas, fresh cilantro, sliced avocado, queso fresco or feta cheese, lime wedges

4. In a dry skillet heated to medium heat, warm the tortillas until they are toasty and pliable, 20 to 30 seconds per side. Or if you prefer, wrap the tortillas in a damp paper towel and warm them in the microwave.

5. Assemble the tacos: Fill the tortillas with the pork and top with cilantro, avocado, and cheese. Enjoy immediately with a squeeze of lime.

pro tips

To keep the pork warm for a party, discard most of the cooking liquid from the slow cooker, then transfer the shredded pork and its juices back into the slow cooker, cover, and set to the warm setting.

Leftover chipotle chiles in adobo can be frozen for future use in a small ziptop bag or ice cube tray.

For more ways to use the chipotle chiles, add a finely diced pepper and/or the adobo sauce to marinades for meat, or stir them into salsa. Add a scant ¼ teaspoon of the adobo sauce to your favorite margarita for a smoky, spicy twist.

market swaps

To Make Chicken Tinga: Swap the pork for 2 to 2½ pounds boneless, skinless chicken thighs. Note that the thighs will cook more quickly—start checking at 4 hours on low for doneness (I do not recommend cooking the chicken on high, as it is likely to dry out). The chicken should reach 165°F on an instant-read thermometer.

ways to serve it

In addition to tacos, pork tinga and your favorite toppings can be used to stuff baked sweet potatoes, fill burritos or quesadillas, make crunchy tostadas or nachos, or turn Blackened Chili-Garlic Sweet Potato Wedges (page 266) into a main event.

curried ginger tofu bowls with coconut rice

ACTIVE TIME:
45 minutes

TOTAL TIME:
55 minutes

YIELD:
Serves 3 to 4

For the Coconut Rice

1 cup brown rice

1 (13.5-ounce) can light coconut milk

¼ cup water

¼ teaspoon kosher salt

For the Tofu Bowls

1 (14- to 16-ounce) package extra-firm tofu

3½ tablespoons canola oil or other neutral oil, such as grapeseed oil, divided

½ teaspoon kosher salt, divided

2 tablespoons minced fresh ginger (about a 2-inch piece), divided

3 garlic cloves, minced (about 3 teaspoons), divided

1½ teaspoons curry powder

½ teaspoon ground turmeric

⅛ teaspoon ground cayenne pepper

1 small yellow onion, thinly sliced (about 1½ cups)

A BYO (build-your-own) adventure of curry-spiced tofu, gingery kale, and simmered tomatoes with rice, this warming, nourishing bowl gives you a reason to look forward to your next meal. The Indian-inspired spices are invigorating, the tender sautéed kale reminds you that you are doing something good for yourself, and the rice stretches your servings. Those who (like me) find pressing tofu a little annoying will especially enjoy this preparation, which skips it. Instead, I break up the tofu in a skillet and sear it until it forms delectable golden chunks. Feel free to swap the rice for other grains, toss in leftover roasted vegetables, or top it off with a drizzle of tahini or blob of plain Greek yogurt for a creamy element.

1. Cook the rice: Place the rice in a mesh sieve and rinse well under cool running water. Place in a medium saucepan. Add the coconut milk, water, and salt. Bring to a boil, then cover and reduce the heat to low. Let simmer for 45 minutes, lowering the heat further if needed so the rice does not boil over. Turn off the heat and let sit, covered, for 10 minutes.

2. While the rice is cooking, prepare the tofu bowls: Drain the tofu, then firmly squeeze to release as much liquid as possible (don't worry if it begins to break apart). Wrap in paper towels and squeeze once more. Roughly chop into 1½-inch pieces.

3. In a large nonstick skillet, heat 3 tablespoons of the oil over medium-high heat. Once the oil is hot and shimmering, add the tofu and ¼ teaspoon of the salt. Stir to combine, then spread the pieces into an even layer. Let cook undisturbed until the tofu begins to turn dark gold underneath, about 4 minutes. With a spatula, break up the tofu into ½-inch pieces. Add 1 tablespoon of the ginger, 2 teaspoons of the garlic, the curry powder, turmeric, and cayenne. Cook, stirring occasionally, until the tofu pieces are crisp all over, about 4 minutes. Transfer to a plate or bowl. With a paper towel, carefully wipe out the skillet.

recipe and ingredients continue

1 medium jalapeño, seeded and finely chopped (about 2 tablespoons)

1 medium bunch curly kale or Swiss chard, stemmed and thinly sliced (about 8 ounces or 6 cups)

1 (14.5-ounce) can fire-roasted diced tomatoes in their juices

⅓ cup chopped fresh cilantro

4. Add the remaining ½ tablespoon oil to the skillet and heat it over medium. Add the onion, jalapeño, and remaining ¼ teaspoon salt. Cook, stirring frequently, until the onion is soft and golden, about 8 minutes. Stir in the remaining 1 tablespoon ginger and 1 teaspoon garlic.

5. Working a few handfuls at a time, add the kale, stirring as you go so it begins to wilt. Pour in the tomatoes. Continue cooking, stirring occasionally, until the kale is tender and most of the tomato liquid has cooked off, about 5 minutes.

6. To serve, place a scoop of coconut rice in each serving bowl. Top with a portion of the kale and tomato mixture, tofu, and a generous sprinkle of cilantro.

do ahead

Every component can be prepared in advance, so do future you a favor and make a big batch, then reheat it for fast, nutritious meals all week long.

bbq chickpea bowls

ACTIVE TIME:
40 minutes

TOTAL TIME:
50 minutes

YIELD:
Serves 3 to 4

For the BBQ Chickpeas and Serving

1 (15-ounce) can reduced-sodium chickpeas, rinsed and drained

¾ cup quinoa or brown rice

1½ cups water

½ teaspoon kosher salt, divided

1 tablespoon extra-virgin olive oil

1 teaspoon chili powder

1 teaspoon smoked paprika

½ teaspoon garlic powder

½ teaspoon mustard powder

1 (8-ounce) can tomato sauce

2 tablespoons pure maple syrup

1 tablespoon apple cider vinegar

1 to 2 ripe medium avocados, sliced or diced

Nonfat plain Greek yogurt

Chopped fresh cilantro

Let's upgrade our humble friend, the garbanzo bean, BBQ-style. Sauced up and spiced, these quick stewed chickpeas are prime for piling onto a baked potato, serving over a hunk of split and toasted cornbread, or my favorite: served up bowl-style with protein-packed quinoa, chili-roasted veggies, and a heap of avocado for good measure. This savory-sweet-smoky main is a vegetarian delight that meat eaters will also enjoy. If your household likes it hot, feel free to add a few pinches of cayenne or swap part of the chili powder for chipotle chile powder. You'll brag about these beans!

1. Spread the chickpeas out on a double layer of paper towels and pat dry. Let them continue to air-dry while you prep the quinoa and vegetables.

2. Cook the quinoa: Rinse the quinoa in a mesh sieve, then transfer to a small saucepan. Add the water and ¼ teaspoon of the salt. Bring to a boil over medium-high heat, then reduce the heat to maintain a gentle simmer. Let simmer uncovered, adjusting the heat as needed, until the water is fully absorbed, 12 to 14 minutes. Remove from the heat, cover, and let rest for 10 minutes. (To cook brown rice, see How to Cook Brown Rice, page 138.)

3. Roast the vegetables: Place racks in the upper and lower thirds of your oven and preheat to 400°F. Place the Brussels sprouts and onion on one large baking sheet and the cauliflower on another. Drizzle the baking sheets with 1 tablespoon oil each, then sprinkle each one with 1 teaspoon chili powder, ¼ teaspoon salt, and ¼ teaspoon pepper. Toss to coat very evenly, then spread the vegetables into a single layer. Bake the pans on the upper and lower racks for 15 minutes, then remove the pans from the oven, use a spatula to turn the vegetables so they cook evenly, and spread them back into an even layer. Return the pans to the oven, switching their positions on the upper and lower racks. Continue baking until the vegetables are tender and beginning to turn dark and crisp in places, 10 to 15 minutes more.

4. While the vegetables roast, make the BBQ chickpeas: Heat a large, deep skillet or Dutch oven over medium-high heat.

recipe and ingredients continue

For the Vegetables

½ pound Brussels sprouts, stems trimmed, brown outer leaves removed, and halved

1 small red onion, cut into 1-inch wedges

3 cups cauliflower florets (about 12 ounces or 1 small head or ½ large head)

2 tablespoons extra-virgin olive oil

2 teaspoons chili powder

½ teaspoon kosher salt

½ teaspoon ground black pepper

Add the oil and heat until it is hot and shimmering but not smoking. Swirl to coat the pan, then add the dried-off chickpeas, chili powder, smoked paprika, garlic powder, mustard powder, and remaining ¼ teaspoon salt. Stir to combine, then let cook, stirring occasionally, until the spices smell ultra fragrant, 2 to 3 minutes. Stand back a little, as the chickpeas will pop.

5. To the chickpeas, add the tomato sauce, maple syrup, and vinegar. Stir to combine, then partially cover the pan to protect from spatters. Bring to a boil, then reduce the heat to a simmer. Let simmer with the pan partially covered until the sauce thickens, about 3 minutes. Remove from the heat, stir, and cover to keep warm while the vegetables finish.

6. To assemble, place a scoop of quinoa in a bowl. Top with a mix of the roasted vegetables, a spoonful of the BBQ chickpeas, avocado, yogurt, and cilantro. Enjoy immediately.

do ahead

Cook quinoa (or brown rice) in big batches, let cool, then freeze in individual portions. Reheat as needed.

The BBQ chickpeas can be refrigerated for up to 5 days. Make them ahead of the rest of the meal, or even double and freeze the second half for later.

next level

Top your bowls with pickled jalapeños for some tang and spice.

For crunch, add a handful of French fried onions.

kale white bean pesto pasta

ACTIVE TIME: **40 minutes**

TOTAL TIME: **40 minutes**

YIELD: **Serves 4**

1 cup raw walnuts, almonds, pecans, or cashews

3 garlic cloves, peeled

4 cups stemmed and chopped kale (about ½ large bunch curly kale or 1 medium bunch lacinato kale), divided

½ cup fresh flat-leaf parsley

¼ cup freshly squeezed lemon juice (from about 1 medium lemon)

¼ cup plus 2 tablespoons finely grated Parmesan cheese (about 1½ ounces), divided, plus additional for serving

1 teaspoon kosher salt, divided

¼ teaspoon ground black pepper

1 (15-ounce) can reduced-sodium white beans, such as cannellini or great northern, rinsed and drained, divided

¼ cup plus 1 tablespoon extra-virgin olive oil, divided

8 ounces long whole wheat pasta noodles, such as linguini or fettuccine

Pinch red pepper flakes

It takes a seriously special recipe for me to bust out my food processor, so know that it is with the utmost sincerity that I say *this recipe is worth it.* This pesto is vibrant and ultra creamy, and unlike more traditional pestos that are made with basil and pine nuts, it uses budget-friendly ingredients you can find year-round. The Swiss army knife of ingredients here is the white beans. A portion is pureed into the pesto to make it thick and rich, and the remainder is stirred into the pasta for satisfying texture and a boost of plant-based protein and fiber. Don't forget to reserve some of the pasta water before draining the noodles. It's necessary to thin the sauce to the right consistency, and the starches in the pasta water help the sauce cling to the noodles.

1. **Toast the nuts:** Warm a large, deep dry skillet over medium heat. Add the walnuts and toast, stirring often and watching constantly, until the walnuts begin to brown and smell toasted and fragrant, 5 to 7 minutes. (Alternatively, you can toast them in the oven: Place a rack in the center of your oven and preheat to 350°F. Spread the nuts in a single layer on an ungreased rimmed baking sheet and bake for 8 to 10 minutes, until fragrant and golden, stirring once halfway through.)

2. As soon as the nuts are toasted, transfer them to the bowl of a food processor. Carefully wipe out the skillet and keep it handy.

3. To the food processor, add the garlic cloves. Pulse in five to six short bursts to roughly chop. Add 1½ cups of the kale, the parsley, lemon juice, ¼ cup of the Parmesan, ½ teaspoon of the salt, the black pepper, and 2 tablespoons of the beans. Pulse in 3-second bursts until the nuts are finely chopped and the mixture resembles a dry paste. Scrape down the sides of the bowl. With the motor running, pour in ¼ cup of the oil through the feed tube. The mixture should look thick and creamy.

4. Meanwhile, bring a large pot of salted water to a boil. Cook the pasta to al dente according to the package instructions. Reserve at least 1 cup of the pasta water (don't forget!), then drain.

5. While the pasta cooks, heat the same large, deep skillet you

recipe continues

used for the nuts over medium heat. Add the remaining 1 tablespoon oil and heat over medium-high heat. Add the remaining 2½ cups kale and ½ teaspoon salt. Sauté until the kale is crisp-tender, 4 to 6 minutes. Add the remaining white beans and stir to warm through.

6. Turn off the heat. To the skillet, add the drained pasta. Scrape the kale pesto into the skillet. With a large spatula, large spoon, or tongs, stir to begin to coat the pasta, adding the reserved pasta water to thin the sauce as needed. Continue to stir—it will take a minute or two to come together. At the end, the ingredients should be nicely combined and the noodles coated with a thick, creamy pesto. Sprinkle with the red pepper flakes and remaining 2 tablespoons Parmesan. Adjust the seasoning to taste. Serve right away with additional Parmesan as desired.

bam bam noodles

ACTIVE TIME:
35 minutes

TOTAL TIME:
35 minutes

YIELD:
Serves 4

For the Noodles

8 ounces stir-fry noodles or similar thin wheat noodle (see Pro Tip)

1 (14- to 16- ounce) package extra-firm tofu

1 tablespoon cornstarch

1 teaspoon kosher salt, divided

3 tablespoons canola oil or other neutral oil, such as grapeseed oil, divided

1 tablespoon low-sodium soy sauce, divided

8 ounces cremini (baby bella) mushrooms, very finely chopped

1 (5- to 6-ounce) container baby spinach, roughly torn or chopped

⅔ cup chopped dry roasted peanuts

For the Sauce

⅓ cup tahini or creamy peanut butter

¼ cup low-sodium soy sauce

3 tablespoons red wine vinegar

This fiery dish is inspired by dan dan noodles, a popular Sichuan street food that migrated over to the United States. I first tasted it at an Asian fusion spot located in an unassuming strip mall a few blocks from our home. In a dark corner booth, I huddled over my plate and employed my finest chopstick work to shovel the addictively spicy, umami rich, and crunchy peanut-topped noodles into my mouth with urgency. This adaptation uses ingredients that are readily available at most grocery stores (though if you have a local Asian market, this recipe is the perfect reason to visit!). For a version truer to the original, instead of sambal for heat, use Sichuan peppercorns, which have the trippy, oddly delightful sensation of making your mouth feel momentarily tingly and numb.

1. Bring a pot of water to a boil and cook the noodles to al dente according to the package instructions. Reserve ½ cup of the pasta water (don't forget!), then drain the noodles in a colander. Rinse the noodles under cool water for a couple of seconds to remove some of the starch (the noodles should stay hot). Set aside in the colander to drain.

2. Drain the tofu, then with your hands, squeeze it gently over the sink to remove as much extra water as you can (don't worry if the tofu breaks into a few pieces). Wrap in a few layers of paper towels and squeeze again to remove as much liquid as possible. Crumble into chunky pieces in a bowl. Sprinkle with the cornstarch and ½ teaspoon of the salt, then use your hands to toss to coat.

3. Prepare the sauce: In a medium bowl or large liquid measuring cup with a spout, briskly whisk together the tahini, soy sauce, vinegar, maple syrup, garlic, ginger, sambal oelek, salt, and cloves.

4. In a large nonstick skillet or wok, heat 2 tablespoons of the oil over medium-high heat. Once the oil is hot and shimmering, add the tofu in a single layer (keep the tofu bowl handy). Let cook undisturbed until golden brown underneath, 4 to 5 minutes. Toss and continue cooking, stirring periodically, until the tofu is golden brown all over. Stir in ½ tablespoon of the soy sauce, then transfer back to the bowl.

recipe and ingredients continue

1 tablespoon pure maple syrup

2 garlic cloves, minced (about 2 teaspoons)

1 tablespoon minced fresh ginger (about a 1-inch piece)

1½ tablespoons sambal oelek (fresh chili paste) or chili oil, plus additional to taste

¼ teaspoon kosher salt

⅛ teaspoon ground cloves

5. Add the remaining 1 tablespoon oil to the skillet. Add the mushrooms and the remaining ½ tablespoon soy sauce. Let cook, stirring periodically, until the mushrooms are nicely browned, about 5 minutes.

6. Return the tofu to the skillet. Pour in the sauce and let simmer for 30 seconds. Stir in the spinach a few handfuls at a time, allowing it to wilt. Add the noodles, and with tongs, toss to coat them with the sauce and combine everything evenly. Add some of the reserved pasta water as needed to loosen the sauce. Stir in the peanuts. Serve hot with additional sambal oelek to taste.

pro tip

Look for thin wheat noodles, sometimes called stir-fry noodles. Whole wheat Italian spaghetti noodles or uncooked chow mein noodles also work well (if using chow mein, make sure it is the kind designed for boiling, not the precrisped kind in a can designed to be added to salads for crunch).

next level

If you have a well-stocked pantry or access to a local Asian market, swap the red wine vinegar for Chinese black vinegar. Add ½ to 1 teaspoon ground Sichuan peppercorns to the sauce to taste, in place of the sambal. Instead of tahini, use Chinese sesame paste. Fresh noodles in place of dried would be fantastic too!

okonomiyaki (savory japanese cabbage pancakes)

ACTIVE TIME:
45 minutes

TOTAL TIME:
45 minutes

YIELD:
4 hearty pancakes

For the Pancakes

1 (14.5-ounce) can low-sodium vegetable broth (or chicken broth if not vegetarian)

8 large eggs, divided

1 tablespoon Worcestershire sauce

1½ cups white whole wheat flour or all-purpose flour

1½ teaspoons kosher salt

1 teaspoon baking powder

½ teaspoon baking soda

½ teaspoon smoked paprika

5 cups shredded vegetable slaw (about 10 ounces), such as Mann's Power Blend, broccoli slaw, Trader Joe's Cruciferous Crunch, or another slaw with a mix of shredded vegetables such as cabbage, Brussels sprouts, and carrots

Japanese okonomiyaki (pronounced "ow-kuh-now-mee-aa-kee") translates to "as you like it." Accept the invitation and make it your own! A bit of a cross between a savory pancake and a frittata, okonomiyaki are usually filled with cabbage and pork belly, but once you have the base recipe, you can use any veggies and protein you like. When we visited Japan a few years ago, it was one of our favorite street foods. I don't see it often in the US, which is a shame because okonomiyaki are delicious, filling, and economical. This recipe is my humble attempt to bring a taste of this wonderful country to your kitchen. For ease and lightning weeknight speed, I use a bag of broccoli coleslaw, but you can certainly swap any finely shredded fresh vegetables or chopped roasted vegetables of your choosing. With a fried egg, this is a super-satisfying main, though should you insist on folding in some cooked, crumbled bacon, I suspect that will be exactly as you like it.

1. If you'd like to keep the pancakes warm between batches, preheat your oven to 200°F and line a baking sheet with parchment paper.

2. In a large bowl, whisk together the broth, 4 of the eggs, and the Worcestershire sauce. Add the flour, salt, baking powder, baking soda, and smoked paprika. Whisk until smoothly combined. It will be the consistency of a loose pancake batter. Fold in the slaw and green onions.

3. Heat ½ tablespoon of the oil in an 8-inch nonstick skillet over medium heat. Once the oil is hot, add one-quarter of the batter, spreading it into an even 6-inch round that is about ¾ inch thick. Do not push down on the mixture; it won't look cohesive at this point but will come together as it cooks. Reduce the heat to medium-low and cook until the pancake is golden brown underneath, 6 to 8 minutes. Flip and cook on the other side until golden brown and set, 2 to 4 minutes more.

recipe and ingredients continue

1½ bunches green onions, thinly sliced (about 1½ cups), plus additional for serving

2 tablespoons canola oil or other neutral oil, such as grapeseed oil, divided

Optional for serving: sesame seeds, nonfat plain Greek yogurt or Kewpie mayo (see Pro Tip)

For the Okonomiyaki Sauce

2 tablespoons hoisin sauce

1 tablespoon low-sodium soy sauce

½ teaspoon sriracha, plus additional to taste

Give the remaining batter a big stir, add another ½ tablespoon oil to the skillet if needed, and continue with the remaining batches, keeping earlier batches warm in the oven on the prepared baking sheet.

4. While the pancakes cook, stir together the hoisin, soy sauce, and sriracha for the okonomiyaki sauce. Prepare any other desired toppings (see Next Level).

5. When you are close to serving, fry the remaining 4 eggs in a nonstick skillet over medium heat, until the whites are set but the yolks are still runny, about 3 minutes.

6. To serve, place each pancake on a plate. Drizzle sparingly with the okonomiyaki sauce, top with a fried egg, then sprinkle with sesame seeds (if using) and green onions. Enjoy hot with yogurt and any other desired accompaniments.

pro tip

Kewpie mayo, which is slightly richer, sweeter, and tangier than standard mayo, is traditionally drizzled on okonomiyaki. I prefer mine with a dollop of Greek yogurt as a healthy swap (and, well, my longtime readers know how I feel about mayo—no thanks!). You can find Kewpie mayo at Asian grocery stores or swap regular mayo.

do ahead

This batter is even better when rested in the refrigerator for 1 hour prior to cooking and can be made up to 1 day in advance.

next level

Do like they do in Japan and top your okonomiyaki with chopped pickled ginger, thinly sliced nori (roasted seaweed sheets), and/or bonito flakes.

lentil kofta

ACTIVE TIME:

45 minutes

TOTAL TIME:

1 hour 15 minutes

YIELD:

18 balls (serves 3 to 4)

For the Lentil Kofta

⅓ cup roughly chopped raw walnuts

1 cup dried green or brown lentils

1 (14.5-ounce) can vegetable broth

1 tablespoon extra-virgin olive oil, plus additional for broiling

1 small yellow onion, finely chopped (about 1 cup)

4 garlic cloves, minced (about 4 teaspoons)

1½ teaspoons ground cinnamon

1 teaspoon ground allspice

½ teaspoon ground nutmeg

¾ teaspoon kosher salt

½ teaspoon ground black pepper

¼ teaspoon red pepper flakes, plus a pinch or two for a spicy kofta

½ cup old-fashioned oats or quick-cooking oats

⅓ cup roughly chopped fresh flat-leaf parsley

1 large egg

Kofta is a bit like a Middle Eastern version of a meatball. Seasoned generously with warm spices like cinnamon and allspice, zippy with garlic and onions, and alive with herbs, koftas can be tucked into pita, served kebab style, dunked with a spicy sauce, or even added to soups. This recipe is a vegetarian spin, swapping the ground meat (usually lamb, beef, or a combination) for hearty lentils. This versatile legume is a powerhouse of nutrients and good source of plant-based protein, and it lends itself well to a wide range of flavors. Be generous with the olive oil when baking. It's key to the lightly crispy exterior and will keep the koftas from tasting dry.

1. Toast the nuts: In a medium dry skillet, place the walnuts. Cook over low heat, stirring often and keeping a close eye on them, until toasted and fragrant, about 5 minutes. (Be patient! Slow and steady wins the race here.) Transfer to a small plate or bowl. Carefully wipe out the skillet and keep it handy.

2. Cook the lentils: In a small colander or strainer, rinse the lentils, picking out and discarding any bits of debris. Place in a medium saucepan. Cover with the vegetable broth, then bring to a rapid simmer over medium-high heat. Reduce the heat so that the lentils gently simmer—you should see some bubbles on the surface, but the lentils in the centermost part of the pan should barely move. Simmer gently until the lentils are tender but still have some

chew, 20 to 25 minutes. Keep an eye on them to ensure they do not dry out—you want the lentils to always be just barely covered with liquid. If the lentils are not yet tender but the liquid has been absorbed, add water as needed. Drain if needed and set aside.

3. Meanwhile, in the same skillet you used for the walnuts, heat the oil over medium-low heat. Add the onion and cook until it is translucent and turning lightly brown, 5 to 6 minutes. Stir in the garlic, cinnamon, allspice, nutmeg, salt, black pepper, and red pepper flakes. Cook for 30 seconds, until very fragrant, then remove from the heat.

4. In the bowl of a food processor, place the oats and parsley. Pulse briefly three times,

recipe and ingredients continue

Warm pita or cooked brown rice, for serving (see How to Cook Brown Rice, page 138)

For the Tahini Yogurt Sauce

½ cup nonfat plain Greek yogurt

¼ cup tahini

2 tablespoons freshly squeezed lemon juice

2 tablespoons water, plus additional as needed

1 tablespoon chopped fresh flat-leaf parsley

½ teaspoon kosher salt

just until the oats break up a little. Add the cooked lentils, onions and any spices and oils that have collected in the pan, and the walnuts. Pulse in three short bursts, until the lentils start to break up. Scrape down the bowl, then crack in the egg. Continue to pulse a few more times, just until the mixture is combined but the lentils still have some texture. Let rest for 10 minutes, or refrigerate overnight.

5. Meanwhile, make the tahini yogurt sauce: In a small bowl, stir together the yogurt, tahini, lemon juice, water, parsley, and salt. If the sauce is thicker than you would like, add a little more water until you reach your desired consistency. It should be smooth and pourable, but not overly runny. Taste and adjust the seasoning as desired.

6. When you're ready to cook the kofta, place a rack in the upper third of your oven and turn the oven to broil. Coat a large rimmed baking sheet generously with nonstick spray. With a cookie scoop or spoon, portion and shape the lentil mixture into balls that are roughly 1½ inches across, about the size of a golf ball. Keep the ball shape or continue to shape them into mini footballs (this is the traditional kofta shape). Arrange them in a single layer on the baking sheet, then drizzle generously with olive oil. Rub gently to coat the koftas with oil on all sides, adding more as needed to ensure each has a complete, light coating. Broil for 6 to 8 minutes, until crisp and browned, flipping once halfway through and keeping a close eye on them. Serve warm with rice or pita and tahini yogurt sauce.

sweet potato samosa pie

ACTIVE TIME:
1 hour

TOTAL TIME:
1 hour 30 minutes (not including making pie crust)

YIELD:
Serves 6

2 pounds similarly-sized sweet potatoes (about 4 medium)

2 teaspoons kosher salt, divided

½ cup green or brown lentils

2 tablespoons extra-virgin olive oil

1 medium yellow onion, ¼ inch diced (about 1½ cups)

2 garlic cloves, minced (about 2 teaspoons)

2 teaspoons ground cumin

1 teaspoon chili powder

1 teaspoon ground ginger

½ teaspoon ground turmeric

½ teaspoon ground black pepper

⅛ teaspoon ground cayenne pepper (optional; increase to ¼ teaspoon for a spicier samosa pie)

1 medium jalapeño, seeded and finely chopped (about 2 tablespoons)

With its enthusiastic warmth, intoxicating aromas, and elevation of vegetables to a feast in their own right, Indian cuisine never ceases to captivate me. One of my favorite dishes is the samosa, a savory fried pastry with a spiced filling, often of potatoes and peas. When I visited India, I relished munching them hot from their paper wrappers, flakes of pastry clinging to my skirt and chin. This recipe is inspired by the popular street food, using similar spices to enliven a fragrant mixture of sweet potatoes, lentils, and vegetables. Top it off with the absolute best pie crust in the world (Bragging Rights Pie Crust, page 297), or make your life a little easier and use store-bought.

1. Place a rack in the center of your oven and preheat to 400°F. Lightly coat a deep 9-inch pie dish with nonstick spray.

2. Scrub the sweet potatoes and place in a large saucepan. Add 1 teaspoon of the salt, then cover with cold water by 2 inches. Bring to a boil over medium-high heat. Continue boiling until a sharp knife easily slides into the center of the sweet potatoes without resistance, 20 to 25 minutes. Drain. Once cool enough to handle, peel and chop into 1-inch chunks.

3. Meanwhile, cook the lentils according to the package instructions. Drain and set aside.

4. Heat the oil in a Dutch oven or similar large, heavy-bottomed pot over medium heat. Add the onion and cook until softened and beginning to brown, about 8 minutes. Stir in the garlic, cumin, chili powder, ginger, turmeric, black pepper, cayenne pepper (if using), and the remaining 1 teaspoon salt. Let cook, stirring constantly, for 30 seconds, until very fragrant.

5. Add the sweet potato chunks and jalapeño. Cook, stirring occasionally, for 5 minutes more. The spices will darken and the sweet potato will break apart, but you should still have some more-intact pieces of sweet potato remaining. Remove from the heat and stir in the peas, cilantro, and lentils. Taste and adjust the seasoning as desired. Spread into an even layer in the prepared pie dish.

6. Roll the pie crust dough into a circle large enough to cover your

recipe and ingredients continue

1 cup frozen peas, no need to thaw

⅓ cup chopped fresh cilantro

½ batch (single crust) Bragging Rights Pie Crust (page 297), or store-bought pie crust (enough for one 9- or 10-inch crust)

1 large egg, beaten with 1 tablespoon water to create an egg wash

dish. Brush the edges of the pie dish with the egg wash, then lay the dough over the top so that it overhangs the sides. Trim the overhang to ½ inch larger than the edge of the dish. Gently press the dough onto the sides of the dish so it sticks, then brush all over the top with a thin layer of the egg wash (discard any excess egg wash). With a sharp knife, cut five slits in the top that are 1 to 1½ inches long.

7. Bake the samosa pie for about 25 minutes, until the top crust is a shiny golden brown. Let cool for a few minutes, then with a big spoon or spatula, slice, scoop, and serve, ensuring each piece has a good portion of the filling and crust.

next level

Crust lovers can add a second pie crust to the bottom of the dish—no need to blind bake it first. Roll the bottom crust to a 12-inch diameter, then fit it into the dish. Add the sweet potato filling. Roll out the second crust, place it over the dish, and trim the overhang of both crusts to ½ inch. Seal the edges by crimping with a fork or your fingers. Brush with the egg wash, slit, and bake as directed.

market swap

For a classic samosa filling, swap the sweet potatoes for the same quantity of russet potatoes.

sweet potato black bean quesadillas

ACTIVE TIME:
35 minutes

TOTAL TIME:
35 minutes

YIELD:
8 quesadillas

2 medium sweet potatoes (about 20 ounces)

1 tablespoon chili powder

1 teaspoon ground cumin

1 teaspoon ground cinnamon

1 teaspoon garlic powder

¾ teaspoon kosher salt, divided

¼ teaspoon chipotle chile powder

1 tablespoon extra-virgin olive oil

1 medium yellow onion, ¼ inch diced (about 1½ cups)

1 medium red bell pepper, ½ inch diced (about 1 cup)

1 medium green bell pepper, ½ inch diced (about 1 cup)

1 (15-ounce) can reduced-sodium black beans, rinsed and drained

8 fajita-size (7- or 8-inch) whole wheat tortillas

Meet how I survived our first year of marriage, plus one of the first recipes ever posted on *Well Plated*! When I started my blog, our budget was tight, and Ben had the appetite of a growing Tyrannosaurus rex. Inexpensive, nutritious food that could be prepared in massive quantities was the move. These sweet, smoky quesadillas were on our menu weekly. Sweet potatoes' natural sugars make them a scrumptious pairing with Tex-Mex spices like the ones you'll find here. The cinnamon adds a signature warmth and is what makes these especially memorable, but if you're shy about it in savory preparations, feel free to dial it back the first time.

1. Scrub the sweet potatoes and cut into 1-inch chunks (see Pro Tip). Place in a large saucepan, cover with water by about 1 inch, and bring to a boil. Continue boiling, adjusting the heat as needed to maintain a steady but not wild boil, until the chunks pierce easily with a fork, about 8 minutes. Remove the pot from the heat and drain the sweet potatoes, then return them to the pot and mash until they are mostly smooth but still have some texture.

2. Stir in the chili powder, cumin, cinnamon, garlic powder, ½ teaspoon of the salt, and chipotle chile powder until well combined. Set aside.

3. Meanwhile, heat the oil in a large nonstick skillet over medium-high heat. Add the onion, red bell pepper, green bell pepper, and remaining ¼ teaspoon salt. Cook until the vegetables soften and the onion starts to brown, about 8 minutes. Scrape the vegetable mixture into the pan with the mashed sweet potatoes.

4. Add the black beans. Stir until all the ingredients are evenly distributed, using a fork to help mix the beans and veggies around as needed.

5. Assemble the quesadillas: Place a tortilla on a work surface. Scoop ½ cup of filling onto half of the tortilla. With the back of a spoon, spread the filling into an even layer over the entire half.

recipe and ingredients continue

2 cups shredded sharp cheddar or Monterey Jack cheese (about 8 ounces), divided

Nonstick spray, butter, or additional olive oil, for cooking the quesadillas

Optional for serving: nonfat plain Greek yogurt (or sour cream), diced avocado, diced red onion, salsa, chopped fresh cilantro

Sprinkle the filling with ¼ cup of the shredded cheese. Fold the empty half of the tortilla over the top. Repeat with the remaining quesadillas.

6. With a paper towel, carefully wipe clean the pan you used to cook the vegetables. Heat it over medium to medium-low heat, adding nonstick spray or a little butter or oil to the skillet if you'd like the tortillas crispier. Place one tortilla in the pan with the folded edge running down the center and the open edge facing outward. Lay a second quesadilla down beside it facing the opposite direction so the two folded edges are next to each other. With the back of a spatula,

lightly press down on the tops so they flatten (don't worry if some of the cheese escapes). Cook on the first side until golden and crisp, adjusting the heat as needed so the quesadillas brown but do not burn, 3 to 5 minutes. Carefully flip and cook the other side until both sides are lightly crisp and golden brown, about 2 minutes more.

7. Transfer the quesadillas to a cutting board and let cool for a few minutes (or transfer to a 200°F oven to keep warm while finishing the remaining batches). With a sharp knife or pizza cutter, slice each quesadilla into pie-shaped wedges. Enjoy hot with desired toppings.

pro tip

While you can peel the sweet potatoes if you like, in most instances I prefer to leave the skins on. From a health standpoint, peels are a source of fiber and nutrients like potassium and manganese. From a culinary standpoint, they give the filling a more dynamic texture and subtle note of earthiness. And from a practical standpoint, skipping the peeling saves you time!

do ahead

The filling can last in your refrigerator for several days and be frozen for several months. Rewarm the portion you need for your meal, cook the quesadilla as directed, then save the rest for future fast lunches and dinners.

stacked butternut squash black bean enchiladas

ACTIVE TIME:
50 minutes

TOTAL TIME:
1 hour 45 minutes

YIELD:
Serves 8

1 (10- to 12-ounce) package frozen chopped spinach, thawed

1 tablespoon extra-virgin olive oil

1 small red onion, ½ inch diced (about 1 cup)

1 medium butternut squash (about 1½ pounds), ½ inch diced (about 3½ cups)

3 garlic cloves, minced (about 1 tablespoon)

2 teaspoons ground cumin

1 teaspoon dried oregano

¾ teaspoon kosher salt

½ teaspoon chipotle chile powder

¼ teaspoon ground black pepper

1 (15-ounce) can low-sodium black beans, rinsed and drained

1 (16-ounce) jar prepared salsa, mild or medium

1 (15-ounce) can tomato sauce

I realize that it won't always work to take two things I love, smush them together, and see what happens (. . . hence, no caramel pickles in this book). But when the results are as outstanding as this lasagna-meets-Tex-Mex mashup, you best believe I'm going to keep throwing noodles (and tortillas) at the wall. Here, core enchilada ingredients—tortillas, spices, plenty of sauce, and beans—are done up lasagna style, all layered together into a slice-and-serve stack of cheesy splendor. This is one of those prized recipes that manages to sneak in a slew of vegetables without actually tasting like it does. Enjoy it on its own, or pair it with Blackened Chili-Garlic Sweet Potato Wedges (page 266) for a comfort dinner with a twist.

1. Place racks in the center and upper third of your oven and preheat to 425°F. Coat a 9 by 13-inch baking dish with nonstick spray.

2. Place the spinach in a mesh sieve or small colander and squeeze out as much water as possible. Place a double layer of paper towels on top and press it further so that the spinach is as dry as possible.

3. Heat the oil in a large, deep skillet over medium heat. Once the oil is hot, add the onion and cook until beginning to soften, 2 to 3 minutes. Stir in the squash, garlic, cumin, oregano, salt, chipotle chile powder, and pepper. Sauté, stirring occasionally, until the squash is tender but not mushy, 12 to 16 minutes. Taste a few pieces of squash to make sure it's the right texture throughout. Add the spinach, using a fork to break it up evenly if needed. Stir in the beans and salsa, then remove from the heat.

4. Assemble the layers: Spread a thin layer of the canned tomato sauce (about ½ cup) on the bottom of the baking dish. Stir the remaining tomato sauce into the butternut squash mixture; taste and adjust the seasoning as desired. Arrange four tortilla halves on top of the tomato sauce so they evenly cover it. Top the tortillas evenly with one-third of the squash mixture.

recipe and ingredients continue

1 cup full-fat plain Greek yogurt, divided

2 cups shredded Monterey Jack cheese (about 8 ounces), divided

6 fajita-size (7- or 8-inch) whole wheat tortillas or regular flour tortillas, halved

Chopped fresh cilantro, for serving

Optional for serving: sliced avocado, chopped red or green onion, plain Greek yogurt

Dollop ½ cup of the yogurt in small spoonfuls over the top, distributing it fairly evenly, then sprinkle with ⅔ cup of the cheese.

5. Add another layer of four tortilla halves, half of the remaining butternut mixture, the remaining ½ cup yogurt, and ⅔ cup of the cheese. Repeat with the last four tortilla halves, remaining butternut squash mixture, and remaining cheese.

6. Lightly mist a sheet of aluminum foil large enough to cover the enchiladas with nonstick spray, then use it to cover the pan, placing it spray side down. Bake the enchiladas on the center rack for 20 minutes. Uncover and continue baking until the filling is hot and bubbly and the tortillas are tender, 5 to 10 minutes more.

7. Transfer the pan to the upper rack and turn the oven to broil. Broil for 2 to 3 minutes to brown the cheese, watching carefully so the cheese and tortillas do not burn. Let stand at room temperature for at least 10 minutes to set up prior to serving. Sprinkle with cilantro. To serve, use a sharp knife to cut the enchiladas, then lift servings onto a plate in big, messy slices. Add additional toppings as desired.

freezing individual portions

For easy grab-and-heat dinners, fully bake, cool, and slice the enchiladas, then wrap and freeze individual portions. Let thaw overnight in the refrigerator, then reheat in a 375°F oven or 350°F toaster oven. Place your leftovers in a baking dish, drizzle about 2 tablespoons of water around your slice, then cover the dish with aluminum foil. Bake for 20 to 30 minutes, depending upon the size of your portion, until the enchiladas are heated through. The enchiladas should reach an internal temperature of 160°F. You can also reheat portions directly from frozen; note that it will take much longer (check your progress at 45 minutes).

variations

Extra Spicy: Use a spicy salsa and/or use pepper Jack in place of the Monterey Jack.

Gluten Free: Swap the flour tortillas for 12 taco-size (6-inch) corn tortillas—since corn tortillas are smaller, you'll need more. Cut the tortillas in half and use eight halves per layer.

red wine mushroom
farro soup page 257

sammies and soups
two of a kind

Despite Ben and I knowing each other for two decades, I never tire of "the question game," in which one of us poses a hypothetical situation to prompt fun conversations (or the more advanced version—you guess the other person's response first). Ben's "if you could open any restaurant" answer is a sandwich shop. The flavor possibilities are expansive, and it's surprisingly difficult to find a great one. The bread must be soft but sturdy, the sauce generous but not sog inducing, and the fillings well seasoned, creative, and substantial. Expand your definition of "sandwich" to include "tasty things on bread," as this chapter does, and your options really are endless.

In addition to the classic bread format—or rather, the open-faced melt format; since things got so deliciously messy, a knife and fork was really the only way to address it—you'll find my favorite fast-food-inspired wrap (page 238), two killer burgers (page 229 and page 232), and even filling *within* bread, in the form of my stepdad Larry's Famous Bierocks (page 235).

Alongside our broadly defined selection of sammies, we have a cache of hearty, big-batch soups. From BTP Creamy Chicken and Wild Rice Soup (page 251) to Warming Chickpea, Kale, and Butternut Squash Soup (page 248), each is designed to be filling and flavorful enough to stand on its own as a full meal. Of course, should you choose to pair your Roasted Eggplant Tomato Soup (page 260) with a Grown-Up Grilled Cheese (*The Well Plated Cookbook*, page 222), I'll do nothing but applaud you . . . and maybe ask you to open a soup and sandwich shop. I'll want to visit **every day**.

....

things on bread

Kale Artichoke Melts

Caprese Cauliflower Melts

Jalapeño Popper Chicken Burgers

Juicy Bison Burgers with
White Cheddar, Caramelized Onions,
and Creamy Dijon Sauce

Larry's Famous Bierocks

Popcorn Chicken Wraps

Slow Cooker Caribbean Beef Sliders

souper!

Ribollita

Warming Chickpea, Kale, and
Butternut Squash Soup

BTP (Better Than Panera)
Creamy Chicken and Wild Rice Soup

Slow Cooker Creamy Corn Chicken
Chorizo Chowder

Red Wine Mushroom Farro Soup

Roasted Eggplant Tomato Soup

btp (better than panera) creamy chicken and wild rice soup

page 257

kale artichoke melts

ACTIVE TIME:
20 minutes

TOTAL TIME:
20 minutes

YIELD:
4 melts

1 (12-ounce) package frozen artichoke hearts, thawed, or 1 (12-ounce) jar, drained

2 tablespoons extra-virgin olive oil

4 cups chopped, stemmed kale (about ½ large bunch curly or 1 medium bunch lacinato)

3 garlic cloves, minced (about 1 tablespoon)

½ teaspoon kosher salt, divided

1 cup water

¼ teaspoon red pepper flakes

1 ripe medium avocado, halved

1 tablespoon freshly squeezed lemon juice

4 slices provolone or Havarti cheese

4 slices thick-cut (¾-inch) good-quality whole wheat bread or sourdough, or your bread of choice

If artichoke dip for dinner sounds like a fabulous time, start licking your lips. Inspired by the dip-of-all-dips, these savory melts pile the good stuff high because—and let's be honest about this—when it comes to artichoke dip, whatever you're eating it with is really just the vehicle. Instead of the typical mayo and sour cream, this wholesome twist uses creamy avocado. It's as rich and cheesy as it should be yet manages to sneak in a redeeming amount of green. Eating your veggies has never been this fun!

1. Pat the artichokes dry, then roughly chop, patting dry once more if needed. Set aside.

2. Heat the oil in a large, deep sauté pan with a lid or a Dutch oven over medium-high heat. Once the oil is hot, add the kale by large handfuls, stirring constantly to allow the kale to wilt. Be careful, as the oil may spatter a bit at first. Cook, stir, and continue adding the kale until it all fits in the pan, 2 to 3 minutes. Add the garlic and ¼ teaspoon of the salt. Stir and cook until the garlic is fragrant, about 30 seconds. Add the water and immediately cover the pan. Reduce the heat to medium.

3. Continue cooking, covered, stirring once or twice, until the kale is wilted, fairly tender, and turns a more vibrant green, about 4 minutes. Add the red pepper flakes and artichokes. Increase the heat to medium-high. Sauté, uncovered, until most of the liquid cooks off and the kale is pleasantly tender but not mushy, about 2 additional minutes. Remove from the heat.

4. Scoop the avocado flesh into a large bowl. With a fork, mash until it is mostly smooth but a few chunks remain. Stir in the lemon juice and remaining ¼ teaspoon salt. Stir in the kale and artichokes. Taste and adjust the seasoning as desired.

5. Place a rack in the upper third of your oven and turn to broil. Place the bread slices on a rimmed baking sheet and toast lightly, about 1 minute per side. Pile the kale-artichoke mixture on top of each slice, dividing it evenly and pressing down lightly so it sticks. Make sure the topping goes all the way to the edges. Lay a slice of cheese on top of each, then broil for 2 to 3 minutes, until the cheese is melted and golden. Let cool a few minutes, then dive in.

caprese cauliflower melts

ACTIVE TIME:
20 minutes

TOTAL TIME:
50 minutes

YIELD:
4 melts

4 slices thick-cut (¾-inch) good-quality whole wheat bread or sourdough, or your bread of choice

1 medium head cauliflower (about 2½ pounds)

3 tablespoons extra-virgin olive oil, divided

2 teaspoons Italian seasoning

1½ teaspoons kosher salt, divided

¼ teaspoon red pepper flakes

3 beefsteak tomatoes

¼ teaspoon ground black pepper

1 cup nonfat plain Greek yogurt

2 cups shredded mozzarella cheese (about 8 ounces), divided

4 tablespoons grated Parmesan cheese (about ¾ ounce), divided

½ cup drained sun-dried tomatoes in oil, patted dry

½ cup thinly sliced fresh basil, divided

In the summer, when tomatoes are at their most majestic and all I want for dinner are things I can assemble mid-Aperol spritz, "caprese" becomes a verb, as in *Let's caprese that!* And *Can we caprese this?* And *Our night was great, thanks—we capresed!* Since summers in Wisconsin are never long enough, I created these yummy melts as a way to caprese year-round. Roasting tomatoes concentrates their flavors so that even in the dead of winter, you can enjoy this hearty meatless main as a cheery pick-me-up.

1. Place racks in the upper and lower third of your oven and preheat to 400°F. Line a large rimmed baking sheet with a double layer of parchment paper, then arrange the bread slices in a single layer on top. Bake the bread on the upper rack for 5 minutes, then flip the slices, return the pan to the oven, and continue baking until the slices are lightly toasted, 4 to 5 additional minutes. Transfer the bread slices to a wire rack and set aside.

2. While the bread toasts, cut off the stem end of the cauliflower head so you have a flat base. Stand it up on the base, then cut it down through the top into four even wedges. Trim away and discard the hard inner core areas, then cut into 1-inch florets (you should have about 6 cups florets). Place the florets on a large rimmed baking sheet and top with 2 tablespoons of the oil, the Italian seasoning, 1 teaspoon of the salt, and the red pepper flakes. Toss to evenly coat, then spread the florets into a single layer. Place on either rack to roast for 25 to 30 minutes, stirring once or twice throughout, until the cauliflower is dark and crispy in places and caramelized in the center.

3. Meanwhile, lay the tomatoes on their sides and cut them into ¾-inch-thick round slices. Discard the stems. Arrange the slices cut side up on the baking sheet that previously held the bread. Drizzle with the remaining 1 tablespoon oil. Sprinkle with the black pepper and ¼ teaspoon of the salt. Place in the oven with the cauliflower. Bake for 15 minutes, then swap the pans' positions on the upper and lower racks. Continue baking the tomatoes until the slices soften and begin to collapse, about 10 minutes more.

recipe continues

Once both the cauliflower and tomatoes are out of the oven, reduce the oven temperature to 375°F.

4. In a large bowl, stir together the yogurt, 1½ cups of the mozzarella, 2 tablespoons of the Parmesan, and the remaining ¼ teaspoon salt. Dice the sun-dried tomatoes and add them to the bowl with the yogurt mixture. Add half of the basil. Stir gently to combine.

5. Let the cauliflower cool for a few minutes, then transfer it to the bowl with the yogurt mixture (no need to clean the pan). Stir gently, ensuring the florets are all nicely coated.

6. Assemble the melts: Place the toasted bread on the baking sheet that previously held the cauliflower (line it with parchment first for easy cleanup). Top each bread slice with a few slices of roasted tomatoes, overlapping them slightly, then divide the cauliflower mixture among the slices, piling it on top. (You'll have a generous 1 cup per melt.) Press down on the cauliflower mixture lightly so it sticks together and spread it all the way to the edges. Top each melt with 2 tablespoons of the remaining mozzarella and ½ tablespoon Parmesan. Bake for 10 to 15 minutes, until the cauliflower mixture is nice and hot and the cheese is melted and turning golden brown. If you'd like to crisp the top further, broil for 2 minutes (watch closely so the bread doesn't burn). Sprinkle generously with the remaining basil and season with a pinch of additional salt. Enjoy immediately.

variations

Pesto: Spread the bread with Creamy Basil Pesto (*The Well Plated Cookbook*, page 100) or your favorite store-bought pesto prior to topping it with the cauliflower mixture.

Balsamic: Drizzle the baked caprese melts with reduced balsamic vinegar.

jalapeño popper chicken burgers

ACTIVE TIME:
40 minutes

TOTAL TIME:
40 minutes

YIELD:
4 burgers

For the Burgers

⅓ cup shredded sharp cheddar cheese (about 1½ ounces), plus 4 cheddar slices for topping the burgers

1 teaspoon kosher salt

½ teaspoon garlic powder

½ teaspoon onion powder

½ teaspoon ground black pepper

¼ teaspoon ground cumin

2 tablespoons extra-virgin olive oil

2 to 3 teaspoons hot sauce, such as Tabasco (spiciest), Cholula, or Frank's RedHot (use more for a spicier burger)

1 tablespoon Worcestershire sauce

1 pound ground chicken

2 tablespoons canola oil or other neutral oil, such as grapeseed oil

4 medium whole grain or brioche buns, lightly toasted if desired

1 jalapeño, very thinly sliced

At the start of every football season, Ben gives me a detailed review of the players' positions in the hope that *this* will finally be the year I understand what a linebacker does. Fifteen years in, this information still hasn't stuck. I like to think it's because my brain is already full of more important information: what constitutes the best football *food*. Jalapeño poppers might be something you've only thought of as a game-day appetizer, but when you taste them in burger form—that is, two crispy, cheddar-laced smash patties sandwiched with jalapeño cream cheese and topped with more cheese—you'll question why they haven't been the main event all along.

1. Prepare the burger patties: In a large bowl, using a fork or your fingers, toss together the shredded cheese, salt, garlic powder, onion powder, black pepper, and cumin, evenly distributing the spices. Add the olive oil, hot sauce, and Worcestershire and stir to combine. Add the chicken and stir very gently to combine, being careful not to compact the meat. Form into eight equally sized round balls; each will be about 2 inches in diameter.

2. Make the filling: In a small bowl, stir together the cream cheese, jalapeño, and salt. Set near the stove, along with a large plate and the cheese slices.

3. Heat a 12-inch cast-iron or similar large, heavy-bottomed skillet over medium-high heat for 2 to 3 minutes, until very hot. Add the canola oil and swirl to coat the pan. Carefully place four of the chicken balls in the pan, spacing them evenly. Immediately, with a sturdy metal spatula or the back of a wooden spoon, press down on the balls until they form thin patties that are 3½ inches across (the patties will be less than ½ inch thick). Cook without disturbing until a deep golden crust forms on the bottom, the very edges start to look a little brown, and the patties release easily from the pan, about 3 minutes. Flip and cook on the other side, until the patties are cooked through and have a nice crust on both sides, 2 to 3 minutes more. Transfer to

recipe and ingredients continue

For the Jalapeño Cream Cheese Filling

3 ounces reduced-fat cream cheese, or Neufchâtel cheese, at room temperature

2 tablespoons minced jalapeño, membranes and seeds removed (about 1 medium)

⅛ teaspoon kosher salt

the large plate, allowing some of the excess oil to drip off the patties back into the skillet. Place the remaining four chicken balls in the skillet, then smash and repeat the cooking process.

4. While the second batch of burgers cooks, top each of the four cooked patties with the cream cheese mixture, dividing it evenly among each. Once you flip the second batch, top each patty in the pan with a slice of cheddar.

5. To assemble, stack the second batch of patties directly on top of the first so that you have a double-stacked smashburger. Serve on buns with jalapeño slices.

do ahead

Form the chicken balls up to 1 day in advance and refrigerate until ready to cook. Mix up the cream cheese filling and refrigerate for up to 3 days.

next level

Top the cooked burgers with French fried onions and/or pickled jalapeños.

juicy bison burgers with white cheddar, caramelized onions, and creamy dijon sauce

ACTIVE TIME:
30 minutes

TOTAL TIME:
50 minutes

YIELD:
6 medium burgers

For the Caramelized Onions

1 tablespoon extra-virgin olive oil

3 medium red onions, thinly sliced

¼ teaspoon kosher salt

For the Creamy Dijon Sauce

½ cup nonfat plain Greek yogurt

1 to 2 tablespoons Dijon mustard

For the Burgers

2 pounds ground bison or 90% lean ground beef

2 tablespoons extra-virgin olive oil

1 tablespoon Worcestershire sauce

1 tablespoon Dijon mustard

1 teaspoon kosher salt, divided

My sisters and I all have first names that start with an "E" (which my mother insists was not intentional . . . but c'mon, Mom). Despite the alliterative start, it's been *cough* suggested *cough* that my "E" stands for "Extra," a designation I have zero inhibition about embracing, especially when I direct my being "extra" to my burger. Sure, we could keep it simple, but why stop there when you can add caramelized onions, white cheddar, and a creamy Dijon sauce? When I'm craving a burger, this is the burger I want. They're ultra flavorful and juicy, and the accoutrements make them restaurant worthy. I love lean ground bison here, which tastes incredibly similar to to beef, though beef works perfectly too if you prefer.

1. Caramelize the onions: Heat the olive oil in a large sauté pan over medium-high heat. Add the onions and salt. Cook until the onions begin to soften and brown, about 8 minutes. Reduce the heat to low and let cook, stirring occasionally, until the onions are very soft and caramelized, 15 to 20 additional minutes. Remove from the heat.

2. Make the creamy Dijon sauce: In a small bowl, combine the yogurt and mustard (add more mustard for a zippier sauce). Set aside.

3. Make the burger patties: Place the bison in a large bowl. Add the olive oil, Worcestershire,

mustard, ½ teaspoon of the salt, and the pepper.

4. With a fork, gently stir to combine, being careful not to compact the meat (handle it as little as possible for the most tender burgers). Gently shape the mixture into six equal patties (they will be about 3½ inches each). Season the outsides with the remaining ½ teaspoon salt and brush lightly with canola oil.

5. Cook the burgers: Heat a gas or charcoal grill to medium-high heat (about 375° to 400°F) or a cast-iron skillet on your stovetop to medium-high heat

recipe and ingredients continue

½ teaspoon ground black pepper

6 slices sharp white cheddar cheese (or 4 if making larger burgers)

Canola oil, for grilling

6 medium whole grain or brioche buns, or English muffins (or 4 larger buns if making larger burgers)

Lettuce and tomato (optional)

(be sure the skillet is hot before adding the burgers). Cook the burgers until slightly charred on the first side, about 4 minutes. Flip and cook on the other side for 3 to 4 minutes more, until the internal temperature of the burger reaches 130° to 135°F (for medium-rare). Do not overcook or the burgers will be dry. Add the cheese during the last minute of cooking (if using the stove, loosely cover the burger with a large skillet lid or aluminum foil to help the cheese melt).

6. If desired, toast the buns on a baking sheet in your oven at 350°F for 5 to 7 minutes. To serve, spread each bottom bun generously with the Dijon sauce. Top with lettuce and tomato (if using), a burger, the caramelized onions, and the top bun. Enjoy!

variations

Fig or Blueberry Brie: Use thinly sliced Brie cheese instead of cheddar; swap the Dijon sauce for blueberry or fig jam.

Pesto Sun-Dried Tomato Havarti: Use Havarti cheese slices instead of cheddar; swap the Dijon sauce for Creamy Basil Pesto (*The Well Plated Cookbook*, page 100) or your favorite store-bought pesto; add 3 tablespoons drained and finely chopped oil-packed sun-dried tomatoes to the burger patties.

Hot Mess Burger: Top burgers with a fried egg and crispy bacon.

larry's famous bierocks

ACTIVE TIME:
55 minutes

TOTAL TIME:
1 hour 30 minutes

YIELD:
**16 bierocks
(serves 6 to 8)**

2 (16-ounce) packages
Pillsbury Hot Roll Mix
(see Pro Tips)

2 cups hot water
(120° to 130°F)

4 tablespoons (½ stick)
unsalted butter, at room
temperature (see Pro Tips)

3 large eggs, divided

1 tablespoon extra-virgin
olive oil

2 pounds ground bison or
90% lean ground beef

2 teaspoons kosher salt,
plus a few pinches

1 teaspoon garlic powder

1 teaspoon onion powder

½ teaspoon ground black
pepper

1 (10-ounce) bag coleslaw
mix with carrots

1 tablespoon water

Grainy mustard, for serving

I was a peak-angst teenager when my mom started dating my step-dad, Larry. I saw exactly zero reason to be friendly, until I found out Larry couldn't just cook . . . he could *cook*. Homemade chicken marsala, Bolognese that would make an Italian nonna proud, and my favorite of all his dinners: bierocks. Pillowy soft dough stuffed with a savory ground meat and vegetable filling, they are a bit like a savory hand pie and can be found across cultures. My mom and Larry have been married for well over a decade, and Larry's bierocks are still my number one request when I come home to visit. These take a little more hands-on time, but the results will win your heart!

1. Prepare the hot roll mix: In the bowl of a stand mixer fitted with a dough hook or in a very large bowl, combine the dry hot roll mix (including the yeast), the water, butter, and 2 of the eggs. Stir until a soft dough forms.

2. Knead the dough for 5 minutes, either with the dough hook on medium-low speed or by hand on a lightly floured surface (see Pro Tips). Cover the dough with a clean towel and let rest while you prepare the filling.

3. Heat the oil in a large sauté pan over medium-high heat. Add the bison, salt, garlic powder, onion powder, and pepper. Cook the meat, breaking it apart with a wooden spoon, until it is turning dark brown in places, fully cooked through, and there is just a little oil remaining in the pan, 5 to 8 minutes.

4. Stir in the coleslaw. Cover the pan, reduce the heat to medium-low, and let the cabbage cook for 4 minutes. Stir, re-cover, and continue cooking until the cabbage is tender, 2 to 4 minutes more. Taste and adjust the seasoning as desired. Remove from the heat.

5. Line two large rimmed baking sheets with parchment paper. Uncover the dough and, if it is not already on the counter, turn it out onto a lightly floured surface; it will be very sticky. Flour the top. With a floured bench scraper or butter knife, divide it into four quarters. Working one quarter at a time, divide each quarter into fourths. Each portion should be about the size of a lemon.

recipe continues

6. Stretch or roll each portion of dough into a rough 5-inch square, adding a small amount of flour as needed so the dough doesn't stick to your hands excessively. Scoop ⅓ cup of the filling into the center. Lift two opposite sides of the dough up toward each other and pinch to seal. Lift up the remaining two sides and pinch into the center. Pinch any remaining seams to create a tidy meat packet. Gently stretch the dough as needed, pinching closed any small holes that tear in the dough. Place seam side down on the baking sheet. Repeat with the remaining dough and filling, leaving 2 inches between each bierock so they can expand. Let rest for 10 minutes, or refrigerate for up to 2 days or freeze for up to 1 month (see Do Ahead).

7. When you're ready to bake, preheat your oven to 350°F. Beat the remaining egg and 1 tablespoon water together to create an egg wash. Brush it over the top of the bierocks, then sprinkle lightly with salt. Bake for 16 to 18 minutes, until the dough is cooked through and the bierocks are golden brown on top. Let cool a few minutes, then enjoy hot with mustard for dipping.

do ahead

Baked and unbaked bierocks are a freezer-meal dream. To freeze, place them in a single layer on a parchment–lined baking sheet and freeze until firm. Transfer to a ziptop bag and seal, squeezing out as much air as possible. Thaw overnight in the refrigerator. Reheat baked bierocks in the oven or microwave. For unbaked, place the thawed bierocks on a parchment paper–lined baking sheet, spacing them 2 inches apart, and let stand at room temperature for 30 minutes. Add egg wash and salt and bake as directed.

pro tips

Forget to soften the butter? For this recipe, it is OK for it to be super soft to slightly melted (it just can't be cold). To quickly soften, cut the butter into a few pieces, place it on a microwave-safe plate or bowl, and microwave it for 10 to 15 seconds, repeating in 10-second bursts as needed.

To knead the dough, with the heel of your hand, press the dough down and away from you. Lift the edge farthest from you up and back toward you, folding the dough over itself. Rotate a quarter turn, then repeat.

Hot Roll Mix is available at many grocery stores in the Midwest, as well as on Amazon. If you can't find it, you can go all out and make your own homemade enriched bread dough, or use frozen roll dough, such as Rhodes (note you won't need the hot water, butter, or 2 eggs used to make the Hot Roll Mix).

popcorn chicken wraps

ACTIVE TIME:
30 minutes

TOTAL TIME:
45 minutes

YIELD:
8 wraps

When it came to eating out in high school, most of the time I was pretty frugal, but if I had an occasion to celebrate (or it was payday), I'd treat myself . . . to KFC. I still have a special place in my heart for their popcorn chicken, though these days I much prefer it in the form of these tasty baked chicken wraps. I like to make a double batch, then reheat the chicken in the oven or toaster oven to enjoy throughout the week in salads, more wraps, or dipped nugget-style.

For the Popcorn Chicken

1 pound boneless, skinless chicken breasts or tenders, cut into 1-inch pieces (about 2 medium breasts)

½ cup white whole wheat flour or all-purpose flour

1 large egg

2 tablespoons nonfat milk or milk of choice

1 cup panko bread crumbs

¼ cup cornmeal

1½ teaspoons paprika

1 teaspoon garlic powder

1 teaspoon onion powder

½ teaspoon dried oregano

¼ to ½ teaspoon ground cayenne pepper

¼ teaspoon kosher salt, plus a few pinches

Nonstick spray or olive oil mister

1. Place a rack in the center of your oven and preheat to 400°F. Line a large rimmed baking sheet with parchment paper.

2. In a large ziptop bag or a bowl, place the chicken pieces. Add the flour and coat the chicken as evenly as possible, either by sealing the bag and shaking or stirring with a large spoon.

3. Set up your dredging stations: In a medium, shallow bowl (a pie dish works well), beat the egg and milk. In a second shallow bowl, stir together the bread crumbs, cornmeal, paprika, garlic powder, onion powder, oregano, cayenne (start with ¼ teaspoon and increase for more spice), and salt.

4. Working in batches, dredge the floured chicken in the egg mixture, then the bread crumb mixture, shaking off the excess flour and egg as you go and lightly pressing the bread crumb

mixture as needed so it adheres. Arrange the breaded chicken pieces in a single layer on the prepared baking sheet.

5. Mist the tops of the chicken with nonstick spray. Bake for 9 minutes, then remove from the oven and flip the pieces over. Mist the tops with spray, then return to the oven and continue baking until the chicken is cooked through, 6 to 7 minutes more—the pieces should no longer look pink in the center when cut in half. As soon as the chicken is removed from the oven, sprinkle lightly with a few pinches of additional salt.

6. In a small bowl, stir together the yogurt and sriracha. Taste and adjust the heat level as desired, either by adding more sriracha to spice it up or more yogurt to cool it down.

recipe and ingredients continue

For Making Wraps

1 cup nonfat plain Greek yogurt, plus more if needed

1 to 2 teaspoons sriracha or hot sauce of choice

8 fajita-size (7- or 8-inch) whole wheat tortillas or wraps of choice

Crunchy lettuce leaves, such as romaine, chopped

Sliced tomato

1 cup shredded sharp cheddar cheese (about 4 ounces), divided

7. Assemble the wraps: Spread each tortilla with about 2 tablespoons of the yogurt sauce. Add the lettuce, tomato, and four to five pieces of popcorn chicken. Sprinkle with 2 tablespoons of the cheese. Roll into a wrap and enjoy immediately.

variation

Chicken Nuggs: For the best-ever homemade chicken nuggets, omit the oregano and cayenne and reduce the garlic and onion powder to ½ teaspoon each. Instead of making wraps, dip the baked nuggets in your sauce of choice: honey mustard (my childhood pick!), BBQ sauce, ketchup, or the sriracha yogurt sauce from this recipe.

slow cooker caribbean beef sliders

ACTIVE TIME:
30 minutes

TOTAL TIME:
6 hours (on high);
9 hours (on low)

YIELD:
30 to 36 sliders or
10 to 12 full-size
sandwiches

For the Beef

2½ to 3 pounds boneless chuck roast, trimmed of large chunks of excess fat

1 medium white onion, ½ inch diced
(about 1½ cups)

2 teaspoons kosher salt

2 teaspoons dried thyme

2 teaspoons ground allspice

1 teaspoon ground ginger

1 teaspoon ground black pepper

¼ teaspoon ground cayenne pepper

1 (14.5-ounce) can fire-roasted diced tomatoes in their juices

6 garlic cloves, minced (about 2 tablespoons)

½ cup seeded and finely chopped jalapeño
(2 to 3 medium-large)

A key to any successful relationship is balancing each other's strengths, and a primary attribute I bring to our marriage is my uncanny ability to remember every dish the two of us have ever ordered at a restaurant. Ben, on the other hand, can't remember what I cooked for dinner two nights ago. (He can, however, give you a play-by-play of every Notre Dame touchdown pass from the past two decades.) Thus, it is no small statement when I say that he never ever forgot about these sliders. Warm, spicy, and juice-drips-down-your-chin tender, this low-and-slow beef is inspired by flavors popular throughout the Caribbean. If you are lucky enough to find Scotch bonnet peppers, you can swap them for the jalapeños for a more authentic flavor (start with 2 to 3 tablespoons chopped Scotch bonnet at most and omit the hot sauce from the beef—they're fiery!). A bright, crunchy lime slaw is the counterpoint that makes these tasty sliders unforgettable.

1. Remove the beef from the refrigerator, pat dry with paper towels, and let sit at room temperature for 15 minutes. Scatter the onion in an even layer in a 6-quart slow cooker. In a small bowl, stir together the salt, thyme, allspice, ginger, black pepper, and cayenne.

2. Place the beef in the slow cooker on top of the onion, then sprinkle the spice mixture all over the beef, rubbing to coat it on all sides (don't worry if some onion sticks to the top as a result). Add the tomatoes, garlic, jalapeños, Worcestershire, vinegar, maple syrup, and hot sauce over top. Zest the lime directly into the slow cooker, then halve it and squeeze in the juice (no need to stir anything). Cover and cook the beef on low for 8 to 9 hours or high for 5 to 6 hours, until the meat is falling apart and shreds easily with a fork.

3. While the beef cooks, prepare the slaw: Place the broccoli slaw in a large bowl. Top with the oil, lime juice, hot sauce, salt, black pepper, and 2 tablespoons of the green onions (reserve the rest for the beef). Stir to combine, then refrigerate for 30 minutes or up to 1 day.

recipe and ingredients continue

1 tablespoon
Worcestershire sauce

1 tablespoon apple cider
vinegar

2 teaspoons pure maple
syrup

1 teaspoon hot sauce,
such as sriracha or Tabasco

1 medium lime, zest and
juice

Slider buns or hamburger
buns (sweet Hawaiian style
if possible)

For the Slaw
1 (10- to 12-ounce) bag
broccoli slaw or coleslaw
mix

2 tablespoons extra-virgin
olive oil

2 tablespoons freshly
squeezed lime juice
(from about 1 medium
lime)

1 teaspoon hot sauce

½ teaspoon kosher salt

¼ teaspoon ground black
pepper

1 small bunch green
onions, thinly sliced
(about 1 cup), divided

4. Once the beef has cooked, transfer it to a large bowl. Use a slotted spoon to scoop as many of the stray vegetables and bits of meat as you can into the bowl. With two forks, shred the beef, discarding any large, chewy pieces of fat. Add the reserved green onions. Stir to combine, adding more of the juices from the slow cooker as needed so the beef is ultra moist.

5. To serve, split the buns. If desired, toast on a baking sheet in your oven at 350°F for 5 to 7 minutes. Pile the shredded beef onto the bottom bun, adding as much juice as you like. Add a scoop of the slaw and the top bun. Enjoy immediately.

ribollita

ACTIVE TIME:

45 minutes

TOTAL TIME:

1 hour 30 minutes

YIELD:

Serves 6

4 large, thick slices
whole-grain bread, or
½ baguette or similar loaf
(about 6 ounces)

3 tablespoons extra-virgin
olive oil

1 medium yellow onion,
½ inch diced
(about 1½ cups)

3 carrots, scrubbed
and ½ inch diced
(about 1½ cups)

2 celery stalks,
½ inch diced (about ⅔ cup)

1 teaspoon kosher salt

¾ teaspoon smoked
paprika

¼ teaspoon ground black
pepper

⅛ teaspoon red pepper
flakes

1 (14.5-ounce) can fire-
roasted diced tomatoes in
their juices

3 garlic cloves, minced
(about 1 tablespoon)

1 tablespoon chopped
fresh sage

1½ teaspoons chopped
fresh rosemary or thyme

Ribollita is Italian for "reboiled," and this soup has the welcome benefit of tasting even better reheated, meaning that future you is going to adore it even more than same-day you—which is saying something because same-day you is going to like it *a lot*. This seriously satisfying Italian soup exemplifies the power of humble, budget-conscious ingredients treated with love. Beans, leftover bread, and Parmesan cheese (I definitely recommend spending a bit more for quality Parmesan) simmer together into something more wonderful than any of them could be alone. This soup is a warm embrace on a cold night.

1. Toast the bread slices in your toaster or toaster oven, then tear into chunks. If using a baguette or other loaf, tear the bread into pieces, spread the pieces on an ungreased rimmed baking sheet, then toast at 400°F for 6 to 8 minutes, until the edges feel lightly dry to the touch. Set aside.

2. Heat the oil in a Dutch oven or similar large, heavy-bottomed pot over high heat. Once the oil is hot and shimmering, add the onion, carrots, celery, salt, smoked paprika, black pepper, and red pepper flakes. Stir to coat the vegetables with the oil and seasonings. Let cook, stirring often, for 2 minutes. Reduce the heat to low and cover the pot. Let the vegetables cook slowly for 20 minutes, uncovering to stir periodically (each time you lift the lid, let the moisture from the lid drip down back inside the pot to help the vegetables cook down). The

vegetables should be very soft and tender. Don't shortcut this step; the flavor you are building is worth it!

3. Increase the heat to medium-high and stir in the tomatoes and their juices, the garlic, sage, and rosemary. Let simmer for 1 minute. Stir in the kale.

4. Add the broth and beans. Increase the heat to high and bring the soup to a boil, then lower the heat to a simmer. Cook, uncovered, for 20 minutes. Stir the soup periodically and adjust the heat as needed so that you maintain a steady but not violent simmer.

5. Remove from the heat and stir in the bread and Parmesan. Let sit uncovered for *at least* 15 minutes (or even better, cool

recipe and ingredients continue

1 small bunch curly kale, stemmed and finely chopped (about 3 cups)

6 cups unsalted vegetable broth

1 (15-ounce) can reduced-sodium cannellini beans, rinsed and drained

¼ cup freshly grated Parmesan cheese (about ¾ ounce), plus additional for serving

Good-quality extra-virgin olive oil, for serving

it completely and/or refrigerate overnight). Just before serving, bring the soup back to a boil to heat it through. Enjoy hot with additional Parmesan and a drizzle of your best olive oil.

next level

Freeze your Parmesan rinds each time you finish a block. Add a rind to the soup with the kale.

market swaps

Let this soup carry you through the seasons! In the spring, it's lovely with asparagus and peas. In the summer, add extra tomatoes, zucchini, and chopped green beans. In the winter, try diced butternut squash and parsnips.

warming chickpea, kale, and butternut squash soup

ACTIVE TIME:
45 minutes

TOTAL TIME:
1 hour 30 minutes

YIELD:
Serves 6

3 tablespoons coconut oil or extra-virgin olive oil

1 large yellow onion, ½ inch diced (about 2 cups)

1½ teaspoons kosher salt

½ teaspoon ground black pepper

3 garlic cloves, minced (about 1 tablespoon)

2 tablespoons finely chopped or grated fresh ginger (about a 2-inch piece)

2 tablespoons curry powder

1 teaspoon chili powder

½ teaspoon ground turmeric

½ teaspoon red pepper flakes (reduce to ¼ teaspoon or omit if sensitive to spice)

2 (15-ounce) cans reduced-sodium chickpeas, rinsed and drained

2 (13.5-ounce) cans light coconut milk

Dinner in the Clarke household goes something like this. Ben: "How long until dinner is ready?" Me: "Thirty minutes." *One hour later.* Ben: "Are we even close?" While I might not be the most timely (or accurate), fortunately Ben is patient, and even more fortunately, it's nearly always worth the wait. This soup came about on such a night. It's loosely based on Alison Roman's internet-famous chickpea stew. The first time I made it, dinner was so late I worried we only inhaled it out of hungry necessity. But I know it wasn't a fluke because we've repeated it so often since. This soup is warm with curry spices, lively with ginger, and creamy with coconut milk. A heaping helping of feel-good greens makes it a nutritious, all-in-one winner.

1. Heat the oil in a Dutch oven or similar large, heavy-bottomed pot over medium heat. Add the onion, salt, and black pepper. Cook, stirring occasionally, until the onion turns translucent and is beginning to brown, about 5 minutes.

2. Stir in the garlic, ginger, curry powder, chili powder, turmeric, and red pepper flakes. Let cook for 30 seconds, until very fragrant. Add the chickpeas and stir to coat in the spices. Let cook for 5 minutes, stirring once or twice.

3. With a wooden spoon or potato masher, roughly mash the chickpeas, leaving some intact. Add the coconut milk and broth.

4. Increase the heat to medium high and bring the soup to a simmer, scraping the spoon or spatula along the bottom periodically. Continue simmering, stirring occasionally, until thickened, about 30 minutes.

5. While the soup simmers, peel the butternut squash and cut into ¾-inch cubes (you should have about 4 cups cubes total). Add to the soup and let simmer, stirring every now and then, until the butternut squash is tender (be sure to taste a few pieces) and the soup has further reduced, about 15 minutes.

6. Stir in the kale, making sure the leaves are submerged.

recipe and ingredients continue

1 (14.5-ounce) can vegetable broth

1 medium butternut squash (about 1½ pounds)

1 medium bunch curly kale, stemmed and chopped (about 6 cups)

2 teaspoons apple cider vinegar

For serving: chopped fresh cilantro, mint, or a mix, and nonfat plain Greek yogurt

Simmer, stirring a few times, until the kale is softened, about 10 minutes. Stir in the vinegar. Taste and adjust the seasoning as desired. Serve hot, with a generous sprinkle of fresh cilantro and/or mint, a dollop of yogurt, and a small pinch of salt to taste.

pro tips

Do not skip the Greek yogurt and herbs. They add an important dimension of flavor and really bring the soup to life.

Serve this soup as it is, over rice, or with naan or pita for dipping.

btp (better than panera) creamy chicken and wild rice soup

ACTIVE TIME:
40 minutes

TOTAL TIME:
1 hour 30 minutes

YIELD:
Serves 6

1 tablespoon extra-virgin olive oil

1 pound boneless, skinless chicken breasts (about 2 medium breasts), cut into bite-size pieces

1 teaspoon kosher salt, divided

4 tablespoons (½ stick) unsalted butter

4 medium carrots, scrubbed and ½ inch diced (about 2 cups)

3 celery stalks, ½ inch diced (about 1 cup)

1 medium yellow onion, ½ inch diced (about 1½ cups)

3 garlic cloves, minced (about 1 tablespoon)

2 teaspoons poultry seasoning

¼ teaspoon ground black pepper

¼ cup white whole wheat flour or all-purpose flour

1 cup wild rice or wild rice blend

One of my coming-of-age moments was when I transitioned my go-to Panera lunch order from the bagel side of the menu (Asiago bagel with chive cream cheese, please!) to the soup side. My reigning favorite: the creamy chicken and wild rice. This recipe has the same cozy tastes-like-home flavor, but it excels where the restaurant original was lacking: the protein and veg departments. You'll find this one thicker, with more chunks of juicy chicken and vegetables in each spoonful, and the ingredients are simple and nutritious. Instead of using heavy cream or processed "cream of" soups, I make a simple roux of butter and flour to give the soup richness and body, all while keeping it healthy dinner approved.

1. Heat the oil in a Dutch oven or similar large, heavy-bottomed pot over medium-high heat. Add the chicken and ½ teaspoon of the salt. Cook, stirring occasionally, until the chicken is browned and cooked through, 4 to 6 minutes. Transfer to a bowl or plate and refrigerate.

2. Reduce the heat to medium-low. Add the butter and let it melt. Add the carrots, celery, onion, and remaining ½ teaspoon salt. Let cook, stirring occasionally, until the vegetables begin to soften, about 10 minutes. Stir in the garlic, poultry seasoning, and pepper.

3. Sprinkle the flour over the top. Cook, stirring constantly, until the flour looks golden and no dry bits remain, about 2 minutes.

4. Stir in the wild rice. Slowly add the chicken broth, stirring as you go to prevent lumps from forming. Add the water. Bring the liquid to a boil, then reduce to a simmer. Continue simmering for 40 minutes, stirring occasionally and adjusting the heat as needed.

5. Stir in the cooked chicken. Continue simmering until the rice is tender, 10 to 15 minutes more, depending upon your brand of rice. Stir every so often to keep the rice from sticking to the bottom of the pot, and add water as needed if the soup

recipe and ingredients continue

4 cups low-sodium
chicken broth

2 cups water, plus
additional as needed

⅔ cup full-fat plain Greek
yogurt (about a 5.3-ounce
container)

Chopped fresh thyme,
chives, parsley, or dill,
for serving

is thicker than you would like.
Remove from the heat.

6. Place the yogurt in a medium
bowl. Add a few spoonfuls of the
soup, stirring to combine (this
will warm up the yogurt and
deter it from separating). Stir the
mixture into the soup. Taste the
soup and add salt and pepper
as desired. Enjoy hot, with a
sprinkle of fresh herbs.

speed it up

Swap 2 to 3 cups shredded store-bought rotisserie chicken for the
sautéed chicken pieces.

next level

After adding the rice, pour in ⅔ cup dry white wine, such as
Sauvignon Blanc or Pinot Grigio, and scrape along the bottom of the
pot to deglaze. Let cook until the wine is reduced by half, then add
the broth.

slow cooker creamy corn chicken chorizo chowder

ACTIVE TIME:
40 minutes

TOTAL TIME:
4 hours

YIELD:
Serves 6

8 ounces chorizo (Mexican-style uncooked ground chorizo, not cured Spanish-style chorizo)

1 tablespoon extra-virgin olive oil

2 poblano peppers, seeded and ½ inch diced (about 1 ½ cups)

1 small yellow onion, ¼ inch diced (about 1 cup)

1 tablespoon smoked paprika

1¼ teaspoons kosher salt, divided

½ teaspoon ground black pepper, divided

2 cups finely chopped cauliflower (about 10 ounces or ½ medium head)

1½ pounds boneless, skinless chicken breasts (about 3 medium breasts)

1 medium sweet potato, peeled and ¼ inch diced (about 2 cups)

1 (14.5-ounce) can low-sodium chicken broth

With the most alliteration-affluent recipe title I've ever created, this chowder embodies the idea of using meat as a complement to, rather than centerpiece of, a dish. Spiced chorizo kicks things off with a punch, but it's the sweet corn, nutty sweet potato, and earthy poblano that do the real heavy lifting here. This sneaky soup packs a hefty amount of cauliflower, but it's chopped so finely, it all but disappears, giving you all the more leeway to serve it to picky eaters. This recipe yields an ample amount and freezes well, so you can feed a crowd, share with neighbors, or stow some away for a future evening.

1. In a large skillet, cook the chorizo over medium-high heat, using a wooden spoon to break apart the meat. Continue cooking until the chorizo is browned and cooked through, about 5 minutes. With a slotted spoon, transfer it to a medium bowl and refrigerate.

2. Reduce the heat to medium. Add the oil, poblanos, onion, smoked paprika, ½ teaspoon of the salt, and ¼ teaspoon of the black pepper. Cook until the vegetables are softened, about 5 minutes. Transfer to a 6-quart or larger slow cooker.

3. Place the cauliflower on top of the vegetables and the chicken on top of the cauliflower. Sprinkle with the remaining ¾ teaspoon salt and ¼ teaspoon black pepper. Add the sweet potato, broth, and corn. Dot the cream cheese over the top. DO NOT STIR. Cover and cook on low until the chicken reaches 155°F on an instant-read thermometer, 2½ to 3½ hours.

4. Transfer the chicken to a cutting board and let rest for at least 10 minutes. Re-cover the slow cooker and cook on high for 20 to 30 additional minutes, until the cauliflower and sweet potato are super tender.

5. With an immersion blender, puree the chowder to thicken it. Stop to stir and check the consistency. You want the chowder to be fairly smooth and creamy but still have some texture to it. If you don't have an immersion blender, transfer a few ladlefuls of the chowder

recipe and ingredients continue

2 (15.25-ounce) cans corn kernels, drained

4 ounces reduced-fat cream cheese, or Neufchâtel cheese

⅔ cup full-fat plain Greek yogurt (about a 5.3-ounce container)

½ cup chopped fresh cilantro, plus additional for serving

to a food processor or blender and puree (be careful—hot food spatters!). Stir the blended portion back in with the rest. Keep pureeing batches until your desired consistency is reached.

6. Dice the chicken and add it to the slow cooker. Add the chorizo. Scoop the yogurt into the bowl you used to hold the chorizo (no need to wash it first), then stir in a few spoonfuls of the soup (this will warm up the yogurt and deter it from separating). Pour the mixture into the slow cooker, stir, then re-cover and cook on high for 5 to 10 minutes more to warm the meat and allow the flavors to marry. Stir in the cilantro, then adjust the salt and pepper to taste. Enjoy hot with a sprinkle of additional cilantro.

market swap

Use 4 to 6 ears sweet corn. After cutting the corn from the cob (see Pro Tip, page 273), add both the kernels and the corn milk that comes away from the cob. DELISH.

red wine mushroom farro soup

ACTIVE TIME:

30 minutes

TOTAL TIME:

1 hour 15 minutes

YIELD:

Serves 4 to 6

For the Soup

3 tablespoons unsalted butter, softened, divided

2 tablespoons extra-virgin olive oil, divided

1 pound cremini (baby bella) mushrooms, sliced (about 4½ cups)

4 to 6 ounces shiitake mushrooms, stemmed and sliced (2 to 3 cups)

1 medium onion, ¼ inch diced (about 1½ cups)

4 medium carrots, scrubbed and ½ inch diced (about 2 cups)

3 celery stalks, ¼ inch diced (about 1 cup)

3 garlic cloves, minced (about 1 tablespoon)

¾ cup semi-pearled farro, rinsed and drained

¾ cup full-bodied red wine, such as Cabernet Sauvignon, Zinfandel, Burgundy, or Côtes du Rhône

4 cups unsalted beef broth (or vegetable or mushroom broth to make it vegetarian)

The world-famous wine might have been the original motivator behind Ben's and my trip to Burgundy, France, but the moment I will remember most is when I sat down to a steaming bowl of one of the region's most celebrated dishes, boeuf Bourguignon, a rich stew of beef slow cooked in an opulent red wine sauce. This full-bodied, velvety stew keeps its luxurious spirit but omits the meat (*l'horreur!*). The trick of mashing softened butter with flour, then stirring it in at the end (called *beurre manié*), is a technique straight from the French cooking playbook. It gives the stew extra thickness and a lush, glossy finish. The Gruyère toasts, while not strictly necessary, are an excellent idea.

1. In a Dutch oven or similar large, heavy-bottomed pot, heat 1 tablespoon of the butter and 1 tablespoon of the oil over medium-high heat. The moment the butter melts, add the cremini and shiitake mushrooms. Cook, stirring occasionally, until the mushrooms are browned but have not yet released their liquid, 5 to 7 minutes. Transfer to a plate.

2. Reduce the heat to medium. Add the remaining 1 tablespoon oil to the pot. Add the onion, carrots, and celery. Cook, stirring occasionally, until the vegetables are softened and the onions are browning, about 10 minutes.

3. Stir in the garlic and farro and let cook, stirring constantly, until the garlic is very fragrant, about 30 seconds. Pour in the wine, and with a wooden spoon or sturdy rubber spatula, scrape the bottom of the pot to remove any stuck-on bits. Let simmer until reduced by half, 2 minutes.

4. Add the broth, tomato paste, salt, pepper, thyme bundle, and sautéed mushrooms.

5. Bring to a boil over high heat, partially cover the pot, and reduce the heat to a gentle simmer. Let simmer, adjusting the heat as needed, until the farro is tender but still has some chew to it, 25 to 35 minutes. Remove from the heat and discard the thyme bundle.

6. In a small bowl, use a fork to mash together the flour and remaining 2 tablespoons butter. Stir into the soup. Let

recipe and ingredients continue

2 tablespoons tomato paste

1½ teaspoons kosher salt, plus additional to taste

½ teaspoon ground black pepper

4 sprigs fresh thyme, tied in a bundle with kitchen twine

2 tablespoons all-purpose flour

For the Gruyère Toasts

½ sourdough or French baguette, cut into ½-inch slices (about 12 slices)

¾ cup shredded Gruyère cheese (about 3 ounces)

simmer for 5 additional minutes. Carefully taste and adjust the seasoning as desired.

7. Make the Gruyère toasts: Place a rack in the upper third of your oven and turn the oven to broil. Arrange the baguette slices in a single layer on a rimmed baking sheet. Broil on each side until lightly crisp, about 2 minutes total (watch closely so the toasts don't burn!). Sprinkle the Gruyère evenly over the slices (you'll have about 1 tablespoon per slice), then return to the oven just long enough to melt, about 30 seconds. Serve hot alongside the soup.

pro tip

Farro will absorb liquid as it sits, so you will need to thin the soup when reheating it. You can also just enjoy the super-thick soup, which is still delicious!

The type of farro you use will impact how quickly it cooks. This recipe calls for semi-pearled farro, though you can use other kinds. If using pearled, it will cook more quickly, in 15 to 20 minutes; whole farro will take 40 minutes or longer.

next level

Save your Parmesan rinds in the freezer, then for an even richer flavor, add one to the soup in step 4.

market swap

Swap the semi-pearled farro for a grain that cooks in a similar amount of time, such as pearled barley. Note that if using hulled (not pearled) barley, you'll need 45 minutes to 1 hour to cook it.

souper!

roasted eggplant tomato soup

ACTIVE TIME:
30 minutes

TOTAL TIME:
1 hour

YIELD:
Serves 6

2 large eggplants
(2 to 2½ pounds),
halved lengthwise

3 tablespoons extra-virgin
olive oil, divided

2 teaspoons kosher salt,
divided

¼ teaspoon ground black
pepper

2 medium onions,
¼ inch diced (about 3 cups)

1 tablespoon paprika

1 teaspoon ground cumin

1 teaspoon dried oregano

½ teaspoon ground
cinnamon

¼ teaspoon ground
cayenne pepper

3 garlic cloves, minced
(about 1 tablespoon)

3 to 4 cups low-sodium
vegetable broth or chicken
broth

1 (28-ounce) can crushed
tomatoes

⅓ cup heavy cream
(optional but highly
delicious and encouraged)

Chopped fresh basil
(optional for serving)

My ultimate comfort food is grilled cheese and tomato soup. For something more elevated that doesn't skip the snuggly contentment, give this roasted eggplant version a try. Even if you're not an eggplant fan (yet), you'll love it here; when roasted and blended, eggplant takes on a creamy texture that gives this soup a luscious, thick body. The warm spices have a Middle Eastern influence that makes this soup unique and worth repeating, but it stays true enough to the classic to pair harmoniously with a good ol' fashioned grilled cheese. Get comfy.

1. Place a rack in the center of your oven and preheat to 425°F. Line a rimmed baking sheet with parchment paper. Place the eggplant halves cut side up on the prepared baking sheet. Brush the cut sides with 2 tablespoons of the oil and sprinkle with ½ teaspoon of the salt and the black pepper. Roast for 20 minutes, until they begin to turn golden brown. Flip the halves over, then return to the oven and continue roasting until they are tender, 10 to 20 minutes more, depending upon the size of your eggplant. Set aside.

2. Meanwhile, in a large Dutch oven or similar large, heavy-bottomed pot, heat the remaining 1 tablespoon oil over medium heat. Add the onions and cook, stirring occasionally, until they are softened but not browned, 6 to 8 minutes. Add the paprika, cumin, oregano, cinnamon, cayenne, and garlic. Stir and cook until fragrant, 30 seconds to 1 minute.

3. Add 3 cups of the broth, the tomatoes, and the remaining 1½ teaspoons salt. Once the eggplant is cool enough to handle, scoop the eggplant flesh from the skins and add it to the pot (discard the skins). Bring to a boil, then reduce the heat to a simmer. Let simmer uncovered for 15 minutes, stirring periodically.

4. Puree the soup until smooth, either with an immersion blender or by ladling it into a blender in batches. (Be careful not to overfill the blender—hot soup spatters. When in doubt, fill it no more than halfway.) Return all the soup to the pot (if using a blender). Stir in the heavy cream (if using). If the soup is thicker than you would like, add the remaining broth until your desired consistency is reached. Taste and adjust the seasoning as desired. Serve hot with basil (if using).

jammy roasted
cherry tomatoes
and onions page 270

sides
somethin' on the side

When it comes to sides, you deserve to have high standards. Since a side isn't the only item on the culinary agenda (by their very nature, they must go along *side* a main), if you are going to go to the effort to cook not one but TWO things, that side dish better be *good* (if it's not, you might as well stick to the one-pan meals, pages 130 to 162).

Of course "good" does not have to be synonymous with "complicated." In fact, if it's a side dish we're talking about (and this is the side dish chapter, so clearly we are), it had better be anything but fussy. We still have that pesky main to worry about, remember?

Enter these stand-out sides. All are simple to make, *and* they deliver where it counts: taste. From Everything Bagel Roasted Asparagus (page 277), to Sage Brown Butter Roasted Squash (page 274), to Salt and Vinegar Smashed Potatoes (page 287), you'll find fun flavor mashups, ideas to elevate everyday veggies, and dinner-party-level sides worth your time and energy.

I've also included a few extra hearty, grain-based sides that have main dish energy. For example, Summery Baked Farro with Zucchini and Tomato (page 279) would taste fabulous served with Green Goddess Chicken Thighs (page 175), but you can just as easily top it with a runny egg or stir in a can of chickpeas to turn it into a filling meatless lunch or dinner.

No matter what else you're serving, here you'll find the right side for your day, **every day**.

salt and
vinegar
smashed
potatoes
page 287

blackened chili-garlic sweet potato wedges

ACTIVE TIME: **15 minutes**

TOTAL TIME: **40 minutes**

YIELD: **Serves 6**

3 medium sweet potatoes (about 2 pounds)

¼ cup extra-virgin olive oil

1 tablespoon chili powder

1 teaspoon garlic powder

1 teaspoon onion powder

1½ teaspoons kosher salt, plus additional for serving

¼ teaspoon ground black pepper

Chopped fresh chives or green onions (optional)

next level

Cheesy Chili Garlic Oven Fries: As soon as the wedges are baked and broiled, remove them from the oven and sprinkle with a pinch of salt and 1 cup of shredded sharp cheddar, Monterey Jack, or pepper Jack cheese, or a mix of cheeses. Bake at 450°F just until the cheese is melted, about 1 minute. Sprinkle with chives and enjoy.

One of the better choices I've made for our marriage is to place my own dang order of sweet potato fries, instead of stealing from Ben's. Peace, equilibrium, and a sense of independence in my fry consumption—it's a win for all. At home, I'm no less of a sweet potato fry fan, but for the sake of eating them more often (and shouldn't we all?), I've embraced the sweet potato *wedge*. Wedges have the same crispy outside and tender inside but—and this benefit is not to be downplayed—are SO MUCH EASIER than cutting a sweet potato into precious matchsticks. I borrowed the spices here from my favorite blackening seasoning (minus the cayenne, but feel free to add a pinch or two if you are feeling spicy). A final pass under the broiler is my trick to getting them magnificently crispy, and the only way you'll want to "wedge" again.

1. Place one rack in the center of your oven and one in the upper third and preheat to 450°F. Line a rimmed baking sheet with parchment paper.

2. Scrub and dry the sweet potatoes (no need to peel). Cut each in half lengthwise. Cut each half lengthwise into 4 long spears of even size. Each spear should be about ¾ inch to 1 inch wide. Place in the center of the prepared baking sheet.

3. Drizzle the oil over the top. In a small bowl, stir together the chili powder, garlic powder, onion powder, salt, and pepper. Sprinkle over the wedges and toss to coat as evenly as possible. Make sure each wedge gets a nice bath of oil and spices.

4. Arrange the wedges into a single layer, being careful that they do not touch (if your pan is crowded, divide the wedges between two baking sheets and bake in the upper and lower thirds of the oven instead).

5. Bake on the center rack for 15 minutes, then flip with a spatula. Return the pan to the oven and bake for another 5 to 10 minutes, until tender when pierced with a fork.

6. Turn the oven to broil. Broil the sweet potatoes on the upper rack for 2 to 3 minutes, until they are crisped at the edges to your liking. The spices will turn very dark (don't worry—they are not burned). Immediately sprinkle with a pinch of additional salt and chives (if using).

charred broccoli with blue cheese and crispies

ACTIVE TIME:
15 minutes

TOTAL TIME:
30 minutes

YIELD:
Serves 4

For the Charred Broccoli

1 pound 1- to 1½-inch-cut broccoli florets (about 2 pounds whole broccoli or 3 medium crowns)

2 tablespoons extra-virgin olive oil

1 tablespoon rice vinegar

1½ teaspoons Dijon mustard

1½ teaspoons low-sodium soy sauce

1 teaspoon onion powder

¼ teaspoon kosher salt

⅛ teaspoon ground cayenne pepper (increase to ¼ teaspoon for more of a kick)

½ small lemon, cut into wedges

⅓ cup crumbled mild blue cheese (about 2 ounces), divided

For the Crispies

1 tablespoon unsalted butter

¼ cup panko bread crumbs

Pinch kosher salt

Tiny pinch ground cayenne pepper (optional)

If you've never used the word "transcendent" to describe broccoli, you haven't yet been to Girl & the Goat, Stephanie Izard's fantastic restaurant in Chicago. I've been haunted (in the best possible way) by the charred broccoli since it opened. I found the recipe published online, and it has approximately forty million steps (no wonder it tastes great!). This recipe is inspired by that tangy, crispy, umami-rich broccoli of my dreams, significantly streamlined for the home chef.

1. Char the broccoli: Place racks in the center and upper third of your oven and preheat to 450°F. For easy cleanup, line a large rimmed baking sheet with parchment paper. Place the broccoli florets in its center.

2. In a small bowl, stir together the oil, vinegar, mustard, soy sauce, onion powder, salt, and cayenne pepper. Pour over the broccoli, then toss to coat the florets evenly, really rubbing the ingredients around so the florets have a nice coating. Spread the florets into a single layer. Bake on the center rack for 15 minutes, then remove from the oven and toss. Return to the upper rack and bake for 5 additional minutes, until they're beginning to turn crisp and dark. If you'd like the broccoli even darker, broil for 1 to 2 minutes to give it a nice final char (keep an eye on it to make sure you don't go from almost burned to actually burned).

3. While the broccoli roasts, prepare the crispies: Melt the butter in a small skillet over medium-high heat, then add the bread crumbs. Cook, stirring very often, until they are dark golden brown and toasted, 3 to 5 minutes. Stir in the salt and cayenne (if using). Set aside.

4. To serve, transfer the charred broccoli to a serving bowl (or scoot the florets into a big pile in one corner of the baking sheet). While the broccoli is still hot, squeeze the lemon over the top and sprinkle with half of the blue cheese and half of the crispies. Toss to coat. Sprinkle with the remaining cheese and crispies. Enjoy immediately.

market swaps

Not a fan of blue cheese? Swap it for another tangy, creamy cheese, such as goat cheese or feta.

jammy roasted cherry tomatoes and onions

ACTIVE TIME:
10 minutes

TOTAL TIME:
35 minutes

YIELD:
Serves 3 to 4

2 pints cherry tomatoes (20 ounces), left whole

1 large red onion, cut into ½-inch wedges

2 tablespoons extra-virgin olive oil

2 teaspoons balsamic vinegar

1 teaspoon honey

½ teaspoon kosher salt, plus additional to taste

¼ teaspoon ground black pepper

1 teaspoon chopped fresh thyme

Save this recipe for the next time: (1) You are staring down a monster haul of summer tomatoes and thinking, *Now what?*; (2) It's the dead of winter and you haven't seen anything more colorful than a potato at the market for months; or (3) You have people coming over, need a side dish NOW, and have zero idea what to make. This recipe does it all! In the oven, cherry tomatoes cook down into juicy, tangy bliss, even out of season. You don't need to slice them prior to roasting, making this recipe especially speedy on prep. Serve these alongside a simple protein (salmon is especially good), mix them with rice to create a yummy grain bowl, or sop up the juices with a slice of crusty bread.

1. Place a rack in the center of your oven and preheat to 450°F. For easy cleanup, line a large rimmed baking sheet with aluminum foil or a double layer of parchment paper.

2. Place the tomatoes and onion wedges in the center of the prepared baking sheet, then top with the oil, vinegar, honey, salt, and pepper. Toss to coat as evenly as possible, then spread into a single layer. Some of the onion layers will come apart, which is absolutely fine.

3. Bake for 25 to 30 minutes, stirring once halfway through, until the onions are tender and the tomatoes have softened and burst and look dark in a few places. Sprinkle with the thyme and an additional pinch of salt to taste. Enjoy warm or at room temperature.

summer squash and blueberry toss with bright lemon dressing

ACTIVE TIME:
20 minutes

TOTAL TIME:
20 minutes

YIELD:
Serves 6

1½ pounds mixed zucchini and yellow summer squash (about 3 medium)

2 ears sweet corn

2 tablespoons extra-virgin olive oil

½ teaspoon kosher salt

⅛ teaspoon ground black pepper

1 garlic clove, minced (about 1 teaspoon)

1 cup fresh blueberries (½ pint, about 5 ounces)

Juice of 1 small lemon (about 3 tablespoons)

½ cup crumbled feta cheese (about 3 ounces)

½ cup thinly sliced fresh basil

I love a good deal, which is why come August, you can't open my refrigerator door without the risk of zucchini and yellow squash tumbling onto the floor (and probably landing on your foot, because the universe is like that sometimes). What to do? Make this squash toss! In addition to being fun to say aloud ("squash toss!"), it is bright, refreshing, and just the light seasonal side to cool you on a hot day. Bring it to all your potlucks and serve it with whatever you are grilling tonight. It's summer in a bowl and will have you stocking up on zucchini all over again.

1. Trim off the ends of the zucchini and squash. Quarter them lengthwise and cut into ½-inch-thick slices. Cut the corn kernels off the cobs (see Pro Tip).

2. Heat the oil in a large, deep skillet over medium-high heat. Once the oil is hot and shimmering, add the zucchini and squash, corn kernels, salt, and pepper. Cook, stirring every minute or so, until the zucchini is crisp-tender, 3 to 4 minutes (the zucchini should be al dente, not completely soft). Stir in the garlic and cook until it is very fragrant, about 30 seconds more.

3. Remove the skillet from the heat and stir in the blueberries, lemon juice, feta, and basil. Serve warm or at room temperature.

pro tip

To cut kernels off a corn cob without making a huge mess, rest one end of the corn on the cutting board and hold the other end so that the cob is at a 45-degree angle (you can hold whichever end feels easiest to you). With a sharp knife, cut down one side of the corn from top to bottom to remove the kernels. Next, lay the cut side of the cob flat on the board so it doesn't roll around. Grip one end and cut away the kernels on top once more. Continue to turn the cob and cut until all the kernels are removed.

sage brown butter roasted squash

ACTIVE TIME:
10 minutes

TOTAL TIME:
35 minutes

YIELD:
Serves 6 to 8

2 acorn squash or similar hard winter squash, such as kabocha or delicata (about 3½ pounds)

2 tablespoons extra-virgin olive oil

2 teaspoons kosher salt

½ teaspoon ground black pepper

3 tablespoons unsalted butter

24 fresh sage leaves

next level

For a festive finish, sprinkle the roasted squash slices with pomegranate arils.

market swaps

Swap the winter squash suggested here with 1 medium butternut squash, peeled and cut into 1-inch cubes, or a different root vegetable, such as sweet potatoes, carrots, or halved baby yellow potatoes.

Once you top oven-caramelized squash with a drizzle of nutty sage brown butter, you realize there's really no other way you can eat it again. With its tender, naturally sweet interior, roasted winter squash is one of the yummiest vegetables you can enjoy any night of the week. The sage brown butter makes it worthy of a holiday occasion.

1. Place the racks in the upper and lower thirds of your oven and preheat to 400°F. Coat two large rimmed baking sheets with nonstick spray.

2. Slice the squash in half and scoop out and discard the seeds (see Pro Tip, right). Cut into ¾-inch-thick slices. Divide the slices between the two baking sheets.

3. Drizzle the squash with the oil and sprinkle with the salt and pepper. Toss to coat, then spread the squash into a single layer. Roast the squash for about 25 minutes, until tender and deeply caramelized. Halfway through the baking time, carefully flip the slices over and switch the pans' positions on the upper and lower racks. Remove the squash from the oven and consolidate onto one baking sheet (it's fine if the slices overlap now).

4. Once the squash is out of the oven, melt the butter in a medium saucepan over medium-low heat. For ease, use a pan with a light-colored interior (such as stainless steel) so it's easier to watch the butter's color change. Let the butter melt slowly; it will take several minutes. It will melt, then crackle and foam. Once the foam subsides, add the sage. Continue cooking until the butter turns clear golden (the crackling will stop), then toasty brown. Swirl the pan periodically. Once the butter begins to smell lightly nutty, stir it frequently, scraping up the browned bits from the bottom. Watch the pan carefully in the last few minutes to ensure that the bits at the bottom do not burn (the color will change fast). As soon as the bits turn pecan colored, immediately pour the butter, along with the sage and toasted bits at the bottom of the saucepan, over the squash. Transfer to a serving bowl or serve directly from the baking sheet. Enjoy warm.

pro tip

The skins of acorn, delicata, and kabocha squash are thin and can be eaten once roasted; if you prefer not to eat them, simply remove after roasting.

everything bagel roasted asparagus

ACTIVE TIME:
15 minutes

TOTAL TIME:
25 minutes

YIELD:
Serves 3 to 4

For the Asparagus

1 pound asparagus

1½ teaspoons extra-virgin olive oil

1½ tablespoons everything bagel seasoning

¼ teaspoon kosher salt

For the Bread Crumbs and Topping

1 slice whole-grain bread, or ½ bagel

1 tablespoon extra-virgin olive oil

1 teaspoon everything bagel seasoning

2 ounces soft goat cheese (about ⅓ cup), crumbled

If vegetables tasted like an everything bagel (or as we call it around here, the EB—OK, no we don't, but maybe we'll start), I think we'd all be excited about eating veggies more often, don't you? This recipe uses the EB's core components—the yummy, garlicky, seedy topping, the creamy cheese, and of course the carbs to elevate a simple pan of roasted vegetables into what will be your forever-favorite way to eat asparagus. The "bagel" part comes in the form of bread crumbs (made from a bagel half if you want extra credit, though any bread will do). The cream cheese is repped by tangy goat cheese, crumbled right over the hot asparagus so it becomes nice and melty. We love this combo with asparagus, but feel free to give the EB treatment to any of your favorite roasted veggies to make them irrefutably delicious.

1. Place a rack in the center of your oven and preheat to 425°F. Line a rimmed baking sheet with parchment paper or lightly coat it with nonstick spray.

2. Snap off the woody ends of the asparagus by holding the top end in one hand and gripping it near the base with the other. Briskly bend; the asparagus will naturally snap in the right place. Discard the stem ends. Alternatively, you can cut off the tough ends with a knife.

3. Arrange the asparagus on the prepared baking sheet. Drizzle with the oil and sprinkle with the everything bagel seasoning and salt. Toss to coat, then spread into an even layer. Bake for 9 to 11 minutes (for thin stalks) or 15 to 20 minutes (for thicker stalks), just until they pierce easily with a fork. Shake the pan once halfway through so the asparagus cooks evenly.

4. While the asparagus cooks, prepare the bread crumbs: Tear or cut the bread into 1-inch pieces (you should have about 1 heaped cup) and place them in a food processor. Pulse a few times until you have coarse crumbs. Heat the oil in a large skillet over medium-high heat, then add the bread crumbs. Cook, stirring often, until the bread crumbs are golden and toasted, 3 to 5 minutes. Watch carefully to ensure they do not burn. Stir in the everything bagel seasoning.

recipe continues

5. Transfer the roasted asparagus to a serving plate. Sprinkle the toasted bread crumbs and goat cheese over the top. Enjoy immediately, ensuring that each serving has a good portion of the bread crumbs and goat cheese.

speed it up

If you don't have time to make bread crumbs or prefer to skip the goat cheese, this recipe is still delicious. Enjoy the asparagus on its own or top it with only the goat cheese or only the bread crumbs.

do ahead

Homemade bread crumbs can be refrigerated for up to 1 month. Make a bigger batch, then add to salads, sprinkle over soup, or use to top just about any roasted vegetable. For max enjoyment, recrisp them for a few minutes on the stovetop or in the oven or toaster oven first. Or, if using for roasted vegetables, sprinkle them on during the last few minutes of cooking.

summery baked farro with zucchini and tomato

ACTIVE TIME:
40 minutes

TOTAL TIME:
1 hour 25 minutes

YIELD:
Serves 4

2 tablespoons extra-virgin olive oil, plus additional as needed

1 small onion, ¼ inch diced (about 1 cup)

1 teaspoon kosher salt, divided

¼ teaspoon ground black pepper

2 garlic cloves, minced (about 2 teaspoons)

¼ teaspoon red pepper flakes, plus additional to taste

¾ pound zucchini or yellow summer squash, quartered lengthwise and cut into ¼-inch-thick slices (about 2 medium)

1 pint cherry tomatoes (about 10 ounces), halved, or 2 cups ¾-inch-diced tomatoes of choice

1½ cups semi-pearled farro, rinsed and drained

½ cup dry white wine, such as Sauvignon Blanc or Pinot Grigio (optional)

3 cups vegetable broth

As much as I love farroto (that is, farro cooked on the stovetop in the manner of a risotto so it becomes starchy and creamy), I flat-out lack the patience to tend to it for 45-plus minutes. Because farro is a whole grain, farroto takes much longer to cook than traditional risotto, which is made with white arborio rice. Enter: the oven. The creamy magic happens while the farro bakes blissfully unattended. This hearty dish is a perfect vehicle for seasonal produce, and while I'm listing it with the sides, it has definite main-dish potential. Top it with a fried egg for a fast, anytime meal, or mix in canned white beans or sautéed Italian sausage for a boost of protein.

1. Place the racks in your oven such that you can fit a deep 3½- to 5-quart ovenproof sauté pan or braiser with a lid on the center rack and preheat to 375°F. Use a pan that is at least 12 inches across and 2½ inches tall.

2. Heat the oil in the pan over medium heat. Add the onion, ½ teaspoon of the salt, and the black pepper. Cook until the onion softens and begins to turn translucent, about 5 minutes. Stir in the garlic and red pepper flakes.

3. Add the zucchini and tomatoes. Increase the heat to medium-high and sauté, stirring periodically, until the vegetables begin to soften and brown, about 8 minutes. If the vegetables begin to stick at any point, add a little more oil as needed.

4. Stir in the farro and coat with the oil. Add the wine (if using) and let it reduce for 2 minutes. Stir in the broth. Bring just to a simmer, remove from the heat, and gently stir in the fontina, half of the basil, and the remaining ½ teaspoon salt (at this point, it will look like a liquidy, cheesy mess, but carry on).

5. Cover the pan (use foil if you don't have a lid) and bake for 30 minutes, then uncover and stir. If the farro looks dry, add ¼ to ½ cup of water or additional broth if you have it. Sprinkle the Parmesan over the top.

6. Return the pan to the oven, uncovered, and continue baking for 10 to 15 minutes, until most of the liquid has evaporated and

recipe and ingredients continue

1½ cups shredded fontina cheese, or Gouda or mozzarella cheese (about 6 ounces)

½ cup chopped fresh basil, divided

⅓ cup finely grated Parmesan cheese (about 1 ounce), plus additional for serving

the farro is cooked through but still has a nice chew to it (farro should not be completely soft). If desired, turn the oven to broil for 2 to 3 minutes to lightly crisp the top. Sprinkle with the remaining basil and enjoy warm with additional Parmesan as desired.

pro tip

Semi-pearled farro is farro that has some but not all of the bran (the fiber- and nutrient-rich outermost layer) removed. This makes it cook more quickly than whole farro, and it also has a slightly higher nutritional content than pearled farro, which has all of the bran removed.

cozy baked farro with butternut squash

ACTIVE TIME:
40 minutes

TOTAL TIME:
1 hour 25 minutes

YIELD:
Serves 4

2 tablespoons extra-virgin olive oil, plus additional as needed

1 small onion, ¼ inch diced (about 1 cup)

1 teaspoon kosher salt, divided

¼ teaspoon ground black pepper

2 garlic cloves, minced (about 2 teaspoons)

¼ teaspoon ground nutmeg

1 medium butternut squash (about 1½ pounds), peeled and cut into ¾- to 1-inch cubes (about 4 cups cubes)

1½ cups semi-pearled farro, rinsed and drained

½ cup dry white wine, such as Sauvignon Blanc or Pinot Grigio (optional)

3 cups vegetable broth

1½ cups shredded Gruyère cheese or sharp white cheddar (about 6 ounces)

2 teaspoons chopped fresh thyme, divided

⅓ cup finely grated Parmesan cheese (about 1 ounce), plus additional for serving

Look familiar? Baked farro is so nice, I've featured it twice! The fall and winter cousin to the summery version on the preceding pages, this harvesty spin is here to warm you on a chilly evening. Cable-knit sweater optional but encouraged.

1. Place the racks in your oven such that you can fit a deep 3½- to 5-quart ovenproof sauté pan or braiser with a lid on the center rack and preheat to 375°F. Use a pan that is at least 12 inches across and 2½ inches tall.

2. Heat the oil in the pan over medium heat. Add the onion, ½ teaspoon of the salt, and the pepper. Cook until the onion softens and begins to turn translucent, about 5 minutes. Stir in the garlic and nutmeg.

3. Add the butternut squash. Increase the heat to medium-high and sauté, stirring periodically, until the squash begins to take on some color but is still too chewy to eat, about 5 minutes. If the squash begins to stick at any point, add more oil as needed.

4. Stir in the farro and coat with the oil. Add the wine (if using) and let it reduce for 2 minutes. Stir in the broth. Bring just to a simmer, remove from the heat, and gently stir in the Gruyère, half of the thyme, and the remaining ½ teaspoon salt (at this point, it will look like a liquidy, cheesy mess, but carry on).

5. Cover the pan (use foil if you don't have a lid) and bake for 30 minutes, then uncover and stir. If the farro looks dry, add ¼ to ½ cup of water or additional broth. Sprinkle the Parmesan over the top.

6. Taste the farro. It should be tender but still have a pleasant chew to it (farro should not be completely soft). If it needs longer, return the pan to the oven, uncovered, and continue baking for 10 to 15 minutes. If the farro is still fairly liquidy, cover the pan and let rest for 10 minutes to absorb further. If desired, prior to serving broil the farro for 2 to 3 minutes to lightly crisp the top. Sprinkle with the remaining thyme. Enjoy warm with additional Parmesan.

cacio e pepe cauliflower mash

ACTIVE TIME:
20 minutes

TOTAL TIME:
30 minutes

YIELD:
Serves 4

6 cups cauliflower florets
(about 24 ounces or
1 medium head)

4 garlic cloves, smashed
and peeled

½ teaspoon kosher salt,
divided

2 tablespoons unsalted
butter, diced

3 tablespoons nonfat milk
or milk of choice, plus
additional as needed

¾ cup finely grated
Parmesan cheese
(about 3 ounces),
plus additional for serving

1 teaspoon coarsely
ground black pepper,
plus additional for serving

Carbs and I have always been on favorable terms, so when the cauliflower-for-president movement started using it in place of carbs in everything from pizza crust to rice, I was skeptical. Since then, cauliflower mash earned my vote. While I can't say this tastes exactly like mashed potatoes (because it's cauliflower), I can attest with absolute confidence that it is *delicious*. Cauliflower is mild, meaning it easily takes on whatever seasonings you use. For our purposes, that's lots of Parmesan cheese and ground black pepper, as inspired by another carby favorite, cacio e pepe pasta. It's hands down one of the tastiest ways you can eat your veggies. I'd campaign on that.

1. Place the cauliflower and garlic in a medium saucepan and add enough cold water to cover the cauliflower by 1 inch (the cauliflower will float, so press it down to the bottom of the saucepan to gauge the amount). Add ¼ teaspoon of the salt, then bring to a boil over high heat. Let boil until the cauliflower is fork-tender, about 6 minutes.

2. Drain, then transfer the cauliflower and garlic to a food processor. Scatter the butter over the top (the heat of the cauliflower will melt it). Add the milk, Parmesan, pepper, and remaining ¼ teaspoon salt.

3. Blend the cauliflower in long bursts, stopping to scrape down the bowl periodically, until the mixture is fairly smooth with just a few small bits of cauliflower here and there—it should look very similar in consistency to mashed potatoes. If it is thicker than you would like, add more milk 1 tablespoon at a time, until your desired consistency is reached. Taste and adjust the seasoning as desired. Serve immediately or transfer to a heatproof bowl and keep warm over a pan of simmering water. Top servings with a handful of additional Parmesan and a few grinds of black pepper.

speed it up

Replace the cauliflower with 24 ounces of steam-in-the-bag riced cauliflower. Reduce the garlic to 1 small clove. Cook the cauliflower according to the package instructions, then add warm to the food processor as directed.

salt and vinegar smashed potatoes

ACTIVE TIME:
15 minutes

TOTAL TIME:
1 hour 15 minutes

YIELD:
Serves 4

1½ pounds baby gold potatoes

1 tablespoon plus ½ teaspoon kosher salt, divided

3 tablespoons extra-virgin olive oil, divided

2 tablespoons apple cider vinegar, divided

½ teaspoon ground black pepper, plus additional for serving

½ teaspoon onion powder

Flaky sea salt, such as Maldon or fleur de sel, for serving

In addition to his-and-hers fries (see Blackened Chili-Garlic Sweet Potato Wedges, page 266), Ben and I each have our personal stashes of chips, if for no other reason than I adore salt and vinegar chips, and he strongly dislikes them. More for me, ha! With their craggy, golden edges and creamy interiors, smashed potatoes are all-out addictive and bring excitement to any meal. If you have salt and vinegar chip lovers at your table, be aware that however many of these potatoes you make, that's how many people will eat.

1. Rinse the potatoes and trim away any small sprouts. Place the potatoes in a large pot and cover them with cold water by 1 inch. Add 1 tablespoon of the kosher salt. Bring to a boil, then reduce the heat to a steady simmer. Let simmer, adjusting the heat as needed, until the potatoes are barely fork-tender, 15 to 20 minutes. Drain the potatoes in a colander and shake off as much water as you can. Let sit for 5 minutes to cool and drain a bit more. Keep the pot you used to boil them handy.

2. While the potatoes boil, place a rack in the center of your oven and preheat to 450°F. Brush a large rimmed baking sheet with 1 tablespoon of the oil.

3. Shake the potatoes once more to remove any remaining water. If the pot you cooked them in is still wet, carefully wipe it

dry. Return the potatoes to the pot. Top with 1 tablespoon of the vinegar, the pepper, onion powder, and the remaining 2 tablespoons oil and ½ teaspoon kosher salt. With a big spoon, stir to coat the potatoes as evenly as possible.

4. Spoon the potatoes onto the prepared baking sheet (leave the extra liquid in the pot for now). With the bottom of a sturdy drinking glass, gently press the potatoes until they are ½ inch thick. Do your best to keep the potatoes in one piece, and if any break apart, use your fingers to gently scootch them back together. They'll look quite thin (and thin = crispy!). Pour the liquid from the pot over the top.

5. Transfer to the oven and roast for 25 to 30 minutes, depending upon the size of your potatoes,

recipe continues

until the potatoes are golden and crisp. Remove the potatoes from the oven and immediately drizzle with the remaining 1 tablespoon vinegar and sprinkle with flaky salt and black pepper. Serve hot.

speed it up

Make regular roasted potatoes: Cut 2 pounds Yukon Gold potatoes into 1-inch chunks. Coat with the oil, vinegar, and spices as directed, then roast in a 425°F oven for 35 to 40 minutes, tossing halfway through. Finish with the remaining vinegar, flaky salt, and black pepper.

next level

For the strongest vinegar punch, swap the apple cider vinegar for malt vinegar.

spiced rice and lentils with caramelized onions

ACTIVE TIME:
30 minutes

TOTAL TIME:
1 hour 15 minutes

YIELD:
Serves 6 to 8

1 cup brown rice

4½ cups water, divided

1 teaspoon kosher salt, divided, plus additional to taste

2 tablespoons extra-virgin olive oil

2 large yellow onions, halved through the ends, then cut lengthwise into ¼-inch-thick slices

1 cup shelled pistachios, or ¾ cup slivered almonds (see Speed It Up)

1 cup green or brown lentils

2 garlic cloves, minced (about 2 teaspoons)

2 teaspoons ground cumin

1½ teaspoons ground allspice

1½ teaspoons ground cinnamon

½ teaspoon ground turmeric

¼ teaspoon ground black pepper, plus additional to taste

This dish is inspired by mejadra, an ancient dish of warmly spiced lentils and rice topped with fried onions that is popular throughout the Middle Eastern world. It's comforting eaten either warm with a dollop of plain Greek yogurt or at room temperature, right from the container at your next picnic. Instead of frying onions, which is more of an endeavor than I'm willing to take on at home, I make sweet caramelized onions, then bring back the crunch with a shower of chopped pistachios. This recipe takes some time to come together, but it happens largely unattended, yields a generous amount that reheats well, and the taste is more than worth it.

1. Cook the rice: Place the rice in a mesh sieve and rinse well under cool water. Place in a medium saucepan. Add 2 cups of the water and ¼ teaspoon of the salt. Bring to a boil, then cover and reduce the heat to low. Let simmer for 45 minutes, lowering the heat if needed so that the rice does not boil over. Turn off the heat and let sit, covered, for 10 minutes.

2. Meanwhile, caramelize the onions: Heat the oil in a Dutch oven or similar large, heavy-bottomed pot over medium-low heat. Once the oil is hot and shimmering, add the onions, separating the layers as you place them in the pot. Add ¼ teaspoon of the salt. Cook, stirring occasionally, until the onions soften and caramelize, 25 to 30 minutes.

3. While the onions cook, toast the pistachios: Place the pistachios in a small dry skillet over medium heat, stirring often, until they are very fragrant and lightly browned, 3 to 4 minutes. Remove from the heat, then stir every so often as the pan cools so they continue cooking evenly. If they are near burning, transfer them immediately to a cutting board to prevent further cooking.

4. Rinse the lentils in the same mesh sieve you used for the rice, picking out and removing any shriveled lentils or bits of debris.

5. Once the onions are caramelized, increase the heat to medium, then add the garlic, cumin, allspice, cinnamon, turmeric, and pepper. Stir

recipe continues

briskly for 30 seconds to bloom the spices and sauté the garlic. Add the lentils and stir to coat with the oil and spices. Add the remaining 2½ cups water. Bring to a boil, then cover the pot, reduce the heat to low, and let simmer gently until the lentils are tender but not mushy, 15 to 20 minutes (you may need a little longer if your lentils are old). Remove the lid (the lentils may still look a little bit watery, which is fine) and stir in the remaining ½ teaspoon kosher salt.

6. With a fork, fluff the rice, then add it to the pot with the lentils. Roughly chop the pistachios, then add. With the fork, stir gently to combine the ingredients evenly. Season with a few pinches of additional salt and pepper to taste. Serve warm.

speed it up

: Purchase pistachios that are already shelled and toasted.

do ahead

: Cooking the rice and caramelizing the onions are the most time-
: consuming parts of this recipe. You can cook both 1 to 2 days in
: advance, storing separately in the refrigerator. When ready to finish
: the recipe, warm up the caramelized onions in a Dutch oven or
: similar large, heavy-bottomed pot with 1 to 2 tablespoons of extra-
: virgin olive oil, then proceed with the recipe as directed.

peanut
butter cup
graham
cracker
ice cream
sandwiches
page 323

desserts
because there's always room

et me let you in on a little secret: when someone says they don't want dessert, very rarely do they mean it. And even if they do, a warm slice of Bourbon-Glazed Apple Galette (page 300) dripping with vanilla ice cream or a sticky Peanut Butter and Jelly Bar (page 306) has a 99 percent effective rate of changing their mind—unless it's the Fudgiest Salted Chocolate Sheet Cake (page 325), in which case the effectiveness rate is exactly 100 percent.

Dessert is meant to be indulgent and a little extra, which is why it's so delectably fun. Wherever possible I've cut down on dishes and appliances (I promise, if I'm asking you to get out the food processor like I do for Bragging Rights Pie Crust, page 297, it will be WORTH IT). You don't need to stress over presentation (messy desserts like Blueberry Cornmeal Crisp, page 309, have always been my favorites; plus, who has time?). No special pans are needed—in fact, for most of these desserts, a cookie sheet or square baking pan will do just fine. Whether you enjoy the baking process or are just here for the end result, you'll love these sweet treats.

peanut butter and jelly bars
page 306

bragging rights pie crust

ACTIVE TIME:
30 minutes

TOTAL TIME:
1 hour

YIELD:
Two 10-inch pie crusts

¼ cup vodka

¼ cup water

¾ cup (1½ sticks) unsalted butter, very cold

½ cup vegetable shortening, such as Crisco

3 cups all-purpose flour

3 tablespoons granulated sugar

1 teaspoon kosher salt

Welcome to the "X" on my pie crust treasure map. It's been a quest! I've researched and tested different fats (vegetable shortening is the flakiest, but butter is the tastiest), gluten inhibitors to make the pie crust more tender (the winner: vodka!), and mixing methods (answer: let the machine do the work). I've tried the "best evers" from the likes of America's Test Kitchen, Queen Ina Garten, church lady cookbooks, people who swear only butter is best, and other people who swear by Crisco alone. The lessons, sticky rolling pins, and flour-spattered countertops have led us here: the only pie crust I'll ever make.

I won't pretend that pie crust is a breeze, but I WILL say it's not as hard as you think it is, and that this one in particular is absolutely worth it. It's perplexingly rich and buttery yet tender and flaky at the same time. When your fork shatters the golden lid on your perfect pie or the sugar-sparkled border of your Bourbon-Glazed Apple Galette (page 300), you'll beam with pride. Pat yourself on the back and brag a little. Then, go in for that second slice. You deserve it!

1. In a small liquid measuring cup with a spout, combine the vodka and water. Place in the freezer while you prepare the other ingredients.

2. Line a cutting board with parchment paper. Place the butter on the parchment and dice it into small pieces (about ¼ to ½ inch each). Dice the shortening on the paper with the butter (if your shortening is in a tub or too soft to dice, use a small spoon and your finger to drop it onto the paper in little blobs). Transfer to the freezer while you prep the dry ingredients, either by lifting the paper with the butter and shortening onto a freezer-safe plate or by placing the cutting board in the freezer directly.

3. In the bowl of a food processor, place the flour, sugar, and salt. Pulse a few times to mix. Scatter the butter and shortening over the top. Pulse six to ten times, until the butter and shortening are roughly the size of peas. Some pieces will be small like pebbles, while others can be as large as your thumbnail. Chunky pieces equal flaky crust, so don't be afraid of them.

4. With the machine running, pour the vodka-water mixture down the feed tube. Stop the

recipe continues

machine, then pulse just until the dough begins to form a ball, about eight pulses. Dump the dough onto a lightly floured work surface and, working quickly, gather it into a ball. If the dough is dry and not holding together when pressed, sprinkle 1 teaspoon of water over it to slightly moisten. Divide the ball into two pieces. If you are going to be making a two-crust pie (such as an apple pie), make one piece slightly larger than the other (the larger one will be for the bottom crust, which needs more dough). Pat each ball into a flat disk that is about 1 inch high. Wrap the disks in plastic and refrigerate for at least 30 minutes or up to 3 days (or put in a ziptop bag and freeze for up to 3 months—let thaw overnight in the refrigerator before rolling).

To Roll:

Set a large sheet of parchment paper on your work surface and flour it lightly. Place the chilled pie dough in its center (if the dough is too cold to roll out, let it sit at room temperature for a few minutes). Lightly flour your rolling pin. Working from the center, roll the dough outward into a circle of your desired size. Always roll from the center out, using the paper to rotate the dough so that you are constantly rolling away from yourself. (Do not run the rolling pin back and forth across the entire crust or it

won't shape properly.) If at any point the dough becomes too sticky to work with easily, pop it into the refrigerator or freezer for a few minutes to rechill the fat.

To Line a Pie Dish:

1. Fold the first circle over the rolling pin, then use the rolling pin to help you unfurl it gently into the dish. Settle it down into the dish so that it is smoothly touching the bottom and sides (don't stretch it or it will shrink back). Trim any overhang to ½ inch beyond the lip of the pan. Tuck the overhang under itself so that the folded edge is flush with the edge of the pan. Crimp the dough evenly around the edge of the pan using your fingers (or use the tines of the fork to do a simple press all the way around; if adding a top crust, wait to crimp). If at any point the dough tears, don't stress—just pinch it back together with your fingers and carry on with your delicious pie.

2. Refrigerate the dough-lined pan until firm, about 30 minutes. If you are using a top crust, roll it out, then keep it in the refrigerator until you are ready to place it on top of the pie. Bake away!

For a Galette:

1. On a sheet of lightly floured parchment paper, roll one disk into a circle that is about ⅛ inch thick. Transfer to the refrigerator and chill while you prepare the filling.

2. If you're using a super-juicy filling (with strawberries or peaches, for example) and want to guard against a soggy bottom crust, lightly sprinkle the center of the dough with a thin layer of bread crumbs, graham cracker or amaretti cookie crumbs, or finely chopped nuts. Add the fruit filling in the center (leave any filling juices in the bowl), leaving a 2-inch border. Dot the filling with a little butter (this makes it extra pretty and shiny), then shape and bake as directed (no need to refrigerate it first).

pro tip

For a pretty sparkle and tasty, subtle crunch on a sweet fruit pie or galette, brush the crust all over with an egg wash made from 1 egg whisked with 1 teaspoon water, or skip the egg and brush with simply milk, heavy cream, or buttermilk. Sprinkle with turbinado sugar or similar sanding sugar. Bake as directed.

bourbon-glazed apple galette

ACTIVE TIME:

30 minutes

TOTAL TIME:

2 hours

YIELD:

Serves 8

1 Bragging Rights Pie Crust (page 297) or store-bought pie crust

1½ pounds mixed sweet and tart baking apples, such as Granny Smith, Honeycrisp, or Braeburn (about 3 large)

3 tablespoons unsalted butter

⅓ cup packed dark brown sugar

¼ cup bourbon or whiskey, dark rum, or apple brandy, or use apple juice or water

½ teaspoon ground cinnamon

⅛ teaspoon kosher salt

1 small lemon

1 tablespoon pure vanilla extract

1 large egg, beaten with 1 tablespoon milk or heavy cream to create an egg wash

1 tablespoon turbinado, demerara, or similar coarse sugar

Vanilla, salted caramel, or butter pecan ice cream or frozen yogurt, for serving

Pies are . . . a lot of work. Galettes? A piece of cake! (Well, technically a piece of galette, but you catch my drift.) Your pie dough is tearing at the edges as you roll? No issue for a galette. You never learned how to crimp? The galette does not care. In fact, the galette's breezy, free-form *"I just threw this together!"* appearance is an integral part of its appeal. You can use any fruit filling for a galette, but it's hard to beat all-American apple . . . unless of course it's all-American apple with bourbon. Now we're talking!

1. Set a large sheet of parchment paper on your work surface and place the chilled pie dough in its center (if the dough is too cold to roll out, let it sit at room temperature for a few minutes). Flour your rolling pin. Working from the center, roll the dough outward into a circle that is ⅛ inch thick and about 12 inches across. Always roll from the center out, using the paper to rotate the dough so that you are constantly rolling away from yourself. (Do not run the rolling pin back and forth across the entire crust.) Don't stress if it's not perfect or if it tears (rustic is the name of the game!). Patch any cracks by pinching the dough back together or pressing small scraps from the edges over any big cracks. Grab the sides of the paper and lift the paper and dough together up and onto a large rimmed baking sheet. Place the baking sheet in the refrigerator while you prepare the apples.

2. Peel the apples, halve each one downward through the stem, and remove the cores (a small knife in combination with a melon baller or small spoon works well). Cut the apple halves crosswise into ¼-inch-thick slices.

3. In a large skillet, melt the butter over medium heat. Add the apple slices, brown sugar, bourbon, cinnamon, and salt. Zest half of the lemon directly into the skillet, then halve it and squeeze in 1 tablespoon of the juice. Stir to combine and dissolve the sugar. Let the liquid come to a simmer. Cook, stirring occasionally, until the apples soften but still have a bit of crispness to them, about 5 minutes. Remove from the heat and stir in the vanilla. With a slotted spoon, transfer the apples to a plate and let cool completely (speed this along in the refrigerator or freezer).

recipe continues

Reserve the cooking liquid in the pan (it's pure gold!).

4. When you're ready to bake, place a rack in the center of your oven and preheat to 400°F. Remove the baking sheet from the refrigerator. Pile the apples into the center of the dough, leaving a 2-inch border all the way around. Leave any juices behind on the plate.

5. Fold the edges of the dough up and over the apple filling, pleating it as you go. Brush the top of the pie dough with the egg wash and sprinkle it with the turbinado sugar. If your oven isn't finished preheating, pop the galette back into the refrigerator until it is.

6. Bake the galette for 40 to 45 minutes, until the crust is a rich golden brown, rotating the pan 180 degrees halfway through. Place on a wire rack to cool.

7. While the galette bakes, add any leftover juices from the plate that held the apples to the skillet with the reserved apple cooking liquid. Simmer over medium-high heat until it is reduced by approximately half, 2 to 3 minutes. Let cool. Once the galette is cool, stir the glaze, then use a pastry brush to brush it generously and evenly over the cooked apples (use it all!). Slice and enjoy with ice cream or frozen yogurt as desired.

cowgirl cookies

ACTIVE TIME:
30 minutes

TOTAL TIME:
1 hour 50 minutes

YIELD:
About 24 cookies

½ cup raw pecan halves

½ cup (1 stick) unsalted butter, cut into four pieces

⅓ cup packed light brown sugar

⅓ cup granulated sugar

¾ cup white whole wheat flour, or ½ cup all-purpose flour and ¼ cup regular whole wheat flour

½ cup old-fashioned oats or quick-cooking oats

¼ cup unsweetened flake coconut

¾ teaspoon baking soda

½ teaspoon ground cinnamon

½ teaspoon kosher salt

1 large egg, at room temperature

1 tablespoon pure vanilla extract

¼ teaspoon apple cider vinegar

¾ cup dark chocolate chips (55% to 72% chocolate)

Flaky sea salt, such as Maldon or fleur de sel

Growing up, did you have a Halloween costume that you couldn't resist dressing up in year after year? For me, it was a cowgirl. I'm not sure if it was the shiny silver star badge that gave me fresh justification to boss my younger sisters around or the shoulder-to-shoulder fringe (or maybe the fact that my mom realized early on that a cowgirl getup could fit easily under a puffy winter coat), but the cowgirl became my go-to Halloween persona.

None of that has anything to do with cookies, except to say that I've spent a good amount of time imagining myself riding into the sunset, and this is the cookie I'd want along with me. Its rough-and-tumble mix of chewy oats, crunchy nuts, chunky chocolate, and toasted coconut make every bite an adventure. You'll see these called cowboy cookies elsewhere, but like any good heroine, I've made them my own, and I hope you do too. Heads up before you giddyap: Don't skip refrigerating the dough. It's critical to ensuring that the dough holds together, the dry ingredients fully absorb the wet ingredients, and the texture of the cookies turns out properly. I promise they are worth the wait!

1. Toast the pecans: Place a rack in the center of your oven and preheat to 350°F. Spread the pecans in a single layer on an ungreased rimmed baking sheet. Bake for 9 to 11 minutes, shaking the pan once halfway through, until the nuts are toasted and fragrant. To ensure that they do not burn (it happens fast!), do not walk away from the nuts toward the end of their cook time. Immediately transfer to a cutting board and let cool. Turn off the oven.

2. In a large microwave-safe bowl, melt the butter in the microwave on low power, or melt it in a heatproof bowl set over a pan of simmering water. Remove from the heat and stir in the brown sugar and granulated sugar until smooth. Set aside to cool.

3. In a medium bowl, whisk together the flour, oats, coconut, baking soda, cinnamon, and salt.

4. Into the bowl with the butter and sugar, whisk the egg, vanilla, and vinegar. Add the dry ingredients. With a rubber spatula or wooden spoon, stir gently until combined. The batter will be loose and wet.

recipe continues

5. Roughly chop the nuts, then add them to the bowl. Add the chocolate chips, then fold to combine. Cover the bowl with plastic wrap, pressing the wrap against the surface of the dough. Refrigerate for at least 1 hour or up to 3 days.

6. When you're ready to bake, remove the dough from the refrigerator and preheat your oven to 350°F. Line a baking sheet with parchment paper or a silicone baking mat (do not leave the sheet unlined—the cookies have the best texture when the pan is lined). With a medium cookie scoop or spoon, portion the dough by rounded tablespoonfuls, then form into balls that are slightly wider than 1 inch. Arrange the balls on the baking sheet, leaving at least 1 inch between each. Sprinkle lightly with flaky salt. Bake for 10 to 12 minutes, until the cookies are golden brown and barely set at the edges and on top.

7. Place the sheet on a wire rack. Let the cookies cool on the sheet for 5 minutes, then gently transfer to them to the rack to finish cooling completely. If the cookies are still too soft to lift with a spatula, carefully slide the sheet of parchment paper or silicone mat onto the rack with the cookies still on it. Repeat with the remaining dough, ensuring your baking sheets are fully cooled between batches or the cookies will spread.

do ahead

Store leftover baked cookies at room temperature for up to 1 week or freeze, tightly wrapped, for up to 3 months.

To freeze unbaked cookie dough: Scoop and shape the cookie dough as directed. Arrange the unbaked cookie balls in a single layer on a parchment paper–lined baking sheet, then place the baking sheet in the freezer. Once the balls have hardened, transfer them to a ziptop bag and freeze for up to 3 months. Bake individual cookies directly from frozen, adding a few extra minutes to the baking time as needed.

variations

Dairy Free: Replace the butter with ½ cup coconut oil; use dairy-free chocolate chips.

Extra Nutty: Replace up to ½ cup of the chocolate chips with peanut butter chips.

peanut butter and jelly bars

ACTIVE TIME:

30 minutes

TOTAL TIME:

1 hour 15 minutes

YIELD:

One 8 by 8-inch pan (12 to 16 bars)

4 tablespoons (½ stick) unsalted butter, at room temperature

¼ cup nonfat plain Greek yogurt

⅔ cup granulated sugar

1 cup creamy peanut butter (see Pro Tip)

1 large egg, at room temperature

1 teaspoon pure vanilla extract

¾ cup white whole wheat flour or ½ cup all-purpose flour and ¼ cup regular whole wheat flour

¾ cup all-purpose flour

½ teaspoon baking powder

½ teaspoon kosher salt

1 cup strawberry jam, or seedless raspberry jam or berry jam of your choice

⅓ cup salted dry-roatsted peanuts, roughly chopped

With two layers of soft, buttery peanut butter cookie sandwiching a sweet layer of strawberry jam, this dessert spin on a classic PB&J is for the big kid inside all of us. Salty and sweet, fruity and nutty, sticky and creamy, they are everything that is wonderful about a PB&J, turned into a pick-up-with-your fingers, take-along-anywhere treat that many generations will love.

1. Place a rack in the center of your oven and preheat to 350°F. Coat an 8 by 8-inch baking pan with nonstick spray. Line it with parchment paper, leaving some overhang on two sides like handles, then coat with spray again.

2. In the bowl of a stand mixer fitted with the paddle attachment or in a large bowl with a hand mixer, beat the butter, yogurt, and sugar on medium speed until pale yellow and fluffy, 1 to 2 minutes. Scrape down the bottom and sides of the bowl. Reduce the mixer speed to low, then with the mixer running, add the peanut butter, egg, and vanilla. Increase the speed to medium and mix until everything is well combined.

3. In a small bowl, stir together the white whole wheat flour, all-purpose flour, baking powder, and salt. With the mixer on low speed, slowly add the flour mixture to the peanut butter mixture. Mix just until the flour disappears.

4. Scoop two-thirds of the dough into the prepared pan, and with a knife or offset spatula, spread it into an even layer. Spread the jam evenly over the dough. Break the remaining dough into small pieces and scatter evenly over the jam (you'll have some bits of jam showing through). Sprinkle the peanuts over the top. Bake for 35 to 40 minutes, until the bars are golden brown. Let cool for 10 minutes in the pan, then, using the parchment paper handles, lift the bars onto a wire rack to cool completely. Slice and serve.

pro tip

I find this recipe works best with shelf-stable peanut butters, such as Jif Natural or Skippy Natural. Drippy-style peanut butter made with peanuts exclusively is my favorite for spreading on toast and snacking, but it does not perform as consistently in baking recipes.

market swap

For a rich, chocolaty version, swap the jam for 1 cup Nutella and sprinkle with chocolate chips prior to baking.

blueberry cornmeal crisp

ACTIVE TIME:

20 minutes

TOTAL TIME:

1 hour 15 minutes

YIELD:

One 9 by 9-inch crisp (serves 8)

For the Filling

4 cups blueberries
(2 pints, about 20 ounces;
see Pro Tip)

¼ cup pure maple syrup

2 tablespoons white whole
wheat flour or all-purpose
flour

½ teaspoon ground
cinnamon

1 medium lemon

Vanilla frozen yogurt, ice
cream, or Greek yogurt,
for serving

For the Topping

¾ cup white whole wheat
flour, or ½ cup regular
whole wheat flour and
¼ cup all-purpose flour

⅓ cup yellow cornmeal,
medium grind if you can
find it

½ cup packed light brown
sugar

½ teaspoon baking powder

½ teaspoon kosher salt

¼ cup nonfat plain Greek
yogurt

4 tablespoons (½ stick)
cold unsalted butter,
thinly sliced

With its maple-sweetened, bubbly blueberry filling and craggy, buttery topping, this is the dessert I imagine enjoying on a wraparound porch some summer afternoon. If you haven't experienced the harmony of blueberry and cornmeal together before, I am ecstatic to be making the introduction. I like to use medium-grind cornmeal for its pleasant bits of texture, but if you can't find it, fine yellow cornmeal works too.

1. Place a rack in the center of your oven and preheat to 350°F. In an 8 by 8-inch or 9 by 9-inch baking dish, place the blueberries, maple syrup, flour, and cinnamon. Zest the lemon directly over the berries, then halve it and squeeze in 2 tablespoons of the juice (about half of the lemon). Stir to combine.

2. Prepare the topping: In a medium bowl, combine the flour, cornmeal, brown sugar, baking powder, and salt. Add the yogurt and use a fork to stir until the ingredients are somewhat moistened. Scatter the butter over the top. Working quickly with your fingertips, pinch and rub the butter into the flour mixture until the butter is in pieces about the size of your thumbnail (some pieces will be larger than others). Scatter the topping over the blueberries (some fruit will peek through).

3. Bake for 40 to 45 minutes, until the filling is hot, bubbly, and thickened and the top is a nice golden brown. Let rest for 10 minutes, then serve hot with a big scoop of frozen yogurt.

pro tip

This crisp also works beautifully with frozen berries. Let them thaw at room temperature for about 2 hours or in the refrigerator overnight (it's OK if they are still a little frozen). Proceed with the recipe as directed, including any juices the frozen berries have released during thawing with the rest of the filling.

market swaps

This topping is scrumptious with a wide array of ripe summer fruit. A blend of peaches and blueberries or a mix of summer berries is especially tasty.

tahini magic bars

ACTIVE TIME:
30 minutes

TOTAL TIME:
1 hour

YIELD:
**One 8 by 8-inch pan
(9 or 16 bars)**

For the Tahini Magic Sauce
½ cup (4 ounces)
sweetened condensed milk

⅓ cup tahini

1 teaspoon pure vanilla
extract

¼ teaspoon kosher salt

For the Crust
10 whole graham cracker
sheets, or 1½ cups graham
cracker crumbs

3 tablespoons granulated
sugar

¾ teaspoon baking powder

¼ teaspoon kosher salt

1 large egg yolk

6 tablespoons unsalted
butter, melted and cooled
(see Pro Tips)

For Topping
¾ cup dark chocolate chips
(55% to 72% chocolate),
divided

½ cup chopped raw pecans

1 cup sweetened flake
coconut

2 tablespoons sesame
seeds

Hello Dolly bars. Seven-layer bars. Magic bars. The midwestern pot-luck staple that inspired this recipe is so good, it needs three different names to encapsulate its magnificence. Sweet, salty, and toasty ingredients like coconut, chocolate chips, and pecans are set atop a graham cracker crust and bound with sweetened condensed milk that acts as the "glue"; the one fatal flaw is that the bars can be cloyingly sweet. This recipe swaps part of the sweetened condensed milk for tahini, giving the bars a subtle, welcome savoriness that renders them all-out impossible to stop eating. Need to win a bake sale? Make these.

1. Prepare the tahini magic sauce: In a small bowl, whisk together the condensed milk, tahini, vanilla, and salt. Set aside.

2. Make the crust: Place a rack in the center of your oven and preheat to 350°F. Lightly coat an 8 by 8-inch pan with nonstick spray. Line it with parchment paper, leaving some overhang on two sides like handles, then coat with spray again.

3. Break the graham crackers into pieces in the bowl of a food processor. Pulse into fine crumbs (you should have about 1½ cups). Add the sugar, baking powder, and salt, then pulse a few times to combine. Pulse in the egg yolk, then with the machine running, pour in the butter. Scrape down the bowl, then continue to process in long bursts until the ingredients are evenly moistened and the mixture begins to form large clumps (see note if you prefer not to use a food processor).

4. Turn out the graham cracker mixture into the prepared pan, then with your fingers or the back of a measuring cup, press it into a firm, even layer. Bake for 5 minutes.

5. Sprinkle the warm crust with ½ cup of the chocolate chips and the pecans. With a small spoon, dollop the tahini mixture all over the crust, then use the back of the spoon to spread it over the chocolate chips and pecans, going all the way to the edges and covering as evenly as you can. Sprinkle on the coconut and lightly press it down to help it stick to the tahini mixture. Sprinkle on the remaining chocolate chips and the sesame seeds. Bake the bars for about 25 minutes, until the toppings are a nice golden brown. Place the pan on a wire rack and let the bars cool completely. Lift the bars onto a cutting board using the parchment overhang and cut to your desired size.

recipe continues

pro tips

To make it easier to pour the butter into the food processor, melt it in a heatproof liquid measuring cup with a spout.

Leftover condensed milk can last in a sealed container for nearly a month in the refrigerator and several months in freezer (do not store it in the can). Try stirring a little into your iced coffee or tea, drizzling it on peanut butter toast, or stirring a few tablespoons into your next pork or chicken marinade.

no food processor?

To make the crust without a food processor: In a large bowl, whisk together 1½ cups ready-made graham cracker crumbs, the sugar, baking powder, and salt. In a separate bowl, combine the egg yolk and melted butter, then add to the crumbs. With a rubber spatula, stir the mixture together until the crumbs are evenly moistened. Proceed with the recipe as directed.

pumpkin gingerbread squares with spiced cream cheese frosting

ACTIVE TIME:
30 minutes

TOTAL TIME:
1 hour 30 minutes

YIELD:
One 8 by 8-inch cake (9 or 16 squares)

For the Cake

½ cup packed dark brown sugar

2 large eggs, at room temperature

¾ cup pure pumpkin puree (not pumpkin pie filling)

½ cup canola oil, or melted and cooled coconut oil

¼ cup unsulfured molasses (not blackstrap)

2 teaspoons ground cinnamon

1¼ teaspoons ground ginger

½ teaspoon unsweetened cocoa powder

¼ teaspoon ground nutmeg

¼ teaspoon ground cloves

½ teaspoon kosher salt

1 small orange

1 cup all-purpose flour

½ cup white whole wheat flour or regular whole wheat flour

1 teaspoon baking powder

½ teaspoon baking soda

One of the rougher parts of being a food blogger is the need to test recipes months in advance. At no time is this more evident than peak summer, when all I want to subsist on is Spicy Tomato and Olive Oil Burrata (page 89) and glasses of ice-cold rosé, but my recipe development calendar requires testing heavy holiday casseroles and desserts. Have you tried enjoying mashed potatoes and gravy when it's 90°F outside?

Thus, when on a steamy August day I went in for a *second* slice of these harvest-spiced squares, I knew I had a keeper! They combine two seasonal greats—pumpkin and gingerbread—into one magically moist, cream-cheese-frosted, highly snackable cake that, while most at home at the holidays, is scrumptious year-round, as I can attest.

1. Place a rack in the center of your oven and preheat to 350°F. Coat an 8 by 8-inch baking pan with nonstick spray. Line the pan with parchment paper so that two strips overhang opposite sides like handles.

2. In a large bowl, whisk together the brown sugar and eggs until pale and foamy, about 1 minute. Add the pumpkin puree, oil, molasses, cinnamon, ginger, cocoa powder, nutmeg, cloves, and salt. Zest half of the orange directly into the bowl (about 1 teaspoon). Reserve the remaining orange to zest for the frosting. Whisk until smoothly combined.

3. Sprinkle the all-purpose flour, white whole wheat flour, baking powder, and baking soda over the top. Whisk until combined and smooth, stirring only as long as needed to incorporate all the ingredients.

4. Scrape the batter into the prepared pan and smooth the top. Gently tap the pan on the counter to remove any air bubbles. Bake the cake for 20 to 24 minutes, until it is puffed, the edges are starting to pull away from the pan, and a tester inserted into the center of the cake comes out clean. Use the parchment overhang to lift the cake onto a wire rack and let cool completely.

5. While the cake cools, make the frosting: In the bowl of a stand mixer fitted

recipe and ingredients continue

For the Spiced Cream Cheese Frosting

6 ounces reduced-fat cream cheese, or Neufchâtel cheese, at room temperature

2 tablespoons unsalted butter, at room temperature

1½ cups powdered sugar, plus a few additional tablespoons as needed

½ teaspoon orange zest (use the same orange from the cake)

½ teaspoon pure vanilla extract

⅛ teaspoon ground cinnamon or pumpkin pie spice

⅛ teaspoon kosher salt

with the paddle attachment or in a large mixing bowl with a hand mixer, beat together the cream cheese and butter at medium speed for 2 minutes, or until very smooth and well combined. Add the powdered sugar, orange zest (zest from the reserved orange directly into the bowl), vanilla, cinnamon, and salt. Beat on low speed for 30 seconds, until the powdered sugar is fairly incorporated. Increase the speed to high and beat until very smooth, creamy, and fluffy, 1 to 2 minutes more. If you'd like a stiffer, sweeter frosting, add an additional 2 tablespoons of powdered sugar at a time until your desired consistency is reached. Spread the frosting on the cooled cake. For easier cutting, transfer to the refrigerator for 20 minutes to allow the frosting to set up (or just go for it). Slice into squares of desired size and enjoy.

pro tips

Make delicious use of your leftover pumpkin puree: stir a few spoonfuls into oatmeal along with a drizzle of maple syrup and dash of cinnamon, add it to smoothies, or blend it with vanilla ice cream, pumpkin pie spice, and milk to make a pumpkin pie milkshake.

This recipe can be doubled and baked in a 9 by 13-inch pan until puffed and golden and a toothpick inserted into the center comes out clean, 30 to 40 minutes.

lemon cloud cookies

ACTIVE TIME:
35 minutes

TOTAL TIME:
1 hour 45 minutes

YIELD:
About 20 cookies

For the Cookies

1¾ cups all-purpose flour

½ teaspoon baking powder

¼ teaspoon baking soda

¼ teaspoon kosher salt

¾ cup granulated sugar

1 small lemon

6 tablespoons extra-virgin olive oil

1 large egg, at room temperature

1 (5.3-ounce) container low-fat or full-fat lemon Greek yogurt, at room temperature

1 teaspoon pure vanilla extract

¼ teaspoon pure almond extract

For the Frosting

2 cups powdered sugar

1 medium lemon

¼ teaspoon pure almond extract

Whenever I think about these airy cookies, I can hear the velvet voice of a 1950s crooner serenading "Come Fly with Me" as I bask in afternoon sunlight and nibble on them. This light, bright dessert has a double hit of lemon from both the zest and juice, a plush melt-in-your-mouth crumb, and a swoosh of creamy lemon frosting. They'll sweep you right off your feet! Heads up: The dough needs to refrigerate for at least an hour before baking but, like all great loves, is worth the wait.

1. In a medium bowl, whisk together the flour, baking powder, baking soda, and salt.

2. In the bowl of a stand mixer fitted with the paddle attachment or in a large bowl with a hand mixer, place the sugar. Zest the lemon right over the top, then with your fingers, rub to combine until the sugar is moist and fragrant. (Save the zested lemon for another use.) Add the oil, egg, yogurt, vanilla extract, and almond extract. Beat on medium-high speed until well combined. With a rubber spatula, scrape down the sides and bottom of the bowl.

3. With the mixer on low speed, slowly add the dry ingredients to the wet ingredients, stopping as soon as the flour disappears. The batter will look thick and creamy. Cover and refrigerate for at least 1 hour or up to 2 days.

4. When you're ready to bake, place a rack in the center of your oven and preheat to 350°F. Line a large baking sheet with parchment paper or a silicone baking mat. Remove the cookie dough from the refrigerator. With two spoons or a cookie scoop, drop the dough by 1½ tablespoonfuls, placing them 2 inches apart on the baking sheet. The dough will be very sticky. For a more smooth-topped cookie, use your fingers to lightly shape any oddly protruding bits of dough into a more uniform round shape (if the dough sticks to your fingers, coat them lightly with nonstick spray).

5. Bake the cookies for 9 minutes, until the bottoms are golden brown. The cookies will still look underdone on top. When you poke the top of a cookie gently with your finger, a slight indent should remain. Place the sheet on a wire rack. Let the cookies cool on the sheet for 5 minutes, then gently transfer to them to the rack to finish cooling completely.

recipe continues

6. While the cookies cool, prepare the frosting: In a small bowl, place the powdered sugar. Zest half of the lemon into the bowl, then halve it and squeeze in 2 tablespoons lemon juice and add the almond extract. Whisk to combine, adding additional lemon juice 1 teaspoon at a time until the frosting reaches a thick but easily spreadable consistency. Spread it over the tops of the cooled cookies.

pro tip

Store the cookies in an airtight container at room temperature, separating layers with wax or parchment paper, for 2 days. Or refrigerate for up to 5 days. The cookies will soften the next day but still taste delicious.

magic brown butter strawberry cobbler

ACTIVE TIME:
30 minutes

TOTAL TIME:
1 hour 25 minutes

YIELD:
Serves 8

For the Filling

1½ pounds whole strawberries, hulled and sliced (about 2½ cups)

¼ cup granulated sugar

2½ tablespoons cornstarch

½ teaspoon pure vanilla extract

For the Cobbler Batter

½ cup (1 stick) unsalted butter

⅔ cup granulated sugar

⅓ cup white whole wheat flour or all-purpose flour

⅓ cup all-purpose flour

2 teaspoons baking powder

¼ teaspoon kosher salt

½ cup milk (I use 1%; Grammy uses whole)

½ cup sliced almonds

Whipped cream, vanilla ice cream, frozen yogurt, or heavy cream, for serving

Grab your wand (er, spatula) and summon your inner culinary wizard! This easy dessert, based on my Grammy's legendary fruit cobbler, is called "magic" because of the way the ingredients switch layers in the oven (no abracadabra needed). The sorcery occurs when the fruit—despite being initially layered atop melted butter and a pancake-like batter—descends to the bottom, while the batter and butter combine into a moist, sticky, cake-like topping above. I take an extra step and brown the butter. While it's not strictly necessary, you'll be glad if you do too.

1. Place a rack in the center of your oven and preheat to 350°F. Keep a 2½-quart baking dish handy—an 8 by 10-inch casserole, deep 9 by 9-inch square, 9- or 10-inch springform pan, or an old Corningware soufflé dish (Grammy's pick) all work.

2. Make the filling: In a medium bowl, stir together the strawberries, sugar, cornstarch, and vanilla. Set aside to macerate while you prepare the cobbler batter.

3. Brown the butter: Melt the butter in a medium saucepan over medium-low heat. For ease, use a pan with a light-colored interior, such as stainless steel, so it's easier to watch the butter's color change. Continue to heat, swirling the pan periodically, until the butter melts completely, foams and crackles, turns clear golden (the crackling will stop),

then turns toasty brown. This entire process will take 3 to 5 minutes, depending upon your pan. Once the butter begins to smell slightly nutty, whisk it frequently, scraping up any browned bits from the bottom. Watch the pan very carefully—butter can burn fast. As soon as the bits in the bottom of the pan turn pecan colored, immediately remove the pan from the heat and pour the butter and any toasted bits that have collected on the bottom of the pan into the baking dish.

4. Make the cobbler batter: In a medium bowl, briskly whisk together the sugar, white whole wheat flour, all-purpose flour, baking powder, and salt. Add the milk and slowly stir until evenly combined. Pour the batter into the dish directly over the butter. Do not stir.

recipe continues

5. Spoon the strawberries and any liquid that has collected in the bowl into the baking dish on top of the batter and butter in an even layer (again, resist the urge to stir). Sprinkle the almonds over the top. Set on top of a parchment-lined rimmed baking sheet to catch any drips, then bake for 45 to 55 minutes, until the topping is deep golden and a toothpick inserted in the middle of the topping (not the filling) comes out clean. The topping will rise above the berries, puff up, and turn deep golden so you have a cake with fruit beneath. Serve the cobbler warm with whipped cream, a scoop of ice cream or frozen yogurt, or our family favorite: a pour of heavy cream.

do ahead

To make it a snap to serve this recipe hot from the oven for dessert, a few hours ahead, stir together the strawberry filling and refrigerate it, then brown the butter and pour it into the baking dish (keep this at room temperature; if the butter solidifies, just pop the dish into the oven as it preheats to melt it). Stir together the dry ingredients, and measure out and refrigerate the milk. An hour before you'd like to serve dessert, preheat your oven, stir the milk into the dry ingredients and pour into the pan as directed in step 4, and proceed with step 5.

market swaps

This cobbler is incredible with any peak-season summer fruit. My Grammy regularly made it with fresh blueberries, cherries, and peaches. If using a less juicy fruit, such as blueberries or cherries, reduce the cornstarch to 2 tablespoons.

peanut butter cup graham cracker ice cream sandwiches

ACTIVE TIME:

30 minutes

TOTAL TIME:

2 hours

YIELD:

8 sandwiches

2 cups peanut butter cup, chocolate, or vanilla ice cream

8 whole graham cracker sheets, each broken into 2 squares

5 tablespoons creamy peanut butter, divided

1 cup dark chocolate chips or chopped dark chocolate (about 6 ounces)

2 teaspoons coconut oil

¼ cup toppings of choice: sprinkles, chocolate cream sandwich cookie crumbs (you'll need about 2 cookies), finely chopped salted peanuts, or a mix!

At my parents' insistence that I play an organized sport, I took up softball, which as far as I know is the only sport where you have enough downtime to paint your nails between the action points (at least when third graders are batting). When my father let out a monster groan as he caught me in the dugout applying my first coat, I assured him that it was fine, because I was painting them purple, our team's color (prize for sportsmanship, please!). The only part of the games I truly relished was our postgame snack, usually some kind of ice cream treat and grape soda (those were the good ol' days). While those formative years didn't exactly foster a love of sports, they certainly solidified an affinity for ice cream sandwiches.

This grownup twist on a childhood favorite is a home run. Serve them at your next party and watch a roomful of adults cheer with delight!

1. Let the ice cream soften at room temperature for 5 minutes. Line a rimmed baking sheet with parchment paper. Rearrange your freezer if needed so that the baking sheet will fit inside.

2. Spread one side of each of the 16 graham cracker halves with a thin layer of peanut butter; you'll need about a heaping ½ teaspoon of peanut butter for each. Arrange eight of the graham crackers on the prepared baking sheet, peanut butter side up.

3. Top each graham cracker square with a ¼-cup scoop of ice cream. Gently press a second graham cracker square on top, peanut butter side

down, pressing lightly so that the ice cream spreads almost to the edges. Repeat with the remaining squares. If any ice cream smooshes out, use the back of a spoon to smooth it neatly into place. Freeze for at least 45 minutes, or until the sandwiches are firm.

4. To dip and decorate: Place the chocolate, remaining 2 tablespoons peanut butter, and coconut oil in a microwave-safe bowl. Microwave for 30 seconds, stir, then continue microwaving and stirring in short bursts, stopping when the chocolate is almost melted. Stir, letting the residual heat melt the chocolate the rest of the way. It should

recipe continues

be smooth and shiny. Get your toppings ready.

5. Remove the sandwiches from the freezer and dip each halfway into the melted chocolate, then return to the baking sheet. Immediately sprinkle with the toppings. Repeat with the remaining sandwiches. Return to the freezer for 30 minutes to allow the chocolate to fully set.

6. Once the chocolate is set, you can devour the ice cream sandwiches immediately or wrap each one separately in plastic wrap or foil. Store them in the freezer for up to 1 month. Eat on repeat!

variations

Nutella: Swap the peanut butter for Nutella. Use vanilla or pistachio ice cream. Top with finely chopped hazelnuts.

Coffee Chip: Use coffee or espresso chip ice cream. Top with finely chopped chocolate-covered espresso beans.

PB&J: Use strawberry ice cream. Top with finely chopped dry-roasted salted peanuts.

the fudgiest salted chocolate sheet cake

ACTIVE TIME: 30 minutes

TOTAL TIME: 1 hour

YIELD: 24 servings

For the Cake

1½ cups finely chopped pecans

1 cup white whole wheat flour, or a 50-50 blend of regular whole wheat flour and all-purpose flour

1 cup all-purpose flour

1 cup granulated sugar

1 teaspoon espresso powder (optional for a more intense chocolate flavor)

1 teaspoon baking soda

½ teaspoon kosher salt

½ cup (1 stick) unsalted butter, cut into a few pieces

⅓ cup unsweetened cocoa powder

½ cup water

¾ cup pure maple syrup

¾ cup full-fat plain Greek yogurt, at room temperature (see Pro Tip)

¼ cup plus 2 tablespoons nonfat milk or milk of choice, at room temperature

2 large eggs, at room temperature

1 teaspoon pure vanilla extract

My great cultural shock moving to Wisconsin wasn't the Cheeseheads or the state's propensity to attach a beer garden to any activity (Little League games, apple picking, you name it). It's the fact that no one here had heard of Texas sheet cake. A tender chocolate cake doused in a hot chocolate pecan icing that seeps down into every crumb, renders the cake impossibly moist, and sets it with a shiny lid, it's the kind of dessert that ends with everyone gobbling cake straight out of the pan with a fork. My version is less cloyingly sweet than the original and incorporates wholesome touches like Greek yogurt, some whole wheat flour, and pure maple syrup. A finishing sprinkle of flaky salt takes it to another dimension. I've yet to serve this cake to a single person and not have them demand the recipe on the spot. My true calling: sheet cake evangelist.

1. Place a rack in the center of your oven and preheat to 350°F. Generously coat an 11 by 17-inch rimmed baking sheet with nonstick spray, or grease and flour the pan.

2. Spread the pecans on an ungreased rimmed baking sheet. Bake for 8 to 10 minutes, tossing once halfway through, until toasted and fragrant. Set a timer and watch closely so the nuts do not burn. Set them aside to cool (if the nuts are on the verge of burning when they come out of the oven, transfer them to a plate or bowl so that the heat of the pan doesn't continue to toast them).

3. Meanwhile, in a large bowl, whisk together the white whole wheat flour, all-purpose flour, granulated sugar, espresso powder (if using), baking soda, and salt. Keep near the stove.

4. Place the butter in a medium saucepan. Melt over medium heat, then whisk in the cocoa powder until smooth. Add the water and heat until bubbling all around the edges, stirring constantly. Remove the pan from the heat, stir in the maple syrup, then pour the mixture into the dry ingredients. With a spatula or wooden spoon, gently stir a few times until about halfway blended (the goal here is to cool the chocolate; you don't need to incorporate it fully). Keep

recipe and ingredients continue

For the Frosting

6 tablespoons unsalted butter

⅔ cup nonfat milk or milk of choice

⅓ cup unsweetened cocoa powder

4 cups powdered sugar, sifted if lumpy

Flaky sea salt, such as Maldon or fleur de sel

the saucepan handy (no need to clean it).

5. In a medium bowl, whisk together the yogurt, milk, eggs, and vanilla until evenly combined; you may have a few specks of yogurt remaining, which is fine. Pour into the chocolate mixture. Whisk gently, stopping as soon as the ingredients are evenly combined and only a few small lumps remain.

6. Carefully pour the batter into the prepared pan and use the back of a spatula to spread it as evenly as possible. Bake for 18 to 20 minutes, until a toothpick inserted in the center comes out with a few moist crumbs but no wet batter clinging to it, rotating the pan 180 degrees halfway

through. Place the pan on a wire rack.

7. As soon as the cake is out of the oven, prepare the frosting: In the same saucepan you used for the cake, place the butter, milk, and cocoa powder. Heat over high heat, stirring constantly, until it begins to bubble rapidly at the edges. Remove from the heat. Stir in the powdered sugar ½ cup at a time, then stir in the toasted pecans from step 2. Immediately pour it slowly and evenly over the warm cake. Quickly spread it into an even layer (a small offset spatula is great for this), distributing the pecans as evenly as you can. Sprinkle the cake with flaky salt and let the frosting set for a few minutes (if you can stand it).

pro tip

If you don't regularly buy full-fat Greek yogurt and don't want to purchase a large container, look for it in a single-serving size, which is usually around 5 ounces. The remaining 1 ounce can come from any variety of plain or vanilla Greek yogurt or sour cream.

next level

Swap the water for coffee for an even more intense chocolate flavor.

acknowledgments

You are holding this book in your hands because a group of smart, dedicated, and unfailing cheerleaders believed I had these recipes inside of me long before I believed it myself.

To my Well Plated readers: For your exuberant support of my first cookbook and your continuous hopeful requests for a second, without either of which this book this would not have been possible. I hope you love it and that it's been worth the wait!

To Maggie Ensing, my right hand in the kitchen: From the moment you said "I'm in" when I asked you if you were up for a second book, I knew it was going to be something special. I treasure our hours together debating the merits of various vinegars and can't imagine these recipes without your touch.

To Ashley McLaughlin: For shooting a gorgeous, inviting cover. You are a godsend, and I am so glad we got to work together!

To Matt Armendariz and Adam Pearson: For shooting the most beautiful interior photos. You captured the joy and spirit of cooking for people you love.

To my editor, Lucia Watson: For your gentle encouragement and insightful inputs, always delivered at just the right time in just the right way. I love being on your team.

To Janis Donnaud, my fearless agent: You were the first person who knew I was going to write more than one book (and told me as much!). Thanks for seeing my potential from the start, for being in my corner when I need you, and for celebrating my successes with me.

To Lottie Lillian, my lifestyle photographer, and Jenna Mickle of Company and Cheer: Your work gives this book genuine personality and life. You made a long day flawless and fun, alleviated my stress, and enabled me to include a piece of myself in this book that would have been missing without you.

To Kenzie Davidovich, Jamie Michalski, and Maggie: Thanks for being the best of girlfriends, both on and off these pages.

To the Avery team: We are two for two! Ashley Tucker, you outdid yourself (again!) with the book's design. Carla Iannone, Alyssa Adler, and Katie Macleod-English, your capable hands helped bring this book to life.

To Caitlin Fultz, my editing guardian angel: Being able to share a part of this process with you again was a blessing.

To my generous recipe testers: Kathryn and Reed Parker, Elaine and Joey Soptic, Erin Hunter and Bryan Bennett, Kate and Conor Kelly, Mary and Garrett Mandeville, Elizabeth Devaney, Meghan Larsen-Reidy, Samantha LaNuez, Megan Hille, Matt Lucci, Laura Davis and Anthony Panozzo, as well as my ultimate MVPs Heather and Tyler Cooksey, Taylor Teppen, and Danielle Clarke. You are one of the most critical parts of the cookbook process. Your time, resources, and thoughtful feedback mean more than I can express.

To Brenna Albritton, Taylor Teppen, Nancy Piran, and Kiersten Frase: You are the best team a girl could ask for. Thanks for sharing the ups and downs of the process with me, for being patient with my space-out moments during deadline weeks (and, okay, in general), and for your essential support with launching this book into the universe.

To my family: Elizabeth, Elaine, Mom, Larry, Danielle, Paul, and Maria. Your unfailing love and belief that I can do anything gives me the confidence to keep on going, even when doubts loom large. Thanks for being my biggest hype people (and for all the cookbooks you've sold to unsuspecting strangers).

And to Ben: To call you my better half does not suffice; you're my whole. Life with you is the most delicious adventure.

index

Note: Page numbers in *italics* indicate photos separate from recipes.